One Mans' Tragedy

One Mans' Triumph

Seven Continents

The Heights of Mt. Everest

The Lows of Death Valley

North of The Artic Circle

South of The Antarctic Pass

Hundreds of Images

One Secret Code

One Amazing Story

I have changed names and places,
other than that the facts are exactly
as I have chosen to remember them

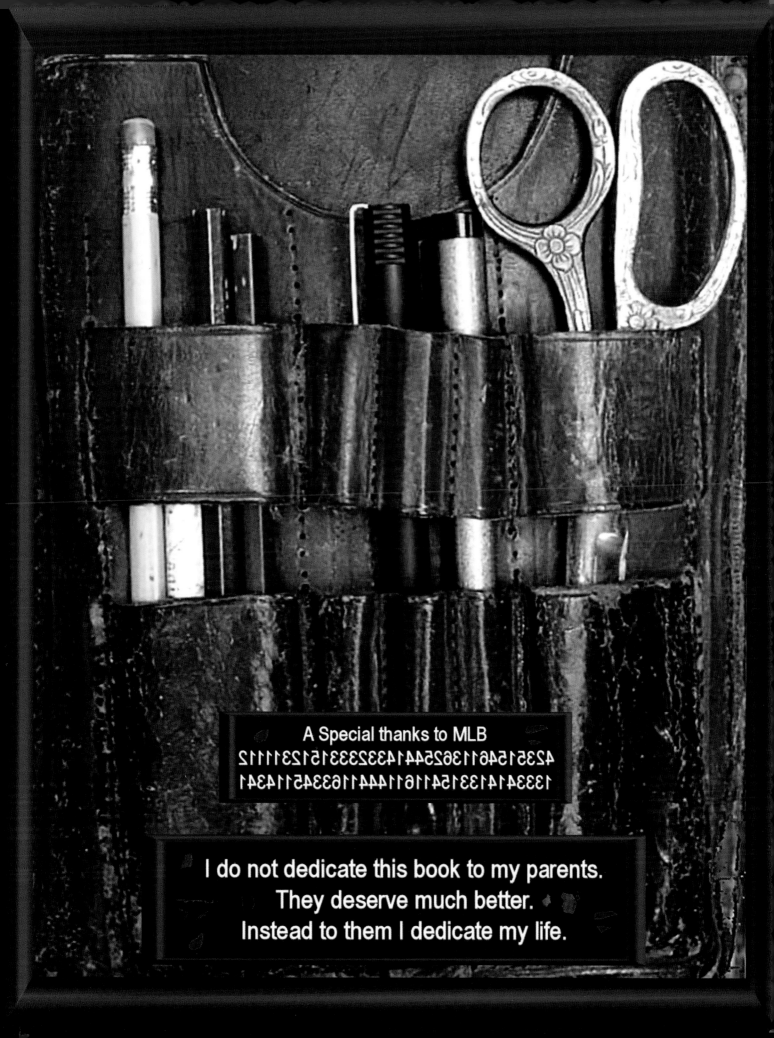

A Special thanks to MLB

I do not dedicate this book to my parents.
They deserve much better.
Instead to them I dedicate my life.

TABLE OF CONTENTS

Mind Safari

TABLE OF CONTENTS

Mind Safari

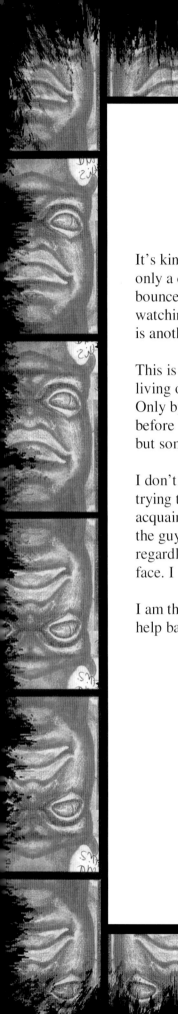

PROLOGUE

JOURNAL ENTRY- (EXHIBIT A)

It's kind of like watching a small child fall on a ski slope. Because a child is only a couple of feet off the ground the fall is never that bad. Children tend to bounce back up barely even noticing the interruption. On the other hand watching a seven footer tumble perilously, ass over tea kettle down the slopes is another matter entirely.

This is how I think of my life. I have lived the best and worst life of any person living or dead that I have ever known, read about or personally encountered. Only by reaching such highs have I been able to fall so far. Unlike so many before me it was not drugs, alcohol, sickness or crime that brought me down but something far more difficult to reconcile…………

I don't think anyone around me even knows I have fallen or how hard I am trying to get back up. I am a rock personally, professionally and even to casual acquaintances. I am the one constant in life those around me can count on. I am the guy you want in your corner when the chips are down. I am the guy who regardless of circumstance always has a confident and settling smile on his face. I am the guy most people think they want to be.

I am the guy who has fallen……and I am the guy who is too big for anyone to help back to his feet.

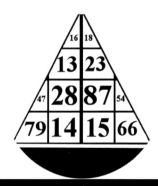

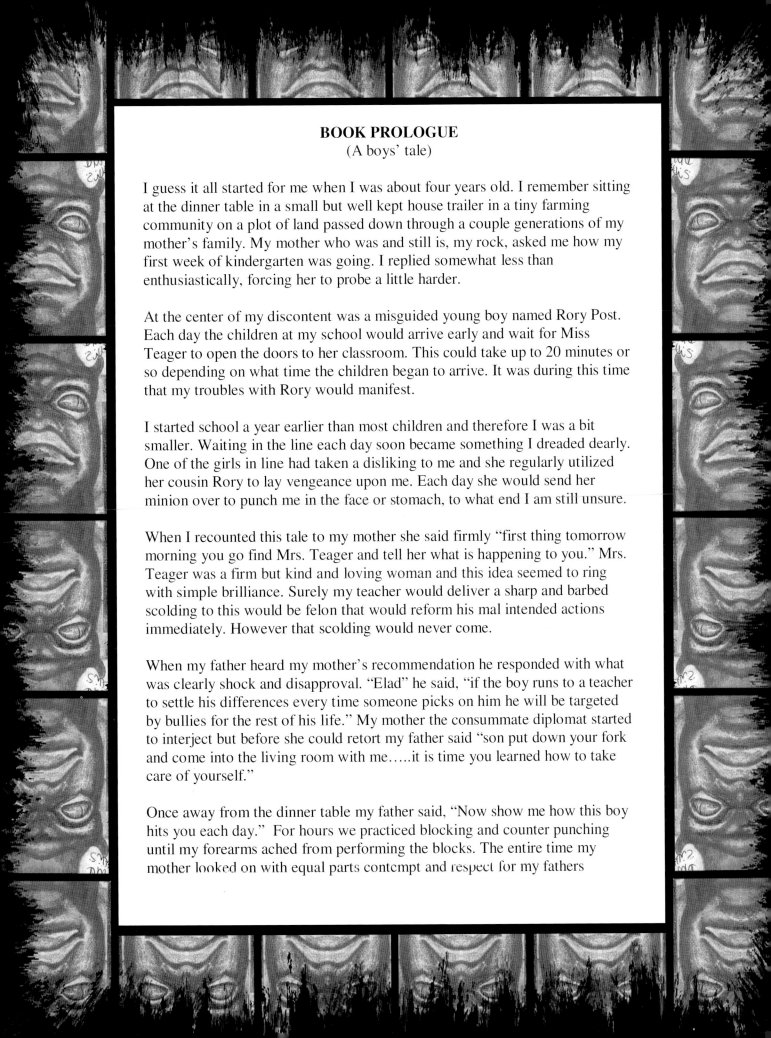

BOOK PROLOGUE
(A boys' tale)

I guess it all started for me when I was about four years old. I remember sitting at the dinner table in a small but well kept house trailer in a tiny farming community on a plot of land passed down through a couple generations of my mother's family. My mother who was and still is, my rock, asked me how my first week of kindergarten was going. I replied somewhat less than enthusiastically, forcing her to probe a little harder.

At the center of my discontent was a misguided young boy named Rory Post. Each day the children at my school would arrive early and wait for Miss Teager to open the doors to her classroom. This could take up to 20 minutes or so depending on what time the children began to arrive. It was during this time that my troubles with Rory would manifest.

I started school a year earlier than most children and therefore I was a bit smaller. Waiting in the line each day soon became something I dreaded dearly. One of the girls in line had taken a disliking to me and she regularly utilized her cousin Rory to lay vengeance upon me. Each day she would send her minion over to punch me in the face or stomach, to what end I am still unsure.

When I recounted this tale to my mother she said firmly "first thing tomorrow morning you go find Mrs. Teager and tell her what is happening to you." Mrs. Teager was a firm but kind and loving woman and this idea seemed to ring with simple brilliance. Surely my teacher would deliver a sharp and barbed scolding to this would be felon that would reform his mal intended actions immediately. However that scolding would never come.

When my father heard my mother's recommendation he responded with what was clearly shock and disapproval. "Elad" he said, "if the boy runs to a teacher to settle his differences every time someone picks on him he will be targeted by bullies for the rest of his life." My mother the consummate diplomat started to interject but before she could retort my father said "son put down your fork and come into the living room with me…..it is time you learned how to take care of yourself."

Once away from the dinner table my father said, "Now show me how this boy hits you each day." For hours we practiced blocking and counter punching until my forearms ached from performing the blocks. The entire time my mother looked on with equal parts contempt and respect for my fathers parenting techniques. When my father was satisfied with my progress he gave me a speech that was almost as long as the lesson itself.

I don't remember all of the details but the message was clear. My father said "son, we are Garners and that means something." "We don't start fights, but we sure as hell don't walk away from them." "Tomorrow, don't wait for this boy to find you….seek him out and tell him that you would rather be his friend than fight with him." If he accepts shake his hand and walk away. If he does not, do exactly as I have taught you.

The next day when I arrived at school I nervously approached the line scanning it diligently for Rory. Before his cousin could issue another attack command I approached him and delivered my speech. It seemed to be working until taunts of "punch him, punch him" came from a familiar and sinister voice somewhere in the line.

I did not have time for another attempt at diplomacy. When Rory delivered his strike I blocked it and scored such a vicious counter punch that one was all it took. As Rory hit the schoolyard gravel in tears the other children's eyes swelled like saucers. Mumbling amongst the line soon ensued and a general consensus was quickly formed…….It might be best, not to screw with the little guy!

Kindergarten was never a source of discontent for me again.

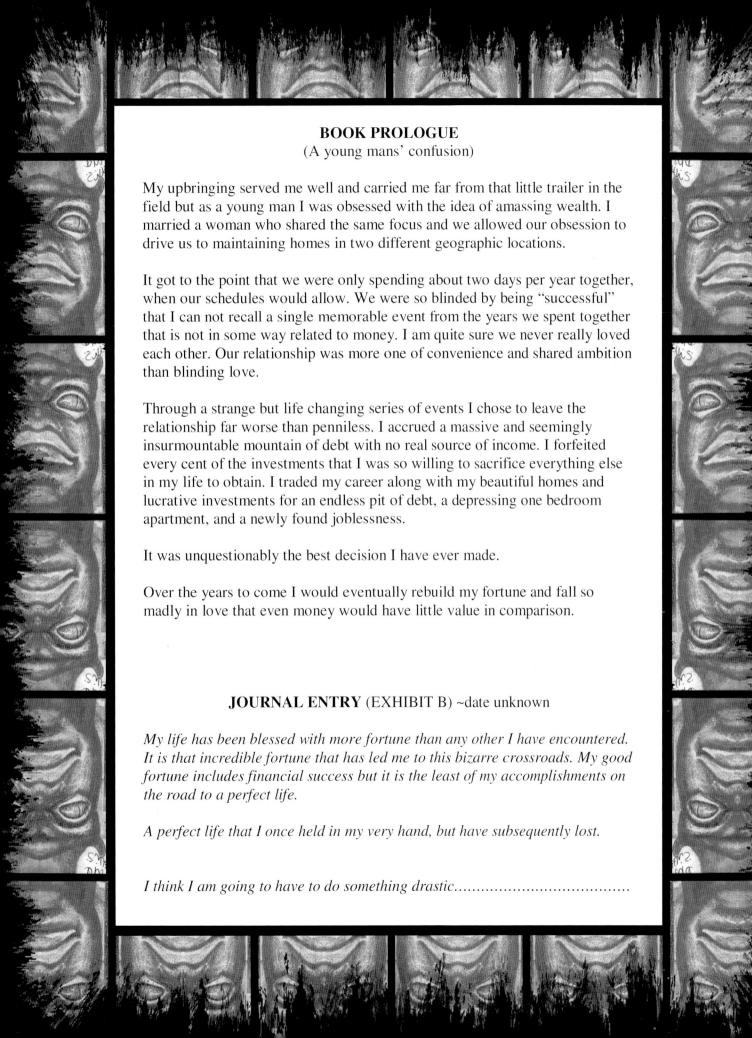

BOOK PROLOGUE
(A young mans' confusion)

My upbringing served me well and carried me far from that little trailer in the field but as a young man I was obsessed with the idea of amassing wealth. I married a woman who shared the same focus and we allowed our obsession to drive us to maintaining homes in two different geographic locations.

It got to the point that we were only spending about two days per year together, when our schedules would allow. We were so blinded by being "successful" that I can not recall a single memorable event from the years we spent together that is not in some way related to money. I am quite sure we never really loved each other. Our relationship was more one of convenience and shared ambition than blinding love.

Through a strange but life changing series of events I chose to leave the relationship far worse than penniless. I accrued a massive and seemingly insurmountable mountain of debt with no real source of income. I forfeited every cent of the investments that I was so willing to sacrifice everything else in my life to obtain. I traded my career along with my beautiful homes and lucrative investments for an endless pit of debt, a depressing one bedroom apartment, and a newly found joblessness.

It was unquestionably the best decision I have ever made.

Over the years to come I would eventually rebuild my fortune and fall so madly in love that even money would have little value in comparison.

JOURNAL ENTRY (EXHIBIT B) ~date unknown

My life has been blessed with more fortune than any other I have encountered. It is that incredible fortune that has led me to this bizarre crossroads. My good fortune includes financial success but it is the least of my accomplishments on the road to a perfect life.

A perfect life that I once held in my very hand, but have subsequently lost.

I think I am going to have to do something drastic.....................................

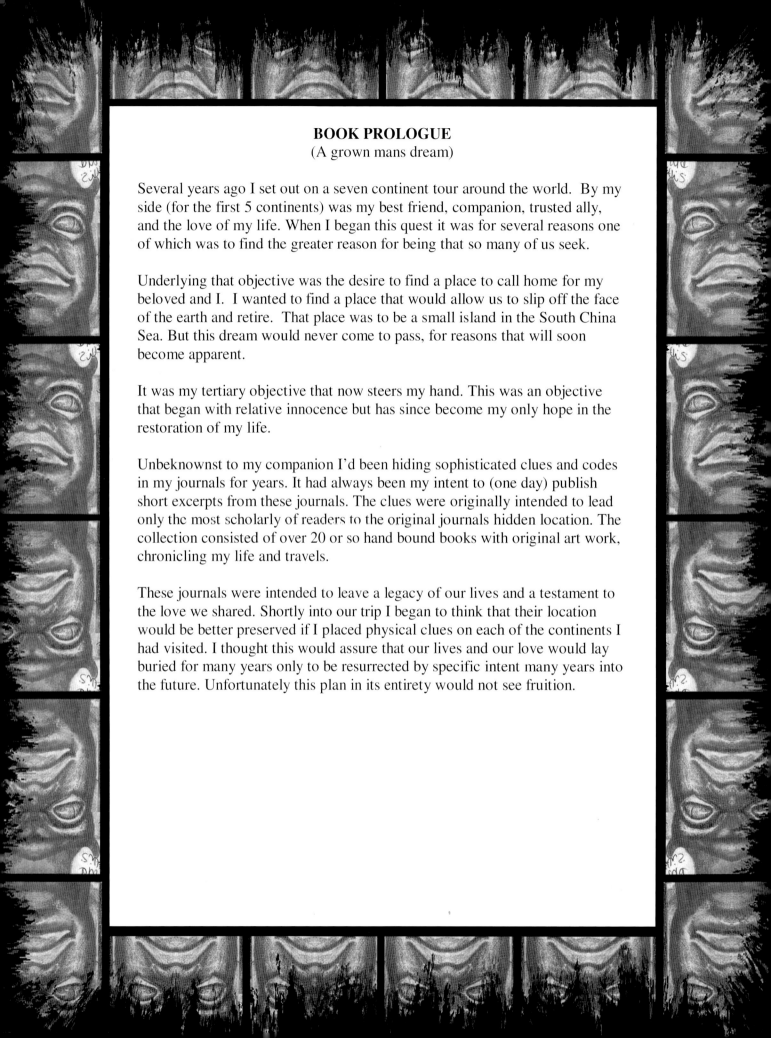

BOOK PROLOGUE
(A grown mans dream)

Several years ago I set out on a seven continent tour around the world. By my side (for the first 5 continents) was my best friend, companion, trusted ally, and the love of my life. When I began this quest it was for several reasons one of which was to find the greater reason for being that so many of us seek.

Underlying that objective was the desire to find a place to call home for my beloved and I. I wanted to find a place that would allow us to slip off the face of the earth and retire. That place was to be a small island in the South China Sea. But this dream would never come to pass, for reasons that will soon become apparent.

It was my tertiary objective that now steers my hand. This was an objective that began with relative innocence but has since become my only hope in the restoration of my life.

Unbeknownst to my companion I'd been hiding sophisticated clues and codes in my journals for years. It had always been my intent to (one day) publish short excerpts from these journals. The clues were originally intended to lead only the most scholarly of readers to the original journals hidden location. The collection consisted of over 20 or so hand bound books with original art work, chronicling my life and travels.

These journals were intended to leave a legacy of our lives and a testament to the love we shared. Shortly into our trip I began to think that their location would be better preserved if I placed physical clues on each of the continents I had visited. I thought this would assure that our lives and our love would lay buried for many years only to be resurrected by specific intent many years into the future. Unfortunately this plan in its entirety would not see fruition.

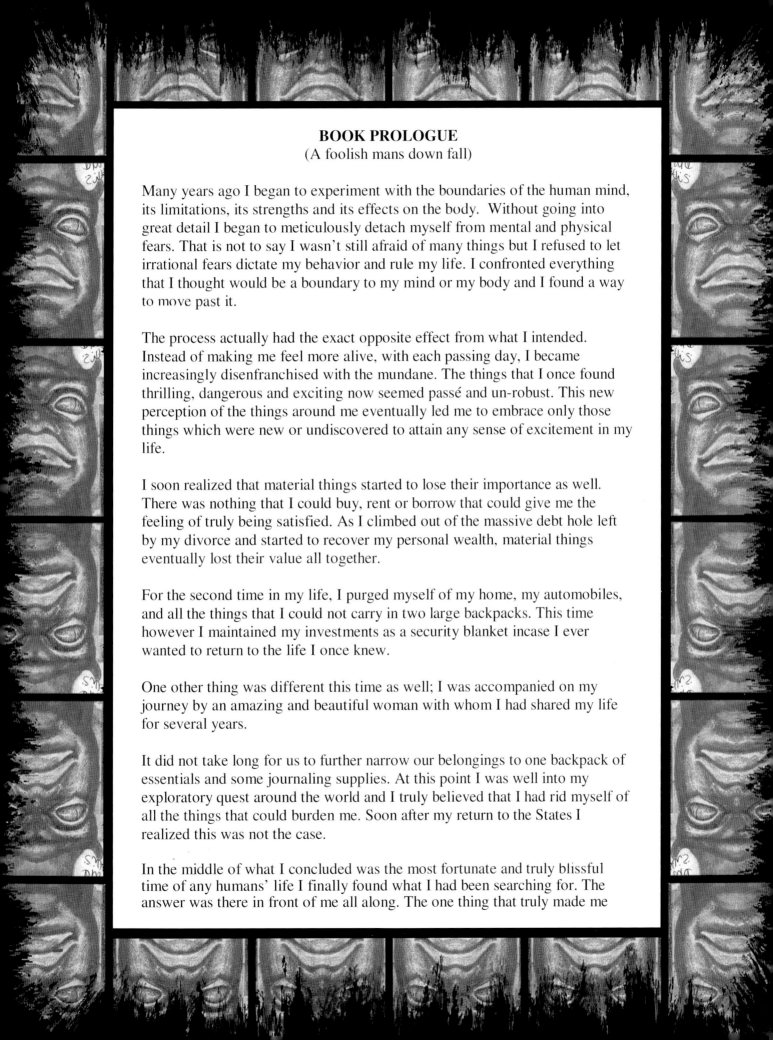

BOOK PROLOGUE
(A foolish mans down fall)

Many years ago I began to experiment with the boundaries of the human mind, its limitations, its strengths and its effects on the body. Without going into great detail I began to meticulously detach myself from mental and physical fears. That is not to say I wasn't still afraid of many things but I refused to let irrational fears dictate my behavior and rule my life. I confronted everything that I thought would be a boundary to my mind or my body and I found a way to move past it.

The process actually had the exact opposite effect from what I intended. Instead of making me feel more alive, with each passing day, I became increasingly disenfranchised with the mundane. The things that I once found thrilling, dangerous and exciting now seemed passé and un-robust. This new perception of the things around me eventually led me to embrace only those things which were new or undiscovered to attain any sense of excitement in my life.

I soon realized that material things started to lose their importance as well. There was nothing that I could buy, rent or borrow that could give me the feeling of truly being satisfied. As I climbed out of the massive debt hole left by my divorce and started to recover my personal wealth, material things eventually lost their value all together.

For the second time in my life, I purged myself of my home, my automobiles, and all the things that I could not carry in two large backpacks. This time however I maintained my investments as a security blanket incase I ever wanted to return to the life I once knew.

One other thing was different this time as well; I was accompanied on my journey by an amazing and beautiful woman with whom I had shared my life for several years.

It did not take long for us to further narrow our belongings to one backpack of essentials and some journaling supplies. At this point I was well into my exploratory quest around the world and I truly believed that I had rid myself of all the things that could burden me. Soon after my return to the States I realized this was not the case.

In the middle of what I concluded was the most fortunate and truly blissful time of any humans' life I finally found what I had been searching for. The answer was there in front of me all along. The one thing that truly made me content, the one thing that had changed my life forever, the one thing that made life worth living was about to be revealed to me.

I had lived like a king in some of the most exotic locations in the world. I lived amongst the Masai Tribes in Africa; narrowly escaped death on Mount Everest, climbed frozen glaciers in New Zealand and dodged gunfire in the South China Sea but none of those things gave me a fraction of the thrill of my next discovery.

Once I finally stopped traveling and stopped searching long enough to look right in front of me I knew I had finally found it. The golden chalice I sought, the reason for my travels, the unattainable state of contentment I had never found was now so obvious.

When I could finally see clearly I realized it was the unparallel and sacred relationship that I had shared with Heather for over ten years that was the true prize in my otherwise un-extraordinary life. When all else was stripped away, I realized it was the Holy Grail I had been searching for all along.

No words can describe how I felt when I realized how the only thing left with any value to me on the entire planet was soon to be gone.

It was not that she had left me for another man, for that I was compassionate. I truly loved her enough to let her go. It was an unimaginable sacrifice, but I was willing to make it if it meant making her happier in the end. I have always said, and truly meant that I would give my life today so that 40 years from now she could have one more hour of happiness added to the end of hers. The chain of events that followed is what has forced me to cut the final tether that binds me to the rules used by the rest of the world.

It was money once again that lay at the root of my undoing. After the break up the legal battles that ensued over my liquid assets left me not only emotionally exhausted, but without purpose or reason to continue living.

Many months passed before I realized what I must do. Instead of my journals buried in a shrine, I must make a bigger commitment to my freedom. I must rid myself of all remaining anchors. It was the money after all that poured the foundation for this particular evil.

If not for the money I could have just let her go. I could still love her from afar to this very day, but I allowed myself to become a pawn to it. It became the ultimate undoing of the only thing that ever really mattered. I could not allow myself to be caught in the snare again. I knew every drop of blood must be drained from the monster, save a few drops to get me through the next year or so. The hole that was once to contain my legacy would become the hole that would set me free.

BOOK PROLOGUE
(A mad mans curse)

The clues are encrypted with the sophistication of mathematicians but the simplicity of a school child. It will not be solely a person of above average intellect who unearths this treasure, but a series of individuals who posses physical and mental strengths and are unencumbered by greed.

For my own protection I have enlisted the help of several individuals and organizations to encrypt the clues. In all cases the names of those involved are unknown to me and my name is unknown to them. Each has a set of legal and intellectual guidelines that prevents them from profiting from the information they hold.

There is a set of simple but elaborate checks and balances that all but guarantee the integrity of the agreement. The clock began to tick on April 21st 2005. 20 years will be the fold and the fold will be 20 years after which all things may come to rest.

I will not disclose the amount or exact nature of the find. I will only say that it is significant by any standard, and I hope that the barer does not fall to its filthy curse, as did I.

Words alone cannot possibly reach a large enough audience to find the rare few, clean hearted enough to bare this prize. I have decided to begin publishing my journals to this end. I hope they provide you with an opportunity to escape from whatever chains may bind you and I hope you do not follow my tracks beyond the cliffs edge.

Today I live as a pauper and I am free from the evil that has been my downfall so many times before. However, new seeds are constantly being planted at my feet and I fear if I don't keep moving they may grow in my presence and bind me once again.

I have left some simple clues in my first publication but never again will I leave such obvious tracks in the snow.

G.D. Garner

throughtheeyesofmadness.com

CHAPTER 1 ....YUCATAN KIDNAPPERS

I had been threatening to cut the cord and disappear out into the world for a number of years before I actually pulled the trigger but like everyone else I was bound by numerous material possessions and responsibilities. I had three different companies in the Seattle area, a home on the ocean, several cars and a massive accumulation of other useless stuff that provided an ample list of reasons to put it off.

When I'd finally made my mind up, the timing seemed right and it took almost no time at all to liquidate the entire lot. Within 30 days I would not set foot in the US or Canada again for a couple of years and never again would I call North America home.

With backpacks in tow we were ready to make the great escape. Up until now I hadn't traveled much internationally so I was unsure of the best means by which to embark upon such a grand journey. I recalled a conversation with a man who patronized my restaurant years earlier. He claimed to have traveled to several different countries using a multi travel ticket that allowed him to circumnavigate the globe with multiple stops for one very reasonable fee.

After a bit of research we confirmed that in fact most airlines were part of one network or another that would allow you to use multiple carriers to travel to different locations on one ticket provided you met certain criteria. I believe the package we chose allowed us to travel 50,000 miles or so, provided we flew in only one basic direction, never stopped at the same airport twice, went all the way around the globe and used all of our miles in a year or less. As our original plan was to travel for only two years this ticket was the perfect way to cement our commitment and get the ball rolling.

With airfare out of the way the only other matter that remained was division of responsibilities. We would be visiting some pretty hostile places and traveling in some inhospitable lands so it was important to have at least a basic plan for our safety and wellbeing before encountering any hardships on the road. I took responsibility for security and finance while Heather handled travel coordination and accommodations.

As far as security went, life and death situations were pretty much the only thing I really wanted to do any pre-planning for. Away from the work environment I was one of the most casual and laid back people you could ever meet. I didn't make or follow a detailed plan in my private life and I was happy to do just about anything with regards to our travels. In fact one of my goals for the journey was to leave the meticulous planner and relentless businessman behind. I just wanted to take my hands off the wheel and let life steer me for awhile.

However I was not so carefree with regards to my responsibility for Heathers' safety. We were both willing to take significant risk but I had a much better understanding of how to manage those risks to a favorable outcome. She had a tendency to trust every person she ever met and seemed to put herself in unforgiving situations more often than necessary. I knew a few simple precautions in the right situations could greatly reduce our risks and help me keep my internal promise, to keep her safe….no matter what that meant for me.

I really wanted our trip to be a mutual, no rules, life changing and spontaneous journey.

It was for this reason that when we started our trip by targeting a small village in the Yucatan Peninsula I did minimal research as to the risks we might encounter during our travels in this part of the world. I did however stumble across an article about the growing sophistication of kidnappers in Central America.

Kidnappings were no longer really random. Kidnappers had learned to focus on wealthy executives who often carried kidnapping insurance or could otherwise afford a healthy ransom. The attackers would often intercept email transmissions to confirm exact travel itineraries, which included arrival times and destinations. They would also use these intercepted transmissions to determine the wealth and amount of ransom for their potential victims.

This was not particularly alarming as I already knew that this was one of the risks with traveling to less developed nations. However by simply avoiding any of these details in our email transmissions and declaring ourselves as an "Artist and a Student" when asked I knew we could lower our risk significantly with very little effort.

Finally D Day had arrived. We took a flight into Mexico where we would set up ground transportation to the Yucatan. I knew that once we got off the plane the transportation would not be very reliable, so I asked Heather to book us a flight that would put us on the ground early enough in the day to avoid traveling by bus at night into an unknown area.

I don't remember the exact time but I think we hit the ground in the early afternoon with plenty of time to make it to Calabar before nightfall. From the very beginning it was clear that the bus ride was going to be an adventure. We wanted to travel "with the people"…….. and boy did we. We took a second or third class bus and, as expected, once we finally found the bus station the bus was running an hour or so late. Once aboard the sweltering vessel we waited another 20-30 minutes for the driver to show up.

Once he was firmly planted in his captains chair we sat for another 30 to 40 minutes baking like raisins in the sun. Even the locals were getting pissed. I could not understand what they were yelling. But one thing is for sure they weren't compliments. Eventually a young man showed up and took his place on the steps by the driver. I later learned that this young fellow was there to chat to the driver and keep him company while he meandered down every back road he could find, arduously filling the bus with more passengers than it was ever intended to hold. But anyway, thank God we could finally get underway and get some air flowing through the oven on wheels.

The bus stopped and stopped and stopped again, it was very clear that there was no chance in hell of being anywhere near on-schedule. The only question that remained was would we make it to our destination before nightfall.

The heat and the bumps really took there toll after a few hours and I just wanted to get there, get to our bungalow, and get some sleep. When I asked Heather how far from the bus stop in Calabar we had to go to reach our house, her answer set off my alarm bells ………………………… "I am not sure," she said.

When I inquired further she said that our contact Sonja was going to meet us at the bus stop when we arrived and drive us to the house. Yes, I said, "that sounds like a great plan but we are going to be several hours late and I doubt she is going to just sit at the bus stop and wait." "You do have the address, right?"
....Heather got that look on her face that let me know I was not going to like what she was about to say.

"No I didn't write the address down because everything was in Spanish, but don't worry Sonja will be there."

I was not pleased with that answer, but I decided not to push. I wanted to focus all of my energy on just getting to the damn village. I passed the time by studying my Spanish book and playing with the little Spanish speaking girl in front of us who was clearly fascinated by our pale white skin and Heather's bright orange hair.

As darkness fell over the bus I was amazed at how people in this part of the world interacted with their children. The children were all very well behaved, no crying, no yelling and screaming and all with no direct supervision from their parents. Many of the children wandered freely around the bus and didn't seem to mind visiting every family they encountered. The little girl in front of us had now joined us in our seat and had been there for a couple of hours without her mother paying her much attention. She was a well behaved little girl but about the only thing that I could understand her say was that her name was Maria. It was also clear that she wanted me to read a book about farm animals to her. We worked out that a cow makes the Moo sound and from there on we pretty much got past the language barrier with all the other animals.

After reading the book by flashlight for what seemed like a hundred times I turned my attention back to my watch. It was now well after ten o'clock and pitch black outside. I couldn't ignore our lack of lodging any longer. I asked Heather if she knew if there was any place else to stay in the village that was near the bus stop. It was clear that we were so late there was little to no chance Sonja would be there to meet us. The answer that she gave to console me was the one thing I did not want to hear.

"Don't worry I emailed her our entire itinerary, flight schedule, bus schedule, what time we would be arriving……. everything."

The one thing I had asked her to avoid……NEVER email anyone our travel itinerary. It was the one thing the article I had read focused on……it just makes it too easy for potential kidnappers to intercept the information and be waiting for you….. right on schedule.

I thought I would enquire more to see just how bad the situation really was. "What else did you say in the email," I asked?

"Oh nothing really just that we would be traveling the world for two years on an around the world ticket and we weren't really sure how long we would need the house for."

Great, now not only did the prospective kidnappers know where we were going and when we would get there, but they also knew that we had enough money to travel the world for two years. That should be just enough incentive for them to do some research and see that I owned three different companies in the worlds' most hated nation.

I tried not to let my imagination get the best of me but this was the one and only restriction I put on the whole damn stop. You can pick the place, you can decide how long we stay, you can decide what kind of place we rent, just don't email the DAMN TRAVEL PLANS!

As we traveled deeper into the darkness I was hoping we would see some city lights or any other sign we were getting close. As the bus slowed in the darkness everyone began to stand. I asked Maria's mother the only Spanish word I knew Calabar? Calabar? She nodded and smiled and motioned with her hands indicating that in two more stops we would be in Calabar at last.

I did not see the city lights that I was expecting. Instead when the bus finally came to rest I saw something straight out of a Clint Eastwood movie. I saw old adobe style buildings with palm branch roofs, dirt streets dividing the buildings and a lone light bulb hanging from a pole about 50 yards from the bus stop. An unsettling darkness covered the town, but it was eclipsed by the unsettling feeling in both of our stomachs.

Immediately off the bus I scrambled for my Spanish book. I strung together a few frantic words for Maria's mother. "Donde esta un Hotel?" She looked at me in a puzzled way, so the second time I asked I used my master charade skills to act out sleeping in a bed while repeating, "Donde esta un Hotel?"

The woman that was so friendly on the bus now seemed curt and impatient. She looked around the streets, grabbed her little girl by the arm and rushed away without even trying to respond. She seemed unsettled to be out on the streets in her own village and even more unsettled to be near me. She rushed away from me in a very unnatural fashion, especially since we basically looked after her daughter for several hours on the infinite bus ride. I began to wonder if maybe she knew something bad was about to happen to us and that is why she made such a brisk effort to get her and her daughter off the street and away from Heather and I.

As I looked to see where she was headed I could not help but notice that even though it was now well after midnight there were several highly suspicious men with machetes standing only a few yards away………. And yep, that's right, no sign of Sonja.

Now Heather was truly beginning to appreciate my concern. As we scanned the town we clung to the only pole with a light bulb. We could see nothing even vaguely resembling a hotel or hostel. What we did see however, was three men heading our way with machine guns. This is not a good feeling. To our

left was a band of guys with machetes and off to our right there were armed gunmen heading straight for us. I can remember thinking to myself that coincidently these unfavorable images were in the only two parts of town lit well enough to see…….God only knows what was waiting for us in the darkness.

My first instinct was to choose the lesser of two evils, with only a second to think, for some reason light seemed like a safer option than darkness (even if it came with machete wielding banditos). We headed for the machete men who were at least stationary and not moving directly toward us but as we got closer to them suddenly darkness did not seem so bad.

We crossed the street and backed ourselves up to an unlit concrete fence adorned along the top with broken beer bottles (to keep people from climbing over). While this side of the street was darker at least it gave us some distance from the would be assailants and a minute to think.

We had two large backpacks and two small day packs. Buried somewhere in one of the packs was a large navy seal knife that I desperately wanted to retrieve. I absolutely did not want to make a scene or give the impression that anything was wrong. All of my maneuvering was done under the guise that this was all part of the plan. I even put my Spanish book away to seem a little bit less lost and touristy. In my mad scramble for my knife I heard Heather say, "I think that man just yelled our names."

I stood up and looked to our right where a small Hispanic man was yelling something in Spanish. I couldn't make out a word he was saying but every so often it did sound a bit like Heather and Gary. I asked Heather to move up the road a bit and stay with the bags so I could see her while I went to talk to the man. When I approached the man I circled around behind him to force him to turn around so I could see Heather while I attempted to talk with him. This seemed to make him a bit nervous but at this point his comfort level was not exactly on the top of my priority list.

I tried my best to understand what the hell he was going on about but it was quite pointless. All I could get out of him was "Gary / Heather" and that was questionable. When I asked about Sonja he did not really respond, but when I said her name repeatedly he would repeat it back to me. He kept motioning for me to get in his car. This was not something that I had a good feeling about. It made perfect sense that if our itinerary had been intercepted he would lure us into his car and haul us off to the cartel to start the bidding war. But there was

also the chance that he had some affiliation with Sonja and was going to take us to our new home. What a dichotomous set of choices.

I went back and talked to Heather about what I had learned from our conversation……NOTHING…..to be exact. Though the guy did not seem particularly threatening and my spider sense was not completely on tilt I didn't feel like he was going to be taking us for tea and crumpets any time soon.

While we were discussing our options I said, "SCREW IT, let's just take our tent and head into the jungle for the night, we can come back here and sort things out in the light of day." We were discussing that very option with this guy yelling in Spanish from a distance when our minds were made up for us. Just as we were about to pull the trigger on the jungle option I looked up only to see the 3 guys with machine guns closing the distance.

At this point any option that got us out of this nightmare of a village and away from the machete militia and automatic weapon toting maniacs seemed like a good idea. ……………………………. We got in the car.

Though we were nervous about the driver and his intentions we were still relieved to be out of that village and away from what seemed like certain death. As the car drove further down the street we could see the light from the poles fade and we felt much better. Better that is until we drove headlong into pitch blackness. Further and further away from anything. Out into the darkness and away from any kind of civilization at all.

After some time we began to whisper to each other in the back. I remember being worried that the driver may only be pretending not to speak English so he could get information from us. We kept our voices below hearing range. I don't remember the nature of our conversation but I know that the consensus was that we were screwed.

In every related movie I had ever seen, they always drove the victims out to some remote location to unleash their evil plot far from prying eyes. This seemed like the perfect way to get to such a place. True to movie form the wind, rain and darkness washed over the swaying palm trees as we passed. The village that seemed like the worst place in the world now seemed like a sanctuary lost. We just wanted to turn around and go back to a place with people and those very wonderful light bulbs hanging from poles.

The entire time we were driving I was leaning into the front seat talking to the driver. I could not understand a single word of his responses but I was trying to gauge his demeanor. I quickly learned as we traveled, to pick up on body language and tone which said a lot more than words you couldn't understand. This fellow however had amazing neutrality about him, a poker face to beat all poker faces. He could have been a school teacher or a henchman I just couldn't tell.

As I leaned back into the seat to whisper to Heather I realized that my knife was once again out of my reach. In our haste to get out of town we threw our backpacks in the trunk and fled. All I had now was the multi-tool in my fleece pocket (which I had been gripping tightly the entire drive). I told Heather that I was going to insist that the driver take us back to town. We were now far away from any houses and any civilization of any kind. Wherever we were it couldn't be good.

As we reached the crest of yet another dark hilltop I told the driver (in my best charades) to take us back to town immediately. I was very firm in my request and the driver could tell something was wrong. He jabbered away in Spanish and pointed over the hill. As we came over the crest of the hill we could see a lone house with a light on at the bottom. It should have given us comfort but it did not. Every development had two possible outcomes. It could be Sonja's house or it could be the safe house where we were being delivered for "processing."

As we approached the house it soon became very clear that it most definitely was not Sonja's house. It was a small unkempt place lit only by a single light in the main room. I was praying that the driver would leave the car running as he pulled over and made his exit from the automobile, but he did not.

Heather and I began to quickly formulate a plan. When and if the driver returned we were going to insist that he return us to town immediately. If he refused we were going to get out and start walking. We thought that this would cut through the communication barrier and help us get down to his true intentions. But before we had a chance to launch our plan, things took a turn for the worse.

Inside the small house we could see the diminutive cab driver's silhouette behind a sheet hanging over the window. He was eclipsed by a huge man who was growing increasingly upset. Once again we could not understand what was being said as the two men began to yell at one another. We watched the scene play out before us, struggling to understand what was being said. I could only make out two words that seemed to be repeating with intensity "La Muchacha and El Dinero"…………… The girl and the money.

This was the first time that I really felt it had come down to life and death, it was clear to me that they were negotiating the amount to be paid for Heather. What nefarious plan they had for her I could not imagine or rather I did not want to imagine. One thing was for sure though…they were about to experience the fight of their lives. Now speculation was finished and my attention was one hundred percent focused on my assault plan. I switched places with Heather so that I was seated directly behind the driver's seat.

My plan was simple but violent. I opened my multi-tool to the longest blade available…..only two and a half or three inches in total but it would have to do. I slipped it handle first inside the elastic sleeve of my fleece with the blade pointed out toward my hand. When the driver returned we were going to refuse to get out of the same car that we wanted so desperately to escape from only minutes ago.

Every scenario that we found to be terrible somehow soon became the lesser of two evils. Every time we got what we wanted it seemed like we were better off with what we had. What had we gotten ourselves into?

Though I was convinced we would soon be fighting for our lives, I still wanted to alleviate the risk of killing an innocent man. I told Heather under no circumstances, not by knife point not by gun point not for any reason were we going to get out of that car. I knew once they took us into that house where they controlled the environment it would be over for us. More importantly I knew that any rational human being would not try to physically force us out of the car just because we couldn't understand what each other were saying. So the plan was simple really if they tried to force us out of the car then they intended to kill us…….and we would reciprocate in kind.

We locked the back doors and waited. There were really only two courses of action they could take and I had a plan for each. They could attempt to force us out here and drag us into the house or they could get in with guns and drive us some place else.

If they tried to force us out I would jump over the front seat and start the car while wildly stabbing anyone trying to prevent me from doing so……at which point we would flee. If they tried to drive us off at gun point I would do in the armed assailant by cutting his throat from behind as we drove. Then I would turn my attention to the driver. My plan was to kill him and then drag his body on top of the dead gunmen so that Heather could climb over and try to get control of the wheel.

It was a pretty messy plan and there was a pretty good likelihood that we would end up shot and/or crashed. Still it was definitely better than going along without a fight. At least this way maybe I could at the minimum buy Heather a chance to escape.

Once the screaming stopped inside the house the driver made a hasty return to our car. He jumped in the driver seat and sped away. This was neither of the scenarios I had planned for. I still could not decisively determine his intentions. Did he get cold feet and suddenly grow a conscience and decide he couldn't go through with it, or had he just successfully negotiated his fee for dropping us off at the safe house.

I now slid the multi-tool out into my hand but still out of sight. I knew that this would be the best opportunity to make our escape……but I was still unwilling to do anything drastic until I knew for sure that this guy was not on our side. Once again when I thought things could not possibly get worse, they did……….

Not more than a quarter mile or so from the house I could see the head lights of an on coming vehicle. The comforting feeling of another human being in our vicinity soon passed as the vehicle turned sideways in the road blocking our path. It was an old pick up truck and it was parked kitty corner in the street in such a way that the headlight glare obscured our view of the driver. We could see several people in the truck but could not make out anymore detail than that.

I was convinced now that the driver had in fact grown a conscience and decided to drive us away from the kidnappers. I knew however that his kind gesture would probably now assure him the same fate as us.

As the gunmen approached our vehicle I was ready to spring my plan into action and with the cab driver now on our side I felt like our chances of success were greatly increased. When the driver of the truck finally came into view I was surprised to see that it was a young, dark skinned, rather attractive woman. While I was taking the whole thing in I heard her say "Gary, Heather is that you?"……it's me Sonja.

I can't describe the overwhelming feeling of relief that poured over me. My heart was still pounding but I finally felt like we might just live to see the morning light and best of all we were going to do it without killing a single person or spending any time in a particularly undesirable foreign prison system.

Sonja spoke a few words to the driver in Spanish handed him some money and motioned for us to come with her. We were still a little skeptical but now we could see several children in the truck and it felt like the best offer we had all night. Very little was said as we drove the next few blocks to our house. When we arrived Sonja opened a chained gate that guarded another cinder block fence adorned with broken glass. She told us to follow her, and we did. She led us up the dark steps to the front door and said, "Whatever you do don't leave anything outside and be sure to lock your doors."

We entered the small house and sat our backpacks on the floor. Sonja said she had some clean drinking water in the truck and she left to retrieve it. We had so many questions for her. Who were the men with machine guns, what was with the driver and how did she find us?

We closed the door to fend off the millions of malaria ridden mosquitoes that were drawn to the light and waited for her to return. We scanned the room while we waited. We quickly noticed that every window and door was heavily guarded by thick iron bars, but other than that the place did not look so bad. There was a couch and although it was completely wrapped in heavy plastic it still looked inviting.

From the entry door we could see the whole place. The kitchen and living area were combined into one small room. The kitchen had no stove but it did have a rusty propane cook top and a small fridge. The tiny bedroom had no door but it did have two small beds with sheets. After the long plane ride, infinite bus trip and brush with the machete militia the two small beds seemed like a suite at the Four Seasons.

All we needed to do was get the low down from Sonja on the safe places in town and our strange trip through the village and we could have some peace of mind on our way to slumber land. We were sure that there must be some logical explanation for it all and once she explained we could sleep like babies. After some time however we began to wonder what had happened to Sonja as she had not yet returned with the water. I opened the door only to find the bottle of water sitting on the steps. Her truck was gone and so was she.

We were both exhausted by our prolonged adrenalin surges lack of sleep and the fact that it had been about 16 hours since we had really eaten anything substantial. We just wanted to get some sleep but we were both excited to check out our new place. We were also both a bit puzzled by Sonja's abrupt departure. We talked it over and decided that it was unlikely that she was part of some bigger conspiracy to kidnap or harm us. It would have been much easier to just subdue us earlier in the evening. Besides why would she bring us water if she were just going to have us killed later? Still her behavior struck us as a bit strange and we never got the answers to some pretty important questions.

It was clear that it was not entirely safe where we were and I secured the door with my backpack lock and chain in addition to the normal locks and paddle lock already on the inside of the door.

The place was a bit spartan to say the least but we were thrilled with it. It was exactly what we had been planning for. No hustle bustle no glitz and glamour just a simple place far from everything where we could figure out life's mysteries. It did not take long to soak the whole place in. There really wasn't much to it and we were about to collapse from exhaustion.

Before turning in I went to the kitchen to wash my hands. As I turned on the water I heard the pipes groan and saw a huge dark colored snake pop his head out of the drain just before a couple of sporadic spurts of dark brown water (that smelled like sewage) spurted out of the faucet. I quickly turned the tap off, made a deal with the snake to leave well enough alone and headed off to bed with dirty hands. I advised Heather not to use the water but did not say why and adjourned to the sweltering bedroom.

The windows had screens but they were riddled with holes and the roof wasn't much better. Even though we had taken a couple of doses of malaria medicine it was still a bit uncomfortable in a house full of unbelievable humidity, sweltering heat and infectious mosquitoes. None the less we were still pretty pleased with ourselves…..we had made it. We weren't living by the rules anymore and we were quite happy about it.

Even though we were completely exhausted it was very hard to sleep. The heat and the constantly marauding mosquitoes were one thing but the wind and noise was another thing all together. The area was surrounded by huge palms and the wind kept smashing the branches against the house. We were still pretty high strung and not sure if we were totally in the clear so each noise set our minds racing. We were not yet use to the sounds of the jungle and each monkey screech sounded like the devil himself at our doorstep. I convinced Heather that most of the sounds were just the wind but I was not so sure. I finally got my knife out of my pack, set it by the bedside and settled in for a much needed night sleep.

I could not have been asleep for more than ten or fifteen minutes when I heard something or someone on the roof. I jumped out of bed grabbed my knife and looked over at Heather. She was sitting straight up and her eyes were as wide as saucers. She raced over to my bed and jumped in. I motioned to my lips for her to be quiet and I got up and crept to the window. I saw nothing. We sat up in bed for another twenty minutes or so before we heard the sound again. What ever it was it sounded massive and it was on the roof again.

Now my imagination was going to work. What could it be…. and then suddenly there it was again. Now that I was fully awake I could tell that it was not someone or something walking on the roof. It was more like something being thrown onto the roof. It sounded like someone was throwing bottles on the roof to lure us out. I snuck over to the window again and sat quietly from a vantage point where I could not be easily seen. I staked the window out for about 15 minutes, my heart once again pounding, before I spotted the culprit.

The wind was blowing so hard it was knocking coconuts down onto the roof of the house. The sound of a coconut on a metal roof is really something the first time you hear it.

(We later learned the house had been unoccupied for a number of years before we came which is probably why the trees were over grown and there were snakes living in the drains). Now that the mystery had been solved we could get back to sleep. Despite the heat there would be no convincing Heather to sleep in her own bed. We crowded in one small bed and struggled to get to sleep.

This time I think I was asleep for about an hour or so before being awoken by a blood curdling scream. It was Heather and she was terrified. She was screaming hysterically "There is a HUGE FRIGGIN …%$!@^&^$#* in here." "Get out here right now!" Still half asleep I grabbed my knife and ran into the living room. When I saw what she saw I immediately knew that I was going to need something much bigger than a knife. I scanned the room for the best weapon possible for the situation.

Against the wall in the kitchen I saw a long handled squeegee used to push water out of the house under the huge gaps beneath the doors when the place was flooded from the rain. It seemed like the perfect weapon for the massive black scorpion stuck to the side of the wall only inches from the light switch to the bathroom. Heather half asleep and surrounded by darkness had just stuck her hand about 3 inches from the thing when she turned on the light to find the bathroom.

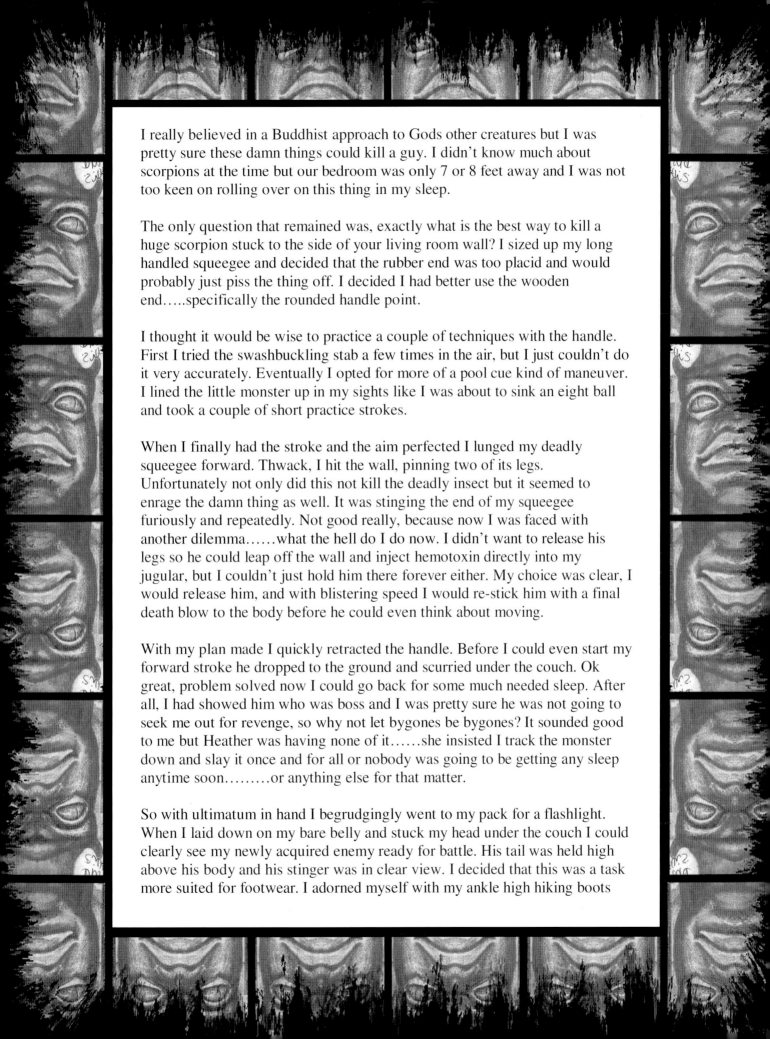

I really believed in a Buddhist approach to Gods other creatures but I was pretty sure these damn things could kill a guy. I didn't know much about scorpions at the time but our bedroom was only 7 or 8 feet away and I was not too keen on rolling over on this thing in my sleep.

The only question that remained was, exactly what is the best way to kill a huge scorpion stuck to the side of your living room wall? I sized up my long handled squeegee and decided that the rubber end was too placid and would probably just piss the thing off. I decided I had better use the wooden end…..specifically the rounded handle point.

I thought it would be wise to practice a couple of techniques with the handle. First I tried the swashbuckling stab a few times in the air, but I just couldn't do it very accurately. Eventually I opted for more of a pool cue kind of maneuver. I lined the little monster up in my sights like I was about to sink an eight ball and took a couple of short practice strokes.

When I finally had the stroke and the aim perfected I lunged my deadly squeegee forward. Thwack, I hit the wall, pinning two of its legs. Unfortunately not only did this not kill the deadly insect but it seemed to enrage the damn thing as well. It was stinging the end of my squeegee furiously and repeatedly. Not good really, because now I was faced with another dilemma……what the hell do I do now. I didn't want to release his legs so he could leap off the wall and inject hemotoxin directly into my jugular, but I couldn't just hold him there forever either. My choice was clear, I would release him, and with blistering speed I would re-stick him with a final death blow to the body before he could even think about moving.

With my plan made I quickly retracted the handle. Before I could even start my forward stroke he dropped to the ground and scurried under the couch. Ok great, problem solved now I could go back for some much needed sleep. After all, I had showed him who was boss and I was pretty sure he was not going to seek me out for revenge, so why not let bygones be bygones? It sounded good to me but Heather was having none of it……she insisted I track the monster down and slay it once and for all or nobody was going to be getting any sleep anytime soon………or anything else for that matter.

So with ultimatum in hand I begrudgingly went to my pack for a flashlight. When I laid down on my bare belly and stuck my head under the couch I could clearly see my newly acquired enemy ready for battle. His tail was held high above his body and his stinger was in clear view. I decided that this was a task more suited for footwear. I adorned myself with my ankle high hiking boots and prepared for combat. I felt like a knight going into the darkened cave of a dragon to slay the evil demon and save the fair maiden. The only problem was that my suit of armor consisted of little more than day old underwear and leather boots and my javelin was a rather modest house keeping utensil. Still………………. I had a job to do.

When I laid back down to look under the couch I had to decide how I was going to get this angry little bastard out into the open. I wanted to stick the squeegee end in first and make a big sweeping motion to the right, forcing him out into the open three or four feet to my right hand side. However, the configuration of the couch made it impossible. Each time I tried I couldn't really get the right angle and the stick just past over his body. I eventually had to lay the stick flat on the floor and use the squeegee end more like a craps dealer retrieving thrown dice. My plan was still to try to bring him out well to my right, but the motion was much more awkward than I envisioned.

In fact the technique didn't really work at all. Instead of angling him off to my right I actually managed to scoop him straight toward my torso. As I lay practically naked on my stomach I was forced to look down and see this beast with its tail raised and stinger poised about two inches from my face. At this point the damn thing could fly and breathe fire for all I knew so I didn't waste any time getting to my feet. In fact, I think I probably shot straight up about five feet in the air. When I landed, I stomped the miserable creature so hard I think I gave myself shin splints……and then I stomped it a few more times just to be safe.

At this point we just couldn't handle anymore drama…….no snakes, no malaria ridden mosquitoes and no God forsaken death bugs. We pushed our beds together and erected our screened jungle tent on top of them. We then crawled inside just as the sun began to rise.

The light of day could mean only one thing…I had survived my first day on the road.

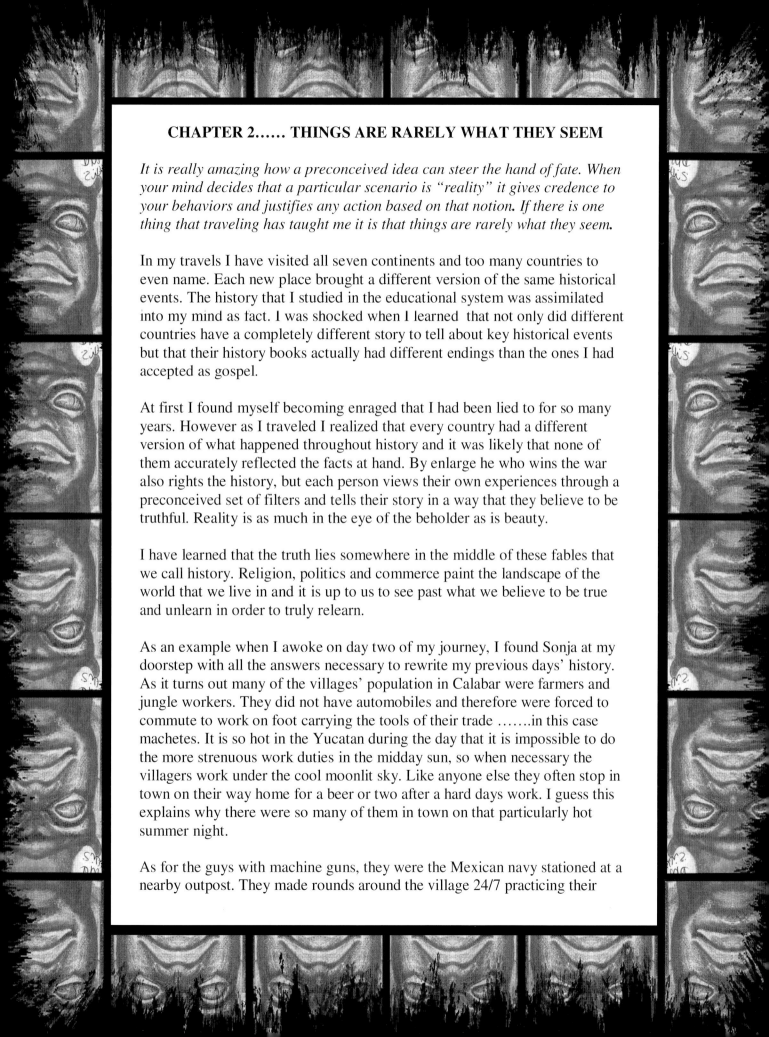

CHAPTER 2...... THINGS ARE RARELY WHAT THEY SEEM

It is really amazing how a preconceived idea can steer the hand of fate. When your mind decides that a particular scenario is "reality" it gives credence to your behaviors and justifies any action based on that notion. If there is one thing that traveling has taught me it is that things are rarely what they seem.

In my travels I have visited all seven continents and too many countries to even name. Each new place brought a different version of the same historical events. The history that I studied in the educational system was assimilated into my mind as fact. I was shocked when I learned that not only did different countries have a completely different story to tell about key historical events but that their history books actually had different endings than the ones I had accepted as gospel.

At first I found myself becoming enraged that I had been lied to for so many years. However as I traveled I realized that every country had a different version of what happened throughout history and it was likely that none of them accurately reflected the facts at hand. By enlarge he who wins the war also rights the history, but each person views their own experiences through a preconceived set of filters and tells their story in a way that they believe to be truthful. Reality is as much in the eye of the beholder as is beauty.

I have learned that the truth lies somewhere in the middle of these fables that we call history. Religion, politics and commerce paint the landscape of the world that we live in and it is up to us to see past what we believe to be true and unlearn in order to truly relearn.

As an example when I awoke on day two of my journey, I found Sonja at my doorstep with all the answers necessary to rewrite my previous days' history. As it turns out many of the villages' population in Calabar were farmers and jungle workers. They did not have automobiles and therefore were forced to commute to work on foot carrying the tools of their trade ....in this case machetes. It is so hot in the Yucatan during the day that it is impossible to do the more strenuous work duties in the midday sun, so when necessary the villagers work under the cool moonlit sky. Like anyone else they often stop in town on their way home for a beer or two after a hard days work. I guess this explains why there were so many of them in town on that particularly hot summer night.

As for the guys with machine guns, they were the Mexican navy stationed at a nearby outpost. They made rounds around the village 24/7 practicing their

formations. This explains why they seemed to be making a bee line right for us…..it was part of their patrol formation and pattern.

The driver was simply a (unmarked) cab driver who did not speak a word of English. Because not many people had cars in the village these guys stayed pretty busy taking people from place to place. Sonja had approached this gentleman earlier and told him that if he saw a couple of strange white people to bring them to her and she would pay him.

The argument with the large gentleman at the house was a result of the cab driver writing down the address incorrectly. The argument was because the driver insisted that a girl (la muchcha) would give him money (el dinero) if he brought the gringos to this address. The guy at the house had no idea what he was talking about and of course refused to pay for a couple of unwanted gringos.

Sonjas' vanishing act the previous night was a result of one of her children getting swarmed by the fire ants in the driveway. I can tell you first hand this is not a pleasant thing and is a good reason to split Dodge unannounced.

Sonja turned out to be a great person and she helped us in every way she could. In the months that we spent in Calabar it proved to be one of the safer places we visited and it provided some life long friendships and unforgettable memories.

Because I had made my mind up about the kind people of Calabar before I really knew them, I nearly murdered a completely innocent cab driver who was just trying to do his job. I am pretty sure that this would not have gone over well with local authorities. My guess is that it probably would have resulted in a less than enjoyable stay for Heather and I………………..Which is exactly what I was trying to avoid in the first place.

My future travels would include some other real eye openers:
- My own near death experience on Mt. Everest
- Watching a man murdered less than five feet away from me
- Being the center of an angry mobs attention in a nation in civil unrest

All of these things would happen in places that I had previously believed to be quite safe and relatively peaceful.

So as I said before "things are rarely what they seem."

One of the best experiences I have had in the Yucatan came on the eve of a surprise rainstorm. I had heard that there was a Mexican couple that served a meal of the day from their home on the ostera. As with everything in Bacalar the exact location was not quite clear. (No one has phones and most people gather) Everything is and hand information and usually it is quite vague we often walk to ... not azul and near as we could tell it ... befor that with a green door. We ... gear and our car ... out on Foot. After about walk around 5:3 ... up quickly and so minutes in ... step before our gear poured so ... zippers for our took perma ... els to get shelter (came ear) W ... saw yet another under a larg ...) we green door ... color for doors) we decided to ... we reached to a door there was a ne ... a string on the front of the locked ga ... s from the house. upon ringing we wait ... in the pouring rain to see if this infact was the correct green door. After a couple minutes time a quite mexican gentle with a full white beard came ... the door. Not yet very strong with the spanish I gestured toward my mouth and rubbed my stomach.

...ouds and cleaning. I believe that as you get a...
machine gets stronger from being exercised, much...
would. As your machine gains more capacity or ability...
additional processing power it allows mo... ...ess to th...
...ailable processing capability...
...hine more?...

entry Friday the thirt-   eenth 2007

I reflected on those events and people that have shaped
...or I have become. I don't necessarily mean monster is an evil
...or like some Franken-   sterian beast patched together
...xperience   Alone. I contemplated
...te   of heredity vs. Ken-
                            man destined, genetically
                            Or is he truly just
                            total of his ex
                            periences. When
                            you cease to ex
                            perience the -
                            previously
unknown, due except the fact that you
have begun to die. Or are you oblivious
that without new experiences and continued
learning your spirit begins to rot like a
soiled carcass in the desert heat. I used to
children, to help me understand the quest for
ledge and innate desire to learn which is so much-
...er in some than others. Now, or atleast lately I
...a become fascinated with those entering the twilight of
...lives. A select few desperately seek un-
...d where they can continue their evolution
...of them seem to realize the true motive
...re value of their actions. Survival instinct
...do not seem as prominent in all people as -
...of the world. Please let me learn from those
...have   learned the
...of -
...allow me to -   learning.
...se this practice
always.

The Vegetables in my mind are starting to fermente nicely.

I planted them with the hope that the pickling process wouldn't corrupt too many

Central nerve functions but now I am not so sure it was a good idea at all. There are subtle signs that this type of unnatural tampering is better left to professionals.

Vancouver Canada June twenty

MAY 20th 2002 ..... BROWNS POINT WASHINGTON
A CERTAIN VACANCY FILLS MY MIND TODAY. I AM
COMMITTED TO FAR TOO MANY MASTER TO SERVE THEM
ALL WELL. PRIORITY IS GIVEN TO THE MONETARY
MONSTER, AND I PAY THE PRICE. WITH THE PROMISE OF
LONG TERM REFUGE FROM THIS BEAST I TRUDGE FORWARD
A LITTLE LESS WILLINGLY EACH DAY. SPOILED BY MODERN
CONVENIENCE I STILL DO NOT REJOICE. I AM PLAGUED
WITH A INNATE QUEST. I MUST UNLOCK THE ONE MYSTERY
THAT HAS ESCAPED MANKIND
ALL TIME. WHAT IS TRUE
AND DOES IT HAVE ANY
ALL TO DO WITH A
SENSE OF HAPPINESS
IT AN [45] UNSOLVEABLE
WHERE KNOWLEDGE
WARENESS ARE ON
SIDE A HAPPINESS
CONTENTMENT ARE
THE OTHER SIDE AND
WO ARE DIAMETRICALLY

THROUGH OUT
CONTENTMEN
THING AT
TRUE
OR IS
FORMU
AND
ONE
AND
ON
THE
OPPOSED

IN GOD WE TRUST

One of many guests in my new home

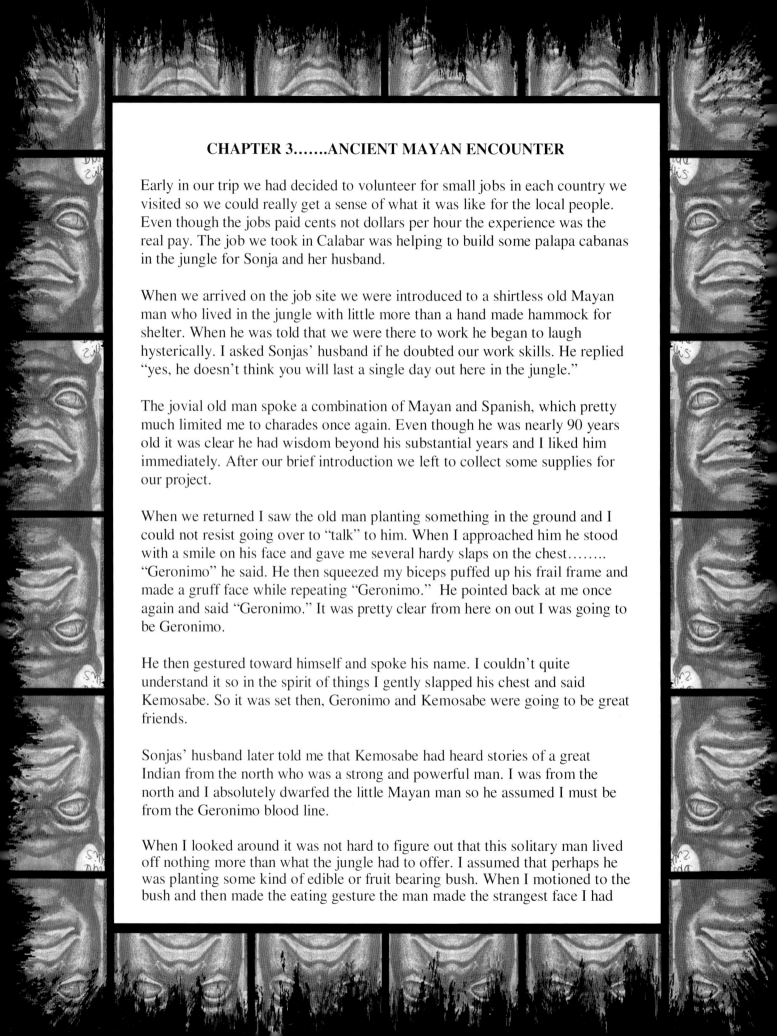

CHAPTER 3.......ANCIENT MAYAN ENCOUNTER

Early in our trip we had decided to volunteer for small jobs in each country we visited so we could really get a sense of what it was like for the local people. Even though the jobs paid cents not dollars per hour the experience was the real pay. The job we took in Calabar was helping to build some palapa cabanas in the jungle for Sonja and her husband.

When we arrived on the job site we were introduced to a shirtless old Mayan man who lived in the jungle with little more than a hand made hammock for shelter. When he was told that we were there to work he began to laugh hysterically. I asked Sonjas' husband if he doubted our work skills. He replied "yes, he doesn't think you will last a single day out here in the jungle."

The jovial old man spoke a combination of Mayan and Spanish, which pretty much limited me to charades once again. Even though he was nearly 90 years old it was clear he had wisdom beyond his substantial years and I liked him immediately. After our brief introduction we left to collect some supplies for our project.

When we returned I saw the old man planting something in the ground and I could not resist going over to "talk" to him. When I approached him he stood with a smile on his face and gave me several hardy slaps on the chest…….. "Geronimo" he said. He then squeezed my biceps puffed up his frail frame and made a gruff face while repeating "Geronimo." He pointed back at me once again and said "Geronimo." It was pretty clear from here on out I was going to be Geronimo.

He then gestured toward himself and spoke his name. I couldn't quite understand it so in the spirit of things I gently slapped his chest and said Kemosabe. So it was set then, Geronimo and Kemosabe were going to be great friends.

Sonjas' husband later told me that Kemosabe had heard stories of a great Indian from the north who was a strong and powerful man. I was from the north and I absolutely dwarfed the little Mayan man so he assumed I must be from the Geronimo blood line.

When I looked around it was not hard to figure out that this solitary man lived off nothing more than what the jungle had to offer. I assumed that perhaps he was planting some kind of edible or fruit bearing bush. When I motioned to the bush and then made the eating gesture the man made the strangest face I had ever seen. It was a combination of shock at my ignorance and concern for my survival. I was relieved to see that it was followed by a paternal like smile of acceptance.

The old man took me by the arm and dragged me out into the jungle. Plant after plant and tree after tree he showed me what could be eaten, what would kill me and what could be used for medicine. I had finally met my charade rival and I had an extremely hard time not laughing as he acted out various sicknesses. I was absolutely in awe of my new friend and I managed to subdue my laughter so as to not interrupt his teachings.

One of the more amazing things he showed me was something I think he called a fire skin tree. Through his charades and a few Spanish words it was clear that you did not even have to touch this tree to feel its bite. The tree apparently gave off a microscopic pollen that assaulted your body so instantly and so fiercely that you felt like your skin had been set on fire.

By showing me the shadow of the tree and gesturing to the sun moving up and down I believe he told me that anywhere that the tree could cast a shadow it could attack you with its pollen. I paid very close attention to what this tree looked like.

He then showed me that within ten paces of this tree there was an antidote tree. According to him these trees always grew within a few feet of each other. Once again I paid close attention to what the tree looked like. Apparently if the first tree got its evil hooks into you, you could rub the leaves of the second tree on your skin for relief of the condition.

I absolutely admired and respected this man for his knowledge of medicine and survival in the jungle. I could not believe that I was fortunate enough to meet such a man and I was sure that I would never meet anyone this knowledgeable about the ways of the jungle again.

The stories I could tell about this interesting old man could go on for pages. As with all the places I have visited there is always more to tell than can fit on a page. The one thing I can say however is that the time we spent on this job gave me a respect and awe for the jungle that I could only really gain through the eyes of a man who had spent a considerable lifetime learning its mysteries. I am grateful for the experience and honored to have been taken under the wing of such a man.

As with the first day of our trip our first job had proven to be a memorable one. When we completed it I had no idea that in a few short weeks we would be putting our lives in the hands of a jungle healer a dozen times more mysterious than the sagely Kemosabe.

CHAPTER 4……….. KEMOSABES' JUNGLE LESSON

Every person I have ever met has taught me something, even if it is what not to do. I have learned more about myself through the actions and behaviors of others than I can ever explain. Taking the time to listen to people's passions, problems and ideas has not only fueled my creativity and enhanced my knowledge of the world but it has probably saved my life on more than one occasion.

Kemosabes' diminutive stature and subtle demeanor made him an easy man to overlook. A little less effort on my part and I may have never gotten to know such a great man. A little less effort on his part and we never would have made it past hello.

I truly believe that everyone has something to teach us and extending ourselves and our ears to a stranger just may open our eyes to something we have never before experienced.

I believe:
When you expect to learn from every person you meet you will learn.
When you expect to grow from each encounter you will grow.
When you expect these opportunities to find you, you will wait in vain.

Kemosabe didn't just teach me about the ways of the jungle plants he taught me about the ways of the jungle life. With little more than a hammock to your name you can still find satisfaction in each day and each new experience.

NOVEMBER 8 — Today we explore ...ncient... Ruins of Chacchoben (Red Corn). The Mayans were an ancient civilization of Architects and Astrologers. Their Hyr- glyphics speak of modern times like 1989 and 2112 when they believe the Sun will have a negative imp[act] on earth. one of their predictions was tha[t] in 1989 the Sun would start to damag[e] the earth with radiation. And in 2112 it would have a much more devastating i[mpact] act on our world. In 1989 plan[ts] began to ...

Quite a Strange Creature the Mayan scarab from below evolution accumulost spirit as you can see the diagram the MEY is very is it is him as though. the of the

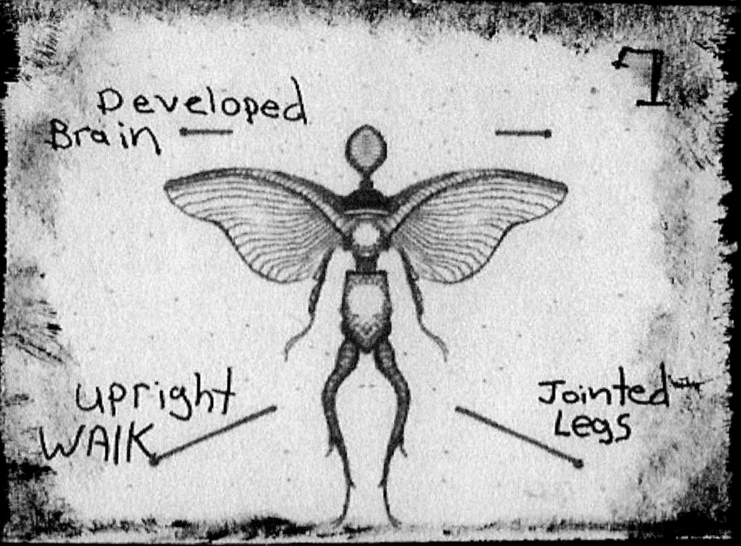

Developed Brain — 7

Upright WALK — Jointed Legs

Mayan People lives on, in this high advanced insect. The series shows the last three stages in re- of evolution the top vers. order. At ous is the croni erea ous.

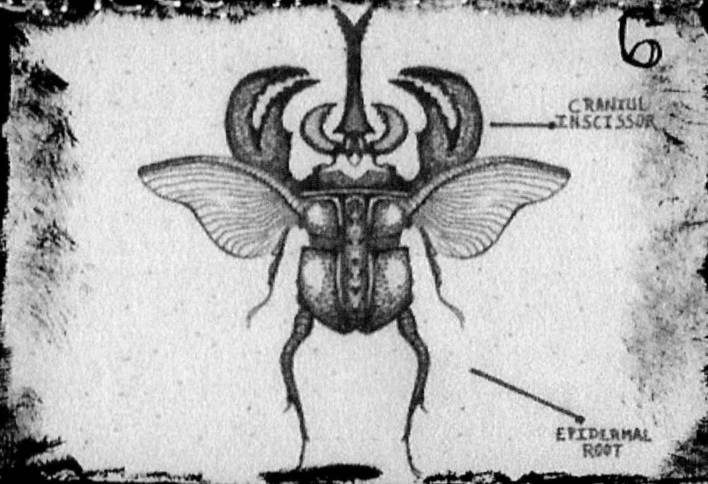

CRANIUL INSCISSOR — 6

EPIDERMAL ROOT

Adult beetles can walk upright and Seem to be Capable of cog nitive thou ght and even the abi lity to rea son. My sketche dont be gin todo thess mag nif

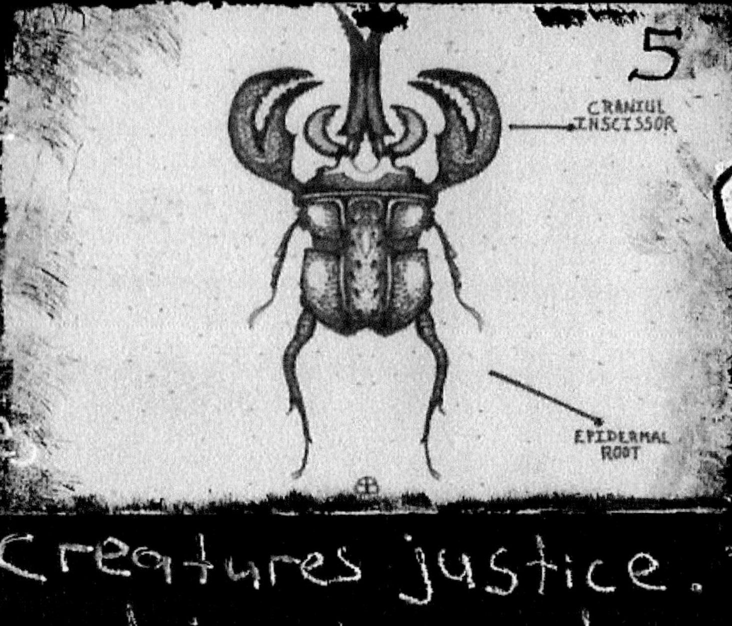

CRANIUL INSCISSOR — 5

EPIDERMAL ROOT

icent creatures justice. They can only be found in direct proximity to this

THE SIMPLE THINGS

NOVEMBER

we normally spend
220 on lunch.

BACALAR TACOS 60¢

The Simple 10¢

Its funny how, when you are traveling the s
leasures go farther then you would imagine.
For example today we traveled to the
city and went to the only modern
grocery stores for many miles. It was
so refreshing, though we didn't buy much
we looked forever. We returned home
on a small bus with about 40
people intended to hold 20 at the
most. Simple pleasure #1 going
to a grocery store. Simple pleasure
#2 Doppinees Pizza. Though we absolutely
love the local cuisine it often makes
us quite Ill. We spent $20.00 today
on the worse Damn Pizza I have ever
had and it was the biggest high
point in the last couple of days.
We had heard that Chetumal
had Pizza but like many other
things around here it was an
unsubstantiated rumor at
best. But the legend was
true. Simple pleasure #3
running water two days in
a row now. Dirty But
Running

Quenca, we use the traditional method of fishing with hand poles. We put about 40 meters of hand gangline baited with a twelve inch and some dead fish fillets. You hold the line and wait for the bite. I can only assume when you actually get a fish on that you... We tell how over hang on the line until you land the fish but the b... cause did not catch on film. But the b... Quenca took... was quite nice none the less. Quenca... for a tour of the coastline in... he got dumbo...

his banana boat racing through... a little by racing through... swells. The love to drink... Even... captain standing of... the boat. Even... trailing through the swell... We love the boat with a... wife who have traveled quite a bit... around the World. His name is... and hers is Connie. They are la... and the Yucatan. The reef in front of... rays, lots of conch some... mad... and wonderful...

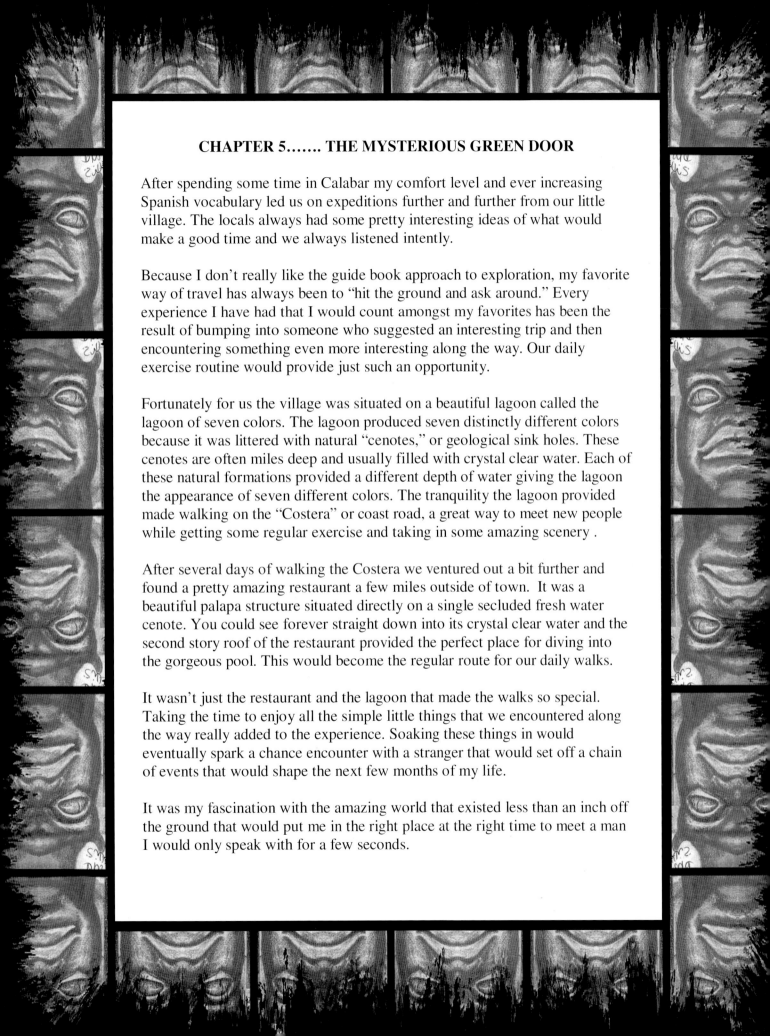

CHAPTER 5……. THE MYSTERIOUS GREEN DOOR

After spending some time in Calabar my comfort level and ever increasing Spanish vocabulary led us on expeditions further and further from our little village. The locals always had some pretty interesting ideas of what would make a good time and we always listened intently.

Because I don't really like the guide book approach to exploration, my favorite way of travel has always been to "hit the ground and ask around." Every experience I have had that I would count amongst my favorites has been the result of bumping into someone who suggested an interesting trip and then encountering something even more interesting along the way. Our daily exercise routine would provide just such an opportunity.

Fortunately for us the village was situated on a beautiful lagoon called the lagoon of seven colors. The lagoon produced seven distinctly different colors because it was littered with natural "cenotes," or geological sink holes. These cenotes are often miles deep and usually filled with crystal clear water. Each of these natural formations provided a different depth of water giving the lagoon the appearance of seven different colors. The tranquility the lagoon provided made walking on the "Costera" or coast road, a great way to meet new people while getting some regular exercise and taking in some amazing scenery .

After several days of walking the Costera we ventured out a bit further and found a pretty amazing restaurant a few miles outside of town. It was a beautiful palapa structure situated directly on a single secluded fresh water cenote. You could see forever straight down into its crystal clear water and the second story roof of the restaurant provided the perfect place for diving into the gorgeous pool. This would become the regular route for our daily walks.

It wasn't just the restaurant and the lagoon that made the walks so special. Taking the time to enjoy all the simple little things that we encountered along the way really added to the experience. Soaking these things in would eventually spark a chance encounter with a stranger that would set off a chain of events that would shape the next few months of my life.

It was my fascination with the amazing world that existed less than an inch off the ground that would put me in the right place at the right time to meet a man I would only speak with for a few seconds.

One night while walking home I took the opportunity to meet the jungles tiniest inhabitants. I was particularly interested in the work habits and discipline of the leaf cutter ants marching past the soles of my boots. They were transporting leaves on their backs using extremely complicated and intersecting multidirectional super highways.

Some of the lanes of ant traffic were for the ants with no leaves on their way to the harvest and some lanes were for the ants returning home with the fruits of their labor in tow. The ants numbered in the millions and the highways went up and down trees, through fields and around every obstacle you could imagine. There was so much traffic that the microscopic little ants eventually wore a foot trail through the blades of grass and weeds that obstructed their path.

It was while watching these little guys do their work that we were approached by a local man named Jose. I think he was compelled to stop and see why I had been bent over for so long staring at the ground.

My Spanish was still pretty weak so asking people about good places to eat or drink always made for the easiest conversation. I could tell Josc enjoyed a good meal and it wasn't long before he said that he had heard that there was a man and woman not far from town that served meals out of their home.

He claimed that the food was more authentic and far cheaper than the cenote restaurant and suggested we give it a try. He had never been there himself, but he had heard good things. He gave us what he believed to be the directions and wished us luck on our travels.

Getting directions from the local people was always an adventure in the making and this would be no exception. We probably made 4 or 5 initial attempts to find the allusive dinner house. Each time we would fail we would stop and ask one of the locals for new directions and try again the next day. Through the language barrier and tribal knowledge only one part of the directions came through clearly each time. The people who did the cooking apparently had a big green door.

With numerous accounts of the alleged green door and several failed attempts at finding the place we made a pact to track down the mystery house of "las camidas." With our commitment set in stone I packed my camera gear, several journaling supplies and some water into a small day pack. Filled with anticipation we set off to find the mysterious green door.

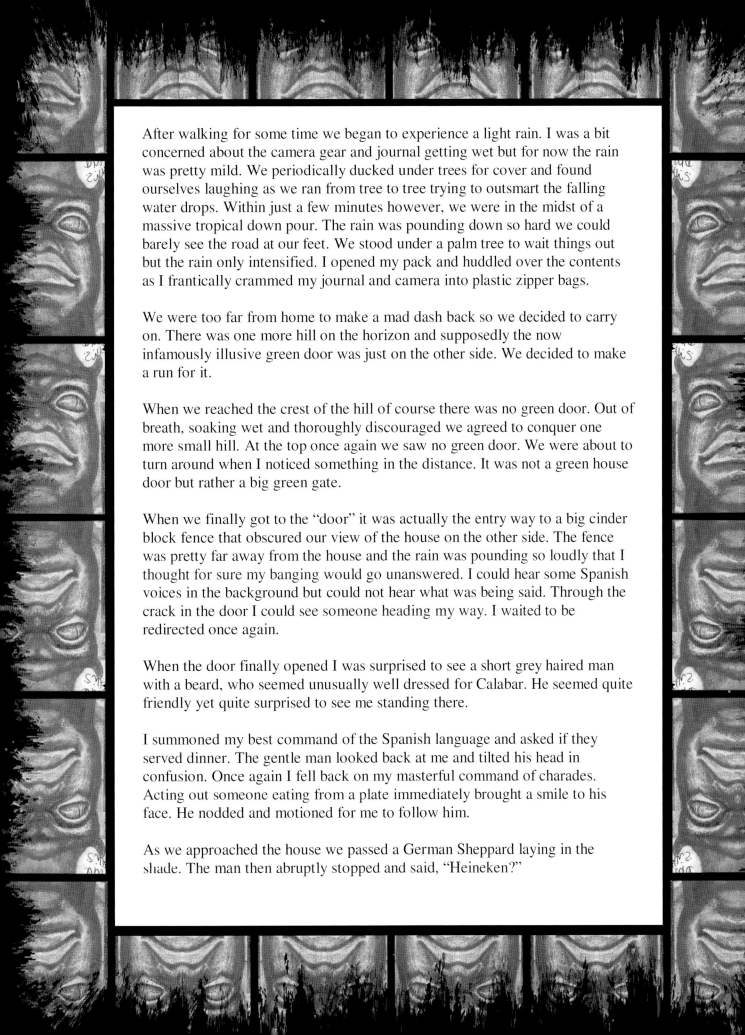

After walking for some time we began to experience a light rain. I was a bit concerned about the camera gear and journal getting wet but for now the rain was pretty mild. We periodically ducked under trees for cover and found ourselves laughing as we ran from tree to tree trying to outsmart the falling water drops. Within just a few minutes however, we were in the midst of a massive tropical down pour. The rain was pounding down so hard we could barely see the road at our feet. We stood under a palm tree to wait things out but the rain only intensified. I opened my pack and huddled over the contents as I frantically crammed my journal and camera into plastic zipper bags.

We were too far from home to make a mad dash back so we decided to carry on. There was one more hill on the horizon and supposedly the now infamously illusive green door was just on the other side. We decided to make a run for it.

When we reached the crest of the hill of course there was no green door. Out of breath, soaking wet and thoroughly discouraged we agreed to conquer one more small hill. At the top once again we saw no green door. We were about to turn around when I noticed something in the distance. It was not a green house door but rather a big green gate.

When we finally got to the "door" it was actually the entry way to a big cinder block fence that obscured our view of the house on the other side. The fence was pretty far away from the house and the rain was pounding so loudly that I thought for sure my banging would go unanswered. I could hear some Spanish voices in the background but could not hear what was being said. Through the crack in the door I could see someone heading my way. I waited to be redirected once again.

When the door finally opened I was surprised to see a short grey haired man with a beard, who seemed unusually well dressed for Calabar. He seemed quite friendly yet quite surprised to see me standing there.

I summoned my best command of the Spanish language and asked if they served dinner. The gentle man looked back at me and tilted his head in confusion. Once again I fell back on my masterful command of charades. Acting out someone eating from a plate immediately brought a smile to his face. He nodded and motioned for me to follow him.

As we approached the house we passed a German Sheppard laying in the shade. The man then abruptly stopped and said, "Heineken?"

Finally someone who could speak my language, a beer is exactly what I needed, so I said, "Si dos cervesas por favor." The man replied, "No………… Heineken." I thought to myself, far be it for me to argue with a man offering me beer. "I'll take whatever you have," I quickly replied with a smile on my face.

The man stared at me and I could tell he was trying to find the words to tell me something that I would understand. He shook his head and carefully spoke the word "DOG" and then "Heineken." I finally understood I was being introduced to a member of the family, Heineken the German Sheppard. Little did I know at the time that I too would soon be part of the family. I reached down and gave Heineken some scratches on the ear and proceeded behind the house.

On a beautiful deck overlooking the lagoon sat a lone table beautifully adorned with a clean table cloth and some fresh flowers. The man motioned for us sit down and we were happy to do so. As we were introducing ourselves a regal dark skinned women with a huge smile on her face came out of the house. I stood up and butchered an introduction in Spanish.

She replied in perfect English, "I am Miim and this is my husband Navi." I knew immediately that these were going to be special people. I could have never guessed that these people would become such a huge part of my life. I could have never guessed that they would set me on a path to one of the most bizarre and yet fascinating experiences of my life. Nor would I have ever guessed that they would open their home to me, house me, feed me and care for me while I lay in their bed so sick from Dengue Fever that I thought death might be an improved alternative.

Right now however all that I could think about was getting some of the food I had heard so much about. After some brief introductions came the question I was waiting to hear. Only I didn't understand it at the time. Navi asked me if I would like some cellas (a word I had never heard before). When I stared back at him blankly, he raised a finger as if to say wait a minute before departing for the kitchen. When he returned he was holding two ice cold bottles of beer.

Over beers Miim returned to explain that they did not have a menu but rather one set meal for the day. As the rain died down Heather and I looked at each other with amazement. We were in the most beautiful setting in the world, with the genuinely nicest human beings you could ever meet and we were about to have a home cooked meal that smelled delicious. This is exactly the kind of experience we had hoped for when we left home.

Part way through our beers the first course arrived……it was simply the best bowl of soup I have ever had. This was the first and last place I would ever eat carrot soup. In my mind this magnificent dish firmly planted Wolfgang Puck in a distant second as the worlds foremost soup chef. This was only the first of five absolutely amazing dishes yet to come…..each one more magnificent than the last.

To add to the beautiful scene, adjacent to the deck was a huge tree swarming with fruit bats that would periodically buzz the table. When I asked about the tree, Miim sent Navi to retrieve a fruit. It was something that I had never heard of before, a fruit called a zapote. Its taste and texture were quite indescribable but it made the perfect post dessert, dessert.

After dinner we stayed and visited for quite some time. I was worried we were overstaying our welcome, but as the sun began to set on the lagoon the whole experience was just too magical to pry myself away from.

With the sun now low enough to reflect all of the colors in the lagoon Navi raised his finger once again. This was a gesture I soon came to appreciate. It meant that he was going to go into the house and retrieve something that I was really going to like. When he came back he held a special bottle in his hand. He looked at the bottle shook his finger and made the money sign by rubbing his fingers together. I immediately understood that I could not buy this drink. What I did not really understand was why he was showing it to me.

Miim soon returned from the kitchen and explained that this was from Navis' private stash, premium label tequila that they were not aloud to sell because they did not have the proper licenses. According to Miim, Navi wanted to share some with me "gratis" because he now considered us friends. It is a moment I will never forget, and today I miss these people with all my heart. The only regret that I have ever had about my travels is that I have lost touch with these wonderful human beings over the years.

As the evening drew to a close the rain began to fall heavily once again and it was time to say goodbye. Navi offered to drive us home but they had already done so much I just couldn't impose. We borrowed a couple plastic bags strapped our flashlights to our heads and started the long walk home.

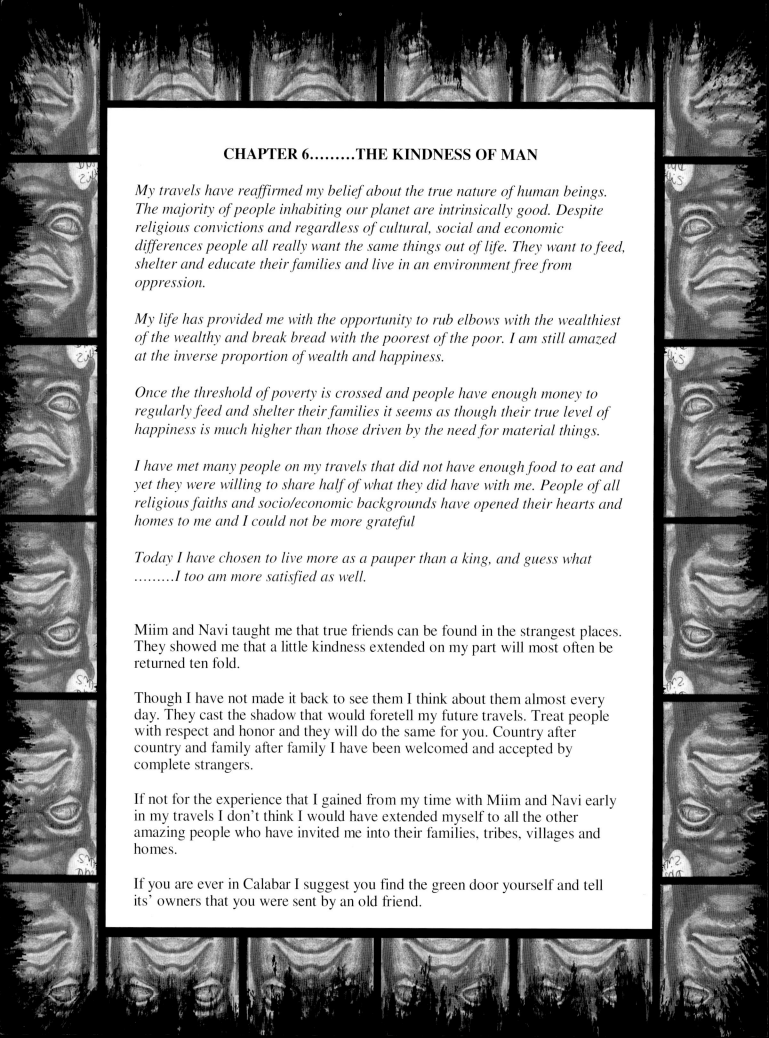

CHAPTER 6.........THE KINDNESS OF MAN

My travels have reaffirmed my belief about the true nature of human beings. The majority of people inhabiting our planet are intrinsically good. Despite religious convictions and regardless of cultural, social and economic differences people all really want the same things out of life. They want to feed, shelter and educate their families and live in an environment free from oppression.

My life has provided me with the opportunity to rub elbows with the wealthiest of the wealthy and break bread with the poorest of the poor. I am still amazed at the inverse proportion of wealth and happiness.

Once the threshold of poverty is crossed and people have enough money to regularly feed and shelter their families it seems as though their true level of happiness is much higher than those driven by the need for material things.

I have met many people on my travels that did not have enough food to eat and yet they were willing to share half of what they did have with me. People of all religious faiths and socio/economic backgrounds have opened their hearts and homes to me and I could not be more grateful

Today I have chosen to live more as a pauper than a king, and guess what ....I too am more satisfied as well.

Miim and Navi taught me that true friends can be found in the strangest places. They showed me that a little kindness extended on my part will most often be returned ten fold.

Though I have not made it back to see them I think about them almost every day. They cast the shadow that would foretell my future travels. Treat people with respect and honor and they will do the same for you. Country after country and family after family I have been welcomed and accepted by complete strangers.

If not for the experience that I gained from my time with Miim and Navi early in my travels I don't think I would have extended myself to all the other amazing people who have invited me into their families, tribes, villages and homes.

If you are ever in Calabar I suggest you find the green door yourself and tell its' owners that you were sent by an old friend.

Ancient Grounds
"A New coffee shop"
Discovery

Telephone Doodle

253-852-8093
"CAFE"

REMOVES USAMA BIN LADEN
CIA
#1 CLEANING AGENT

DEC 17

114336423515461141

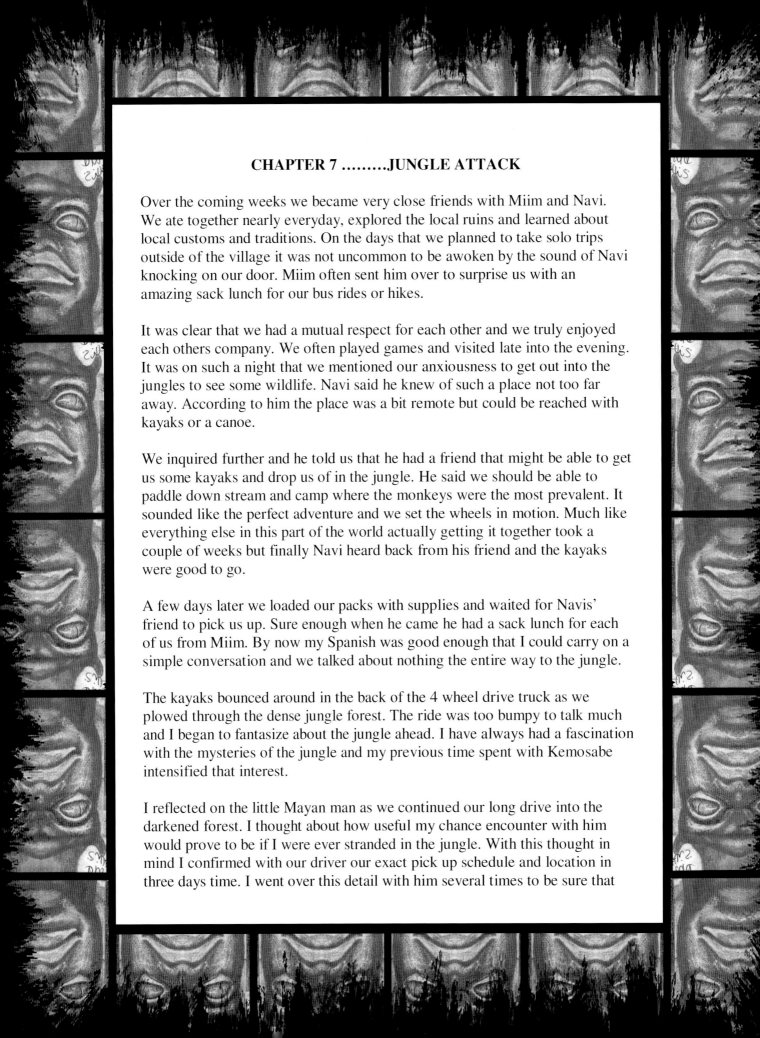

CHAPTER 7 ....JUNGLE ATTACK

Over the coming weeks we became very close friends with Miim and Navi. We ate together nearly everyday, explored the local ruins and learned about local customs and traditions. On the days that we planned to take solo trips outside of the village it was not uncommon to be awoken by the sound of Navi knocking on our door. Miim often sent him over to surprise us with an amazing sack lunch for our bus rides or hikes.

It was clear that we had a mutual respect for each other and we truly enjoyed each others company. We often played games and visited late into the evening. It was on such a night that we mentioned our anxiousness to get out into the jungles to see some wildlife. Navi said he knew of such a place not too far away. According to him the place was a bit remote but could be reached with kayaks or a canoe.

We inquired further and he told us that he had a friend that might be able to get us some kayaks and drop us of in the jungle. He said we should be able to paddle down stream and camp where the monkeys were the most prevalent. It sounded like the perfect adventure and we set the wheels in motion. Much like everything else in this part of the world actually getting it together took a couple of weeks but finally Navi heard back from his friend and the kayaks were good to go.

A few days later we loaded our packs with supplies and waited for Navis' friend to pick us up. Sure enough when he came he had a sack lunch for each of us from Miim. By now my Spanish was good enough that I could carry on a simple conversation and we talked about nothing the entire way to the jungle.

The kayaks bounced around in the back of the 4 wheel drive truck as we plowed through the dense jungle forest. The ride was too bumpy to talk much and I began to fantasize about the jungle ahead. I have always had a fascination with the mysteries of the jungle and my previous time spent with Kemosabe intensified that interest.

I reflected on the little Mayan man as we continued our long drive into the darkened forest. I thought about how useful my chance encounter with him would prove to be if I were ever stranded in the jungle. With this thought in mind I confirmed with our driver our exact pick up schedule and location in three days time. I went over this detail with him several times to be sure that there was no confusion. Little did I know at that time that the pick up would never occur.

After a long drive to get to the jungle entry point and a long and slow drive into the jungle itself we finally reached a clearing in the woods. It was a beautiful spot nestled up to the river and we unloaded our kayaks. He explained that about 4 miles down river there should be a great place to see and photograph the wildlife… especially the monkeys.

We shook hands and once again I confirmed the pick up details. As he drove away we had a great feeling about our adventure to come. We quickly set up camp, had some lunch and made our plan for the next couple of days. We would camp here for the night and head out by kayak in the morning.

With camp made I could enjoy one of my guilty pleasures …….. a good nap. Napping is the one time that I really get to be alone with my mind and it makes me feel like I am getting away with something, so I sneak one in whenever I can. Therefore it came as no surprise to Heather when I suggested that we take a nap in the tent with the river gurgling in the background and the shade perfectly perched over our heads. We really didn't have much else to do anyway so it was an easy sell.

As I drifted off I did not realize how short lived my tranquility would be. Unlike when I was awoken by screams of terror from the scorpion encounter, this time I was awoken by deep uncontrollable sobbing. Not fear……. but the aftermath of fear, the kind of crying that lets you know the terrible thing has already happened. Heather was a pretty tough girl and she didn't randomly breakdown without cause so I knew something was really wrong.

As I sat up in the tent it took me a minute or two to take it all in. I couldn't quite understand what she was saying through all of the tears. She was holding her arm with tears running down her face and I thought that she said something about being shot. When I regained my focus I could see that her arm was covered in a thick black tar like substance.

Through her deep sobbing I could now make out something about being attacked and something about shots…..but that was about it. I consoled her and got her to take some deep breaths. I just wanted her to tell me what happened so we could deal with it in the best way possible. Once she calmed down and I woke up fully I could better understand her and I got the full story.

Apparently she awoke from the nap before I did and went outside for a short walk. She stopped to pee in some bushes and as she was pulling up her pants, from out of nowhere, a big black dog attacked her. It chomped onto her arm and began to shake its' head ferociously. It opened up a pretty nasty wound and Heather was clearly traumatized by the whole thing.

It finally hit me……I knew what she meant about getting shot. It wasn't that she had been shot that had her so upset, it was that she hadn't.

Months earlier before we left the States we visited a travel doctor to get vaccinations for all the countries we were going to visit. Normally it's no big deal but when you are traveling around the world there are countless shots required. We went to the travel doctor pretty late in the game so whatever shots we were going to get, we were going to get that day.

Some shots were required, without proof of these shots you can't get into certain countries. Other shots were strongly recommended and some shots were optional. We got all of the required ones and pretty much all of the recommended ones. With so many shots in one day we were both a little nervous about getting pumped full of these crazy drugs all at once. The fact that some of them carried some undesirable side effects made us even more apprehensive. We weighed our choices carefully and decided which things we would be at risk for and which shots we could skip. Of course rabies is one of the shots we decided we would not need.

I distinctly remember the doctor telling us that there is no treatment for rabies…..once you have contracted it you die……just that simple. I had no idea that rabies was such a serious condition but getting bit by a rabid animal still seemed pretty unlikely so we were confident in our decision.

"If you do get bitten you still have a chance," the doctor said. He went on to explain that as long as you are not stuck in a remote location when you get bitten you may be able to get post bite treatment. Getting to a doctor immediately for shots could still save your life if the shots are administered before the symptoms of rabies start to manifest.

One of the only damn shots we didn't get and we were in the most remote of locations…..this was not good, but it did explain Heathers' concern.

I now knew what she meant by "shots" but I still could not quite piece together the rest of her story. I thought that maybe she was in shock because what she was telling me just did not make sense. She said that she let out a scream when

she was attacked and a strange woman came out of the jungle and got the dog off of her. That part was believable enough but the rest of the story was a bit hard to follow at first.

Apparently the woman put her hands on Heathers' shoulders and forced her to sit on the ground. Heather insisted that she get up and come to find me immediately but the woman was very forceful. She reached out and placed both of her hands on Heathers' head. When she did this Heather said that her feet immediately started to get very warm and then extreme heat began to travel up her body and into her head. The last thing she remembered before going unconscious was an extremely bright flash of white light.

When she awoke she was lying on her back and the woman was rubbing this tar like substance on her wounds. She winced from the pain causing the woman to place her hand directly on the wound. The heat that her hand generated was tremendous and Heather said that it felt like her skin was going to blister. When the woman removed her hand however the heat and the pain were completely gone. The woman then finished applying the tar which immediately sealed the wounds. She then motioned for Heather to come with her. Heather now fully awake stood and ran back to the tent immediately.

At this point in her story all kinds of things were going through my head…was Heather delirious, did she hit her head and have some sort of semi lucid dream? As I was pondering the possible explanations I fixed my sight on her arm covered in a thick black pitch….it must have come from somewhere?

The first thing I remember was reflecting on the doctors' advice. In the rare event we did receive a bite we could greatly reduce the risk of contracting rabies by cleaning and sterilizing the wound. That was good news. But he also said you have to get to a hospital immediately and get the shots. If the rabies set in the shots won't help. YOU HAVE TO GET THE SHOTS BEFORE YOU GET RABIES….IF YOU GET RABIES YOU WILL DIE!

As I scrambled for my medical kit I could see a silhouette approaching from outside the tent. Sure enough it was the strange medicine woman from the jungle. She told me something about giving Heather some more medicine, but the language barrier made it hard to understand exactly what she was saying. She began apologizing to me for "using too much power"…..which I didn't really understand at first. As she went on it became clear that she was referring to putting her hands on Heathers' head. She said that sometimes she can't control it and if she uses too much power, then the white light comes and people fall asleep.

I could barely believe what I was hearing and I wanted to ask her a million questions but I was extremely worried about Heather so I stayed focused on the task at hand. I did not want to be disrespectful of the lady or her medicine but I knew I had to clean and sterilize the wound. I could tell that the woman didn't like it when I began to remove the tar but out of respect for me she did not say anything. I thoroughly cleaned and sterilized Heathers' arm and with the tar gone I could see that it was a pretty nasty bite.

Without the black goo the wound began to bleed quite badly. The woman shook her head as to say of course dumb ass that is what the tar was for….but she didn't say a word. I think she could tell that we were both very concerned as I bandaged the arm.

I asked her if there was anyone with a car or telephone nearby……. as expected she said, "no." She then said that she would be happy to take care of Heather here in the jungle and that we should relax because everything was going to be OK.

Not that I disrespected her healing skills but I just didn't think she understood the whole rabies risk, so we declined.

With the wound cleaned I now turned my attention to getting out of the jungle and into the closest hospital I could find. I knew that this was not going to be an easy task. My immediate concern was getting out of the jungle before nightfall. I already knew that there were trees that could practically eat me alive. Lord only knows what other demon spawn was waiting to arise from the depths of the jungle floor under the cloak of darkness.

When I looked down at Heathers' watch to see how much daylight we had remaining I noticed that the second hand had stopped moving. Before I could say a word the woman interjected with another apology….. "I am sorry about the clock"….. "That happened once before when I used too much power, it should restart again in a few minutes."

For some reason after all that had happened that was the one thing that kind of gave me the chills…..but at the same time it added some credence to Heathers' story.

I didn't have time to stop and think about the strange power or the woman who was so eager to help. I was focused on beating darkness out of the jungle and getting some sort of non witch doctor treatment for Heather. I threw our things together and slung my pack onto my back.

Heather could walk just fine but I did not want her heart beating any faster than necessary. I thought an accelerated heartbeat might speed the introduction of rabies into her blood stream so I put her pack on frontwards and we began to make the long hike out of the jungle. After a few minutes of hiking Heather checked her watch once again and sure enough just as the woman had predicted it was working just fine.

I don't really remember much about the hike through the jungle. I was just focused on keeping a ferocious pace and beating the darkness. I remember thinking about all the weight in just one single pack. We had seriously over packed expecting that most of the time our gear would be stowed in or strapped to the kayaks not carried for long distances.

I was lugging two of these heavy monsters and I considered jettisoning some of the gear but I was not sure what we might encounter. In fact I was not sure if Heather would be able to make it the whole way out so I wanted to keep everything on hand just in case. At this point Heather was having a hard time keeping up with my fevered march anyway so making me faster would not really gain us anything.

As dusk fell on the jungle I could hear the sounds of passing traffic in the distance. I knew the road was close and our next major obstacle would soon be at hand. Even though we were almost out of the jungle, Calabar was miles away. Convincing anyone to stop for a couple of sweaty foreigners in the middle of nowhere could prove to be quite a challenge. I knew that if we did make it back to Calabar the nearest hospital was still miles away.

I had hoped to flag down a car or truck but there was not much traffic on this lonely road at nighttime. Much to my surprise after only a mile or so I saw a bus approaching in the distance. I stood in the middle of the road so he could not help but to stop. Once onboard I explained that Heather needed a doctor quickly. He said he was headed straight for Calabar with no more stops……a miracle in and of itself. These buses usually stop a few times every block or so to pick up or drop off passengers. An expeditious return to Calabar was quite unexpected.

We were able to get the driver to drop us off near Miim and Navis' house. Navi immediately drove us to the nearest hospital a couple of hours away. When we arrived it was truly a sight to behold. It was the only trauma center

for miles around and it was over run with bleeding people and chaos. It was a gruesome scene, people screaming and blood everywhere. Dirty blood soaked instruments were haphazardly thrown into piles and no one was available to help us for at least another hour and a half. I explained our sense of urgency but no one really took us seriously. I guess this was understandable. We were there for a dog bite and the man waiting next to us had a huge hole in his head.

When the chaos finally subdued we were taken back to see the doctor. I was very uncomfortable with the state of things in this place. Again more bloody instruments lying about and a general state of un-cleanliness and disorder everywhere.

We explained our situation to the doctor and requested the rabies treatment. He looked at us in a bewildered way and asked, "Do you have rabies now?" Once again we told him our tale and explained that our doctor in the States said that once you get rabies it is too late for treatment and that we should get shots immediately if bitten.

He scoffed and asked how long ago the bite had occurred. We added it up in our heads and calculated several hours. He examined the wound, wrapped it in some fresh bandages and said that the treatment would not be necessary. He said if we showed any signs of rabies we should come back. Even though this was the exact opposite advice we received in the States, he insisted that he had treated many dog bites and no one had ever asked for a series of rabies shot.

The idea of getting a shot in a place where we were convinced that they probably went down an assembly line of patients refilling and reusing the same syringe, wiping it off on their shirt sleeves in between injections, did not particularly appeal to us. The doctor was quite adamant and Heather seemed fine so we decided to wait on the shots.

In the end everything was fine and I guess the woman in the jungle was right after all. We should have just relaxed, left the black tar on and stayed in the jungle.

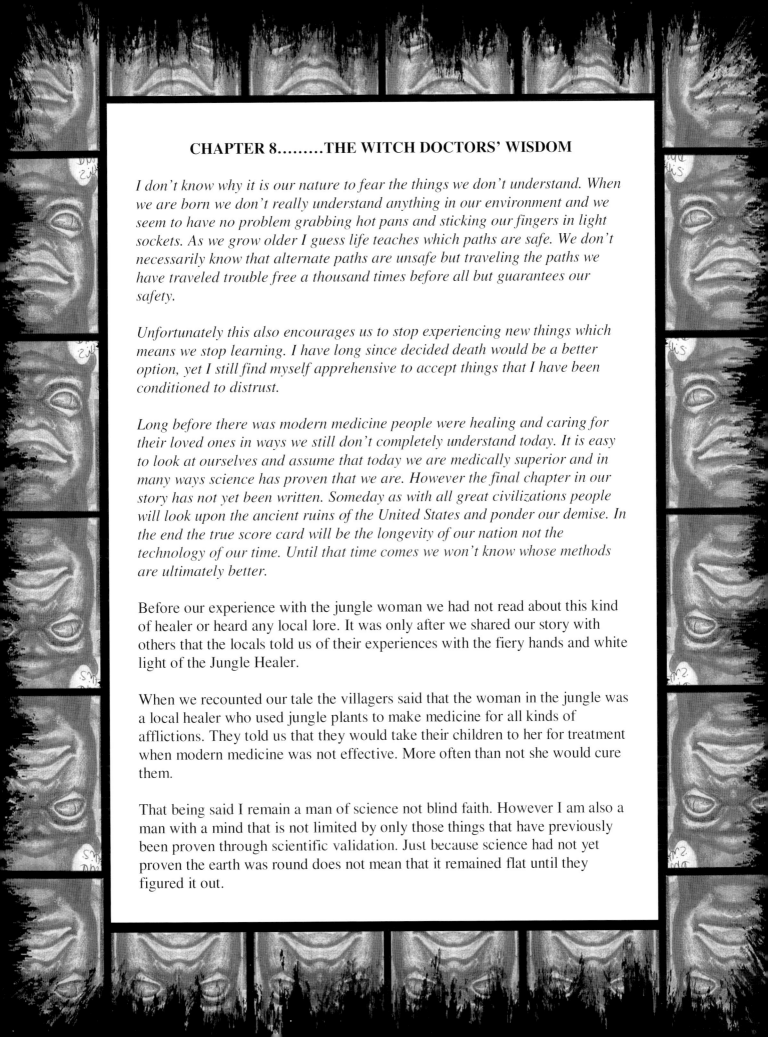

CHAPTER 8.........THE WITCH DOCTORS' WISDOM

I don't know why it is our nature to fear the things we don't understand. When we are born we don't really understand anything in our environment and we seem to have no problem grabbing hot pans and sticking our fingers in light sockets. As we grow older I guess life teaches which paths are safe. We don't necessarily know that alternate paths are unsafe but traveling the paths we have traveled trouble free a thousand times before all but guarantees our safety.

Unfortunately this also encourages us to stop experiencing new things which means we stop learning. I have long since decided death would be a better option, yet I still find myself apprehensive to accept things that I have been conditioned to distrust.

Long before there was modern medicine people were healing and caring for their loved ones in ways we still don't completely understand today. It is easy to look at ourselves and assume that today we are medically superior and in many ways science has proven that we are. However the final chapter in our story has not yet been written. Someday as with all great civilizations people will look upon the ancient ruins of the United States and ponder our demise. In the end the true score card will be the longevity of our nation not the technology of our time. Until that time comes we won't know whose methods are ultimately better.

Before our experience with the jungle woman we had not read about this kind of healer or heard any local lore. It was only after we shared our story with others that the locals told us of their experiences with the fiery hands and white light of the Jungle Healer.

When we recounted our tale the villagers said that the woman in the jungle was a local healer who used jungle plants to make medicine for all kinds of afflictions. They told us that they would take their children to her for treatment when modern medicine was not effective. More often than not she would cure them.

That being said I remain a man of science not blind faith. However I am also a man with a mind that is not limited by only those things that have previously been proven through scientific validation. Just because science had not yet proven the earth was round does not mean that it remained flat until they figured it out.

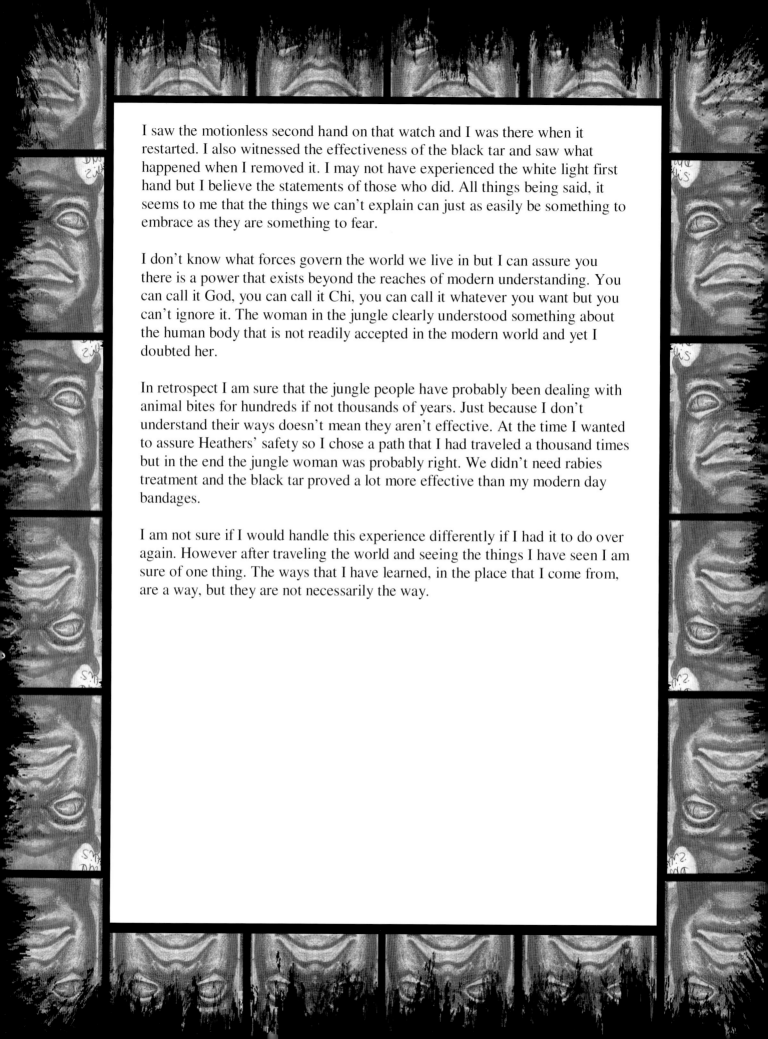

I saw the motionless second hand on that watch and I was there when it restarted. I also witnessed the effectiveness of the black tar and saw what happened when I removed it. I may not have experienced the white light first hand but I believe the statements of those who did. All things being said, it seems to me that the things we can't explain can just as easily be something to embrace as they are something to fear.

I don't know what forces govern the world we live in but I can assure you there is a power that exists beyond the reaches of modern understanding. You can call it God, you can call it Chi, you can call it whatever you want but you can't ignore it. The woman in the jungle clearly understood something about the human body that is not readily accepted in the modern world and yet I doubted her.

In retrospect I am sure that the jungle people have probably been dealing with animal bites for hundreds if not thousands of years. Just because I don't understand their ways doesn't mean they aren't effective. At the time I wanted to assure Heathers' safety so I chose a path that I had traveled a thousand times but in the end the jungle woman was probably right. We didn't need rabies treatment and the black tar proved a lot more effective than my modern day bandages.

I am not sure if I would handle this experience differently if I had it to do over again. However after traveling the world and seeing the things I have seen I am sure of one thing. The ways that I have learned, in the place that I come from, are a way, but they are not necessarily the way.

CHAPTER 9 .....IN THE PATH OF AN ERUPTING VOLCANO

Before I left the States I spoke with a friend of mine about traveling to Guatemala. He was born there and was eager to put me in contact with his uncle. He said he would have his uncle pick me up at the airport and show me around.

When I told him that I would not be flying but rather traveling by bus from the Yucatan he reacted quite harshly. He said that the country still had many rebel fighters and even the local people would not be safe on such a journey. He insisted that I fly and when I refused he retracted the offer of putting me in touch with his uncle.

This was my first sign that things might be a little sketchy in this part of the world. Still the lost civilization of the Mayans and one of the most significant ruins on the planet were in Guatemala and before long I would be too.

His warnings about the bus gave me some cause for concern but I knew that if I cancelled my plans every time there was a risk of danger I would never go anywhere. Now that I was in the Yucatan it seemed silly to fly the whole way and miss the amazing jungle scenery and adventure that I knew would accompany the bus ride. Because Miim could help me get over the Spanish barrier, she called around and researched the safest bus route for us to take.

We had heard about a Guatemalan woman who boarded people in her home and I contacted her by phone to see if we could use her house as a base camp for exploring the country. When she agreed we decided to take the bus the majority of the way to her house.

For the final leg into Guatemala City we had two choices. The first was an additional seven hours through bumpy jungle terrain on an un air-conditioned bus. We were expecting to spend a good 20 hours on the bus getting to that point so when we found a small cargo plane that could make the journey in about an hour for around 70 dollars it was not a difficult decision.

The bus ride was seemingly endless but it did provide some amazing scenery. There were a couple of adrenaline pumping encounters and some sketchy border crossings but all in all things didn't get really interesting until we got off the plane.

Once on the ground the pilot didn't even stop the engines. He gestured for us to get out on a seemingly abandoned runway and nearly ran us over as he taxied off. I could see a couple of buildings in the distance and assumed that they must be the terminal.

When we finally reached the buildings it was clear that finding a taxi or airport shuttle was not going to be an option. After combing through several vacant buildings I found the airports only inhabitants. After some brief negotiations with the two men one of them agreed to call someone to come and pick us up.

When the driver arrived I could see he was a young outgoing man about twenty or so years in age. I described our destination and he said that he would be happy to take us there. I piled into the front of his van after loading our packs and Heather climbed in right behind me.

He explained that when we hit Guatemala City, traffic would be quite bad so the trip may take some time even though we were not going all that far. I knew Guatemala City was quite large so I envisioned a massive metropolitan city with all the modern trappings.

I was not prepared for what the city was about to show me. I had already heard that it was not a particularly safe place but I assumed that it was still well organized and somewhat clean. What I didn't imagine was the chaos that would exist in the dirty streets of this polluted metropolis. The pollution was so thick that I was forced to roll up my window despite the heat. There were developed streets but they might as well have been one big parking lot. Traffic was moving in any and all directions possible and the horns were used like turn signals as people forced their way in and out of every available crack.

The only thing I had to compare with the buses here was an earlier trip where I had spent 9 hours standing up on a bus that was designed to hold 44 people. On that trip I lost track of my counting at 106 when a spooked chicken mauled my face. That was nothing compared to Guatemala.

At least on my earlier bus trip all of the people were on the inside of the bus. Guatemala City however was different. It was full of brightly colored (Partridge Family) busses stuffed way past capacity on the inside and then loaded down with dozens more people on the outside. People hung from every open window with their feet pressed against the outsides of the bus to keep them from falling off. A dozen more sat on the hood leaving a small hole in the crowd for the driver to see through. Countless people packed onto the roof as

though they were on a British double decker…… minus the walls and windows.

One thing was for sure I was damn glad I was not on one of those buses.

In any event it was clear that it was going to take a while to get out of the city. As we approached the outer city limit I could see a strange wall of darkness in the distance. I asked our driver if we were expecting a big tropical storm or some heavy rain. He replied in Spanish, "Yes much rain."

We talked about his family and the ruins at Tikal as our journey carried us out of the city. I could tell he was kind of a hip urban kid but he seemed to have a good heart and I enjoyed talking with him as we traveled. As the thick curtain of blackness grew near I could not imagine it being rain. It was clear that at some point we were going to drive from obvious daylight into total darkness.

I could not help but to ask the driver once again "Are you sure that is rain up ahead?" He suddenly had a look of clarity on his face. "Oh I forgot," he casually replied, "Mt. Fuego is erupting."

I immediately began to ask some pretty important questions.

First of all……………….. "Is it dangerous?"

"Si si esta muy peligroso," he replied.

"OK great………….now that I know it is very dangerous, I need to know how close to the erupting volcano my new home will be."

Our driver calmly explained that the address I gave him was not much farther and we should be there soon. This was not my question. My question was how close to the God Damn volcano were we going to be.

He replied happily "muy cerca."

Great "very close"……but why are you so happy about that?

As I probed deeper I learned that my house was at the base of the volcano and he suspected it was very close to the lava flow. His excitement was based on the fact that he knew I was here to take some pictures and he figured I should be able to get some great shots as the molten lava hurled toward our small wooden house.

I asked him if perhaps it would be wise to find another place to stay. He assured me that this would not be necessary. He said that there were four levels of severity used to rate the volcanic ferocity….and we were only at level three. At level four the government would do a forced evacuation of the area and that was not likely to occur for several more days.

OK…………. well now that I knew my well being was safely in the hands of the Guatemalan government I felt much better. As we drove deeper and deeper into the blackness finally I could see some light up ahead. But it wasn't the sun….it was Mt. Fuego angrily spewing molten lava straight into the blackened sky. As we pulled up to the address the driver was clearly excited about his next proposal.

For a small fee he could return in a few hours and drive me up the angry mountain to a spot where I could get some great shots of the flaming lava rivers. Provided I was still alive in a few hours I thought this sounded like a great idea. We agreed on a time and I unloaded our packs before paying him and sealing our deal with a handshake.

The city that we stayed in had some of the most beautiful and eclectic architecture I have ever seen. The volcano had destroyed the city numerous times and the locals always sifted through the rubble to salvage a mish mash of reusable pieces. These pieces were the cornerstone of their rebuilding which made each structure a beautiful Frankenstein of bits and pieces from different eras.

The home we were to stay in exhibited some of the same creative architecture. The façade was mostly comprised of a huge wooden door that had clearly been tested by time. It guarded an adobe wall that provided protection for the roofless part of the home. This part of the home housed a long adobe hallway leading to another outside area adjacent to a covered kitchen.

I knocked on the massive door and was soon greeted by a tiny but stern woman who I guessed to be about 55. She welcomed us to her home and invited us to have a seat in the kitchen before we could even stow our packs. I was excited about the proposition of a hot meal after a day and a half in transit and gladly took my place at the table.

The diminutive woman spoke quickly and curtly and I had a hard time understanding her Guatemalan accent and slang. Still I could tell she was happy to have us and that we were most likely in good hands. She gave us a bowl of soup and some water straight from the tap. I didn't want to offend but water straight from the tap was never a good idea.

Before I would be forced to make my choice about the water I would have another important decision to make. As I looked down at my bowl of soup it began to form rings and then the entire house started to tremble. Before I could get out a single word the power and lights went out completely.

Our host had a live in helper named Rosa. Rosa was the smallest woman I have ever met she was half the size of the tiny woman who greeted us and at least twice as feisty. When the lights went out Rosa and Mrs. Gomez began to chatter feverishly. They were speaking so fast I could not understand a word they were saying.

As I had done before I focused my attention on their tone instead of their words. Around the table in total darkness in a place where I couldn't really understand the language there was a feeling of concern but not panic. This gave me the opportunity to ask a few questions before making a mad dash for the first non molten high ground I could find.

I first asked if it was the volcano, knowing full well that it was. Once that fact had been established I asked if we should abandon the house, both women seemed to think this was a great idea. As we felt our way through the darkened obstacle course towards the massive door I could hear one of the women scurrying around the kitchen in an effort to locate something.

Once out of the door I was sure we would follow some well established evacuation protocol. I expected we would line up out front as the aid trucks rushed in to sweep us to safety. Of course this was not the case.

The women led us down a narrow alleyway behind the house to an adjacent building. At this point it became clear that Rosa had salvaged a candle from the kitchen as we made our hasty retreat. She lit the candle and we could see a small rickety handmade ladder at our feet as she lowered the light. She struggled to raise the ladder so I attempted to help. I could tell immediately by her growling that she did not want help.

She propped the ladder up against a make shift shed and then scurried up it to the roof of the shed where she erected yet another cobbled ladder. From here she went straight up to the roof of the house and held the candle so we could see the pathway up. Mrs. Gomez motioned for us to go first and she followed close behind.

While I was not sure how much protection this ancient house made from 400 year old wood was really going to offer against a raging volcano, it did seem better than standing in the street at ground level and being incinerated on impact. As we all reached the roof I was anxious to see what our next move would be.

It quickly became apparent that we were not on the roof to escape the fury of the mountain, but rather to soak in its' beauty. Mrs. Gomez directed us to the sky where we could clearly see lava being exploded into the heavens. Rosa banged me on the arm as to say hey knuckle head this is beautiful so pay attention. Both women then went on in Spanish about how beautiful this gift of God was and how lucky we were to be able to witness its' awesome power and beauty.

After watching for thirty minutes or so we adjourned back to the house. Inside the women assured us that it was nothing to worry about and showed us to our room. At this point the night was still young and we had not yet met up with the driver for our lava photos so we decided to walk into the blackened town and get a feel for things.

Each place we approached exhibited no sign of life. With the sky filled with black smoke and the whole town empty the place had kind of a spooky feel. After passing several streets we seemed to be running out of town to explore. On our last corner we turned to see a dull glow coming out of a building at the end of the block. When we approached it we could see a blood red flickering of light coming from inside. The sounds coming from the building were unmistakable…….it was some sort of pub.

When we entered the building we were overwhelmed with the beauty of the scene. During the day the deep red walls and beautiful ancient wooden accents were probably amazing. But on a night like tonight, lit only by a dozen or so candles the place was absolutely magical.

We sauntered inside bellied up to the bar and had a few drinks while waiting for our driver. We did our fair share of visiting and then headed back to the house. When we arrived at the house the young man was already there waiting for us. Instead of the confident young man who had driven us through the city, we were presented with an almost sick looking fellow with deep regret in his eyes. This was a look I would come to know well as we visited places in various states of civil unrest. It was a look of fear and discouragement.

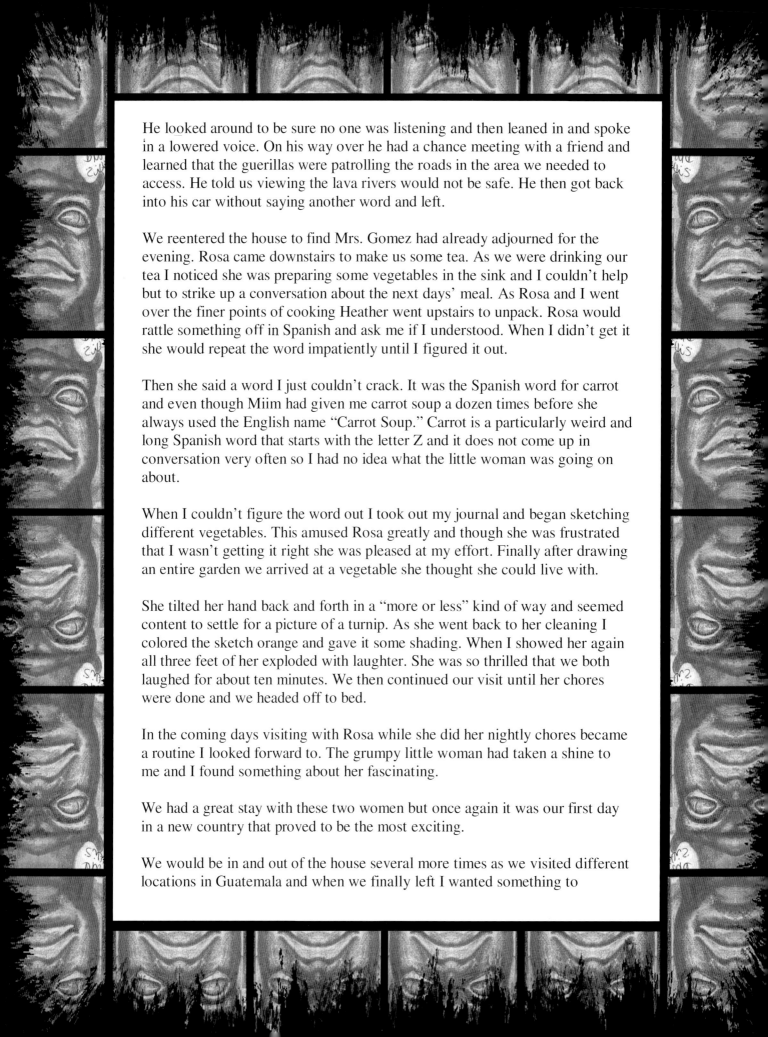

He looked around to be sure no one was listening and then leaned in and spoke in a lowered voice. On his way over he had a chance meeting with a friend and learned that the guerillas were patrolling the roads in the area we needed to access. He told us viewing the lava rivers would not be safe. He then got back into his car without saying another word and left.

We reentered the house to find Mrs. Gomez had already adjourned for the evening. Rosa came downstairs to make us some tea. As we were drinking our tea I noticed she was preparing some vegetables in the sink and I couldn't help but to strike up a conversation about the next days' meal. As Rosa and I went over the finer points of cooking Heather went upstairs to unpack. Rosa would rattle something off in Spanish and ask me if I understood. When I didn't get it she would repeat the word impatiently until I figured it out.

Then she said a word I just couldn't crack. It was the Spanish word for carrot and even though Miim had given me carrot soup a dozen times before she always used the English name "Carrot Soup." Carrot is a particularly weird and long Spanish word that starts with the letter Z and it does not come up in conversation very often so I had no idea what the little woman was going on about.

When I couldn't figure the word out I took out my journal and began sketching different vegetables. This amused Rosa greatly and though she was frustrated that I wasn't getting it right she was pleased at my effort. Finally after drawing an entire garden we arrived at a vegetable she thought she could live with.

She tilted her hand back and forth in a "more or less" kind of way and seemed content to settle for a picture of a turnip. As she went back to her cleaning I colored the sketch orange and gave it some shading. When I showed her again all three feet of her exploded with laughter. She was so thrilled that we both laughed for about ten minutes. We then continued our visit until her chores were done and we headed off to bed.

In the coming days visiting with Rosa while she did her nightly chores became a routine I looked forward to. The grumpy little woman had taken a shine to me and I found something about her fascinating.

We had a great stay with these two women but once again it was our first day in a new country that proved to be the most exciting.

We would be in and out of the house several more times as we visited different locations in Guatemala and when we finally left I wanted something to remember Rosa by. On our last visit the women were hosting a chemical engineer from the States. She was there to work on some local pollution issues and she decided to stay with the ladies to learn to speak Spanish.

On the morning that we were to leave for the final time I was sitting in the kitchen having breakfast when the woman came into the kitchen with a camera and pointed it directly at Rosa.

Rosa ran from the kitchen screaming as the woman refused to put the camera down. It did not take Rosa long to return with a broom and a few swats quickly cleared the room of both the woman and her camera. At this point I pretty much figured out that a photo was out of the question.

That evening I caught Rosa alone in the kitchen and told her that I would be honored if she would write or draw something in my journal. She confessed to me that she couldn't really write or draw but she watched me doodling in that journal every morning and thought that it would be fun to try. She took great care and time scratching a few marks and a couple of illegible words onto the pages. She then proudly handed it to me and went upstairs. To this day it is one of my favorite journal entries.

Later that evening we said our goodbyes to the ladies and left for our next destination which just happened to pass through the same guerilla country the driver warned us to avoid.

CHAPTER 10.......A CONFLICT WITHIN

As a young man I had strong opinions and convictions on any subject you would care to discuss. To me everything was black and white, right or wrong, good or evil. As I have traveled I have learned that very few things are that simple.

I have reversed my opinions on things I swore I would defend to my grave and I have learned to be an effective arguer for both sides of many issues. I have realized that there are some things in this world that I just don't have the answer for and yet other things that are unanswerable all together.

I have visited many war torn nations and places in various states of civil unrest. I have found myself siding with the government only to learn that they are oppressing the people and I have found myself siding with the "freedom fighters" only to learn they are killing the very people they claim to be liberating.

I can make the best argument for war that words can conjure and yet I wish that such things would never again be necessary. I am a soldier at heart but peace runs through my veins. I am conflicted in every way when it comes to resolving disputes with those blinded by madness, greed and religion.

When you take the time to unlearn what you think you know and truly examine both sides of a conflict the borders begin to blur and the blacks and whites often become a single shade of grey.

The only thing I know for sure is that killing innocent people to draw attention to your cause hardly seems an effective way to win the support of those whose moral votes have not yet been cast.

After I had seen the ancient ruins of Tikal and toured the beautiful cities of rural Guatemala I wanted to visit a mountain village that I had heard a lot about. According to numerous accounts there was an active underwater volcano in one of the mountain lakes that created an amazing underwater habitat and diving experience.

Some quick research on available transport led me to the conclusion that a ten person mini bus would probably be the most practical means of travel. We had heard that the roads into the mountains could sometimes be dangerous but we hadn't heard of any reports of recent guerilla activity in the area so we assumed that our route would be safe enough for a quick entry and exit.

As we gained altitude on our way up the mountain we saw a few military men standing by some broken glass and debris on a particularly sharp switchback. We didn't think much of it and assumed they were cleaning up another accident on the treacherous and windy mountain roads.

When we reached our destination we bumped into some other travelers and soon found ourselves engaged in some casual conversation. They had been in the village for a few days and gave us a quick briefing on the dos and don'ts. When they learned that we had just arrived they asked us if we had seen the guerilla attack on the road as we came into town.

According to them they were eating in their regular breakfast haunt when they overheard some military guys being dispatched. The soldiers abandoned their breakfast around ten o'clock and left to deal with a tourist bus that had been attacked by guerillas.

We thought about our timing and realized that we probably passed those same military guys at the "accident" scene around eleven. We asked around town several times but no one seemed to know anything about it.

These kinds of things aren't exactly good for tourism and people are discouraged from talking about them. In addition to the obvious impact on tourism people in conflict ridden regions are often afraid to speak openly about rebel activities. The government often promotes the silence because they do not want to lend credence to these attention getting acts of defiance. In areas of conflict it is not uncommon for the military to hastily clean up such a scene and pretend the whole thing never happened.

By plan we left Guatemala a couple of days later and never heard another word about the incident. A few weeks later we ran into some travelers in Nicaragua that were headed for Guatemala. They said that they were doing some research on the internet when they ran across a small article about ten Austrian tourists being mowed down in a small van on its way into the mountains just a few weeks ago.

It was not until then that we realized the story we had heard earlier was probably true. If we had left just an hour earlier it could well have been us on the other end of that gunfire.

I have never really researched the facts and I don't know what prompted the alleged attack. I don't really even have any idea what the true issues are that lie at the foundation of the struggles between these rebels and their government. But I can tell you it is unlikely that taking the lives of innocent people got them any closer to a resolution.

rica Elephants - w...
Darbet (bird) - Tawny Eagl...
now (?) - Re...oxpecker...

sa Elephants - w...
-set (bird) - Ta...
foul Pied ox...
pelica...

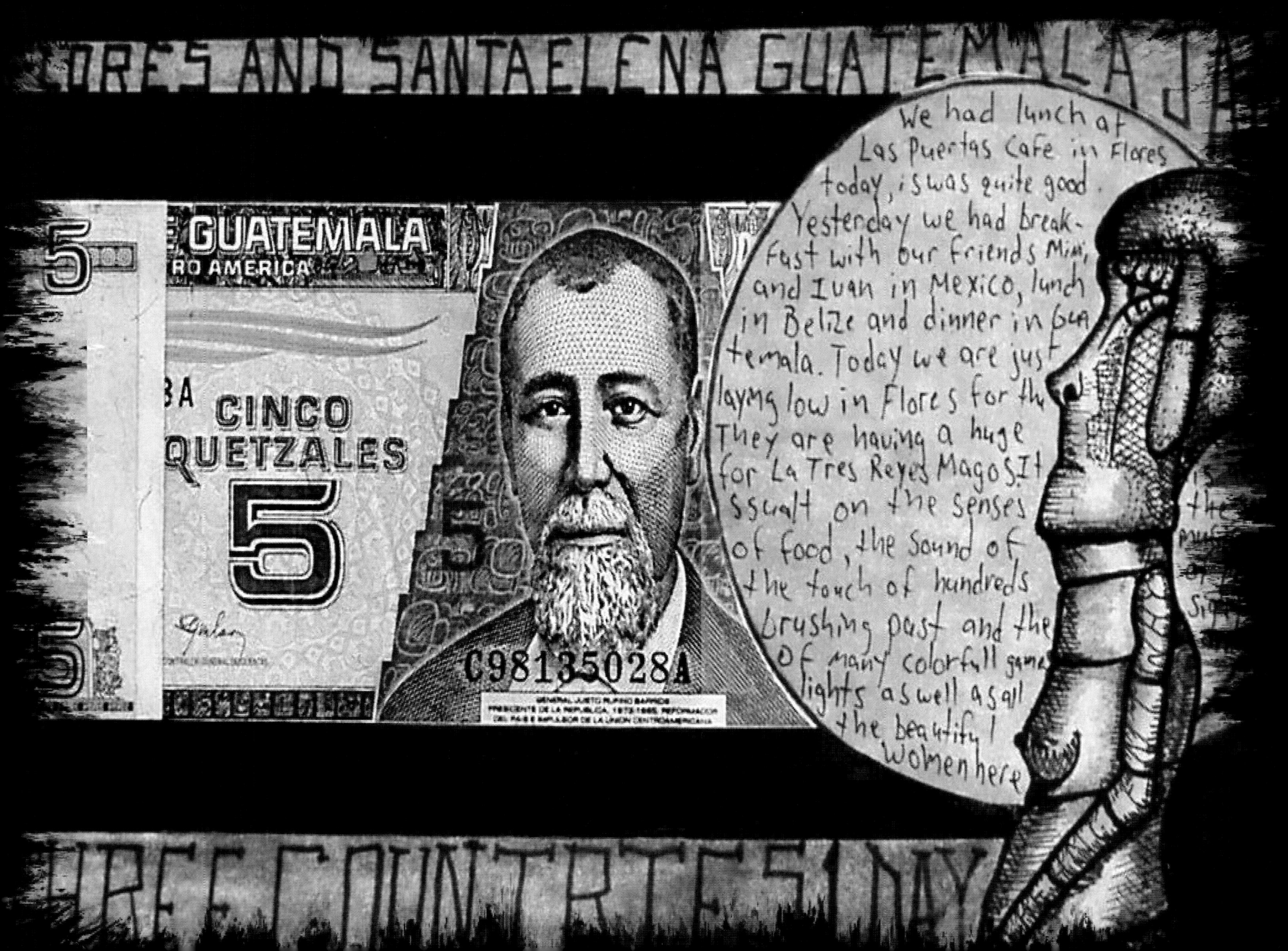

We had lunch at
Las Puertas Cafe in Flores
today; it was quite good.
Yesterday we had break-
fast with our friends Mimi
and Ivan in Mexico, lunch
in Belize and dinner in Gua
temala. Today we are just
laying low in Flores for the
They are having a huge
(for La Tres Reyes Magos) I
sscraft on the senses
of food, the sound of
the touch of hundreds
brushing past and the
of many colorful give
lights as well a sall
the beautiful
Women here

GUATEMALA
RO AMERICA

BA CINCO
QUETZALES

5

09813 5028 A

February 1st Another day of doing absolutely nothing in Nicaragua. We have been here for three days and I have really enjoyed just staying put and doing nothing. Yes terday I painted a small mural on one of the doors at our hotel for the manager, a wild and easy going girl from Argentina. At night I hang out with a local girl and play games or watch MTV. Las Spanish night for we played hangman of hours, with the names Latino and En glish artists the night befor

we played jacks for chille sauce. shots of tequila and with stars in Arlen is a girl many her eyes and dreams I suspect.

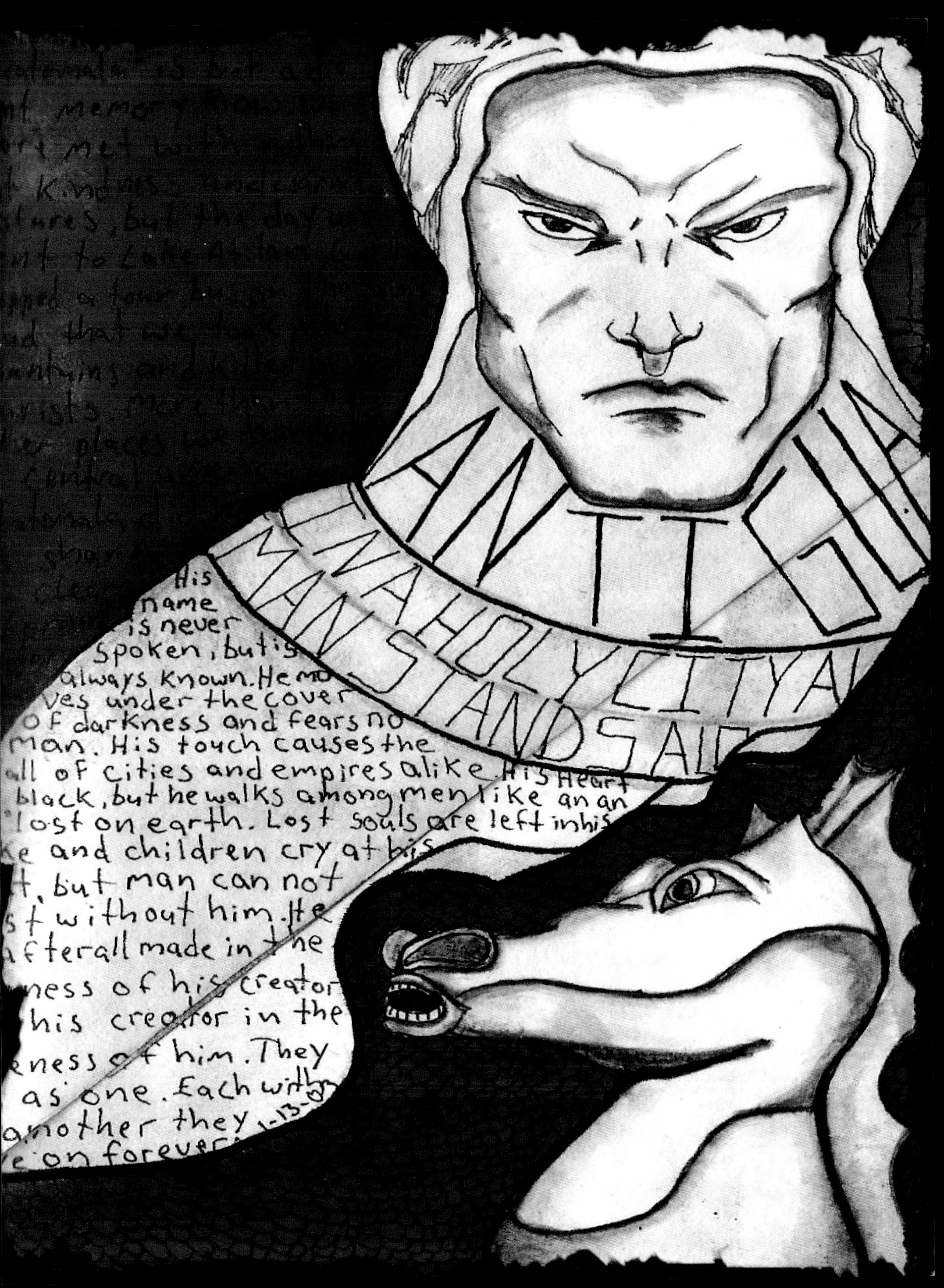

memory flows we
met with nothing
kindness and cert
tures, but the day we
nt to Lake Atilan. Cert
pped a four brion
nd that we took
ntains and killed
rists. More than
her places we
central
aterials
shar
clea

ANTI GU

MA HOLY CITY A
MAN STAND SAL

His name is never spoken, but is always known. He mo
ves under the cover of darkness and fears no
man. His touch causes the
all of cities and empires alike. His Heart
black, but he walks among men like an an
lost on earth. Lost souls are left in his
ke and children cry at his
t, but man can not
without him. He
afterall made in the
ness of his creator
his creator in the
ness of him. They
as one. Each with
another they   1-13-0
e on forever.

nnur

e of

namandalam
nikrishnan Nambiar among others, gave
an example of how versatile the mizhavu is as
a percussion instrument.
Tradition and transformation with special
reference to Kerala Kalamandalam wa

the actor at Hyderabad in the not very distant
past, I felt that Madhu was below his usual
form. Margi's great endeavour at revival of
the play Mayasitankam, dedicated to late
Appukuttan Nair in the presentation, need
a more experienced Sita. Even Rama a

CHAPTER 11…….. AMBUSHED AND ROBBED IN COSTA RICA

Shortly after arriving in Costa Rica I met a Columbian family that invited us to stay in a three bedroom hotel that they ran out of their home. They welcomed us with open arms and regularly invited us to family functions. It was not uncommon for them to treat us to special fiestas complete with Columbian music, ethnic dancing and magnificent barbeque. Their home made the perfect base camp for us as we explored the rest of Costa Rica and Central America.

After experiencing the amazing beauty of the Pacific side of Costa Rica we stowed half our gear with the Columbians and set out for the Caribbean region. Words can not begin to describe the beauty of the countryside we witnessed as we traveled by bus through the jungles, banana plantations and mountains of Costa Rica.

When we arrived in our first Caribbean village it was clear that we were in a whole different Costa Rica. Reggae rang out from the local pubs and surfers littered the beaches. I immediately took a liking to my new surroundings as the Rastafarian vibe and mellow attitude poured over the little village.

After a few days of relaxing on the beach we decided to plan our next adventure. We had heard that the jungles were teeming with monkeys and after striking out in the Yucatan I could not wait to have another shot at seeing the beautiful creatures in their natural habitat. It did not take us long to hatch the plan for another monkey safari.

As we lay on the beach sipping pina coladas and planning our trip I had no idea that within a couple days time I would be ambushed, robbed and forced to return to the village with very little dignity. For now however, I was quite excited about our new surroundings and I thought the idea of a monkey safari seemed like a capitol idea.

Though I was excited, I didn't let my enthusiasm blind me to the risks involved in traveling that far off the beaten path. I knew the new home I so enthusiastically embraced was a great place for the jobless of the world to congregate and "chill out" but I also knew it had a reputation for lawlessness.

The place we were headed was a long way down the coast and we knew it would be a good idea to get some advice from the locals before heading off into the jungle on our own. During our inquiries we learned that a few miles down shore there had been reports of tourists being robbed at knife point. We wanted to avoid any such complications at all cost.

Because the robberies were predominantly on the beach and not in the jungle we thought we could probably avoid any altercations by walking on the beach up to a certain point and then traveling through the jungle and around the troubled area. During our inquiry one of the locals pointed to a distant outcropping on the beach and made a head bashing motion while repeating the words "lugar peligroso." A little more conversation made it clear that the bandits would drop down from those particular rocks, bonk you on the head and steal everything you owned. It was clear that this was the spot to avoid…..a lugar peligroso indeed.

As the next morning broke we loaded our packs and headed out on foot down the beach. I had my Navy seal knife at the ready, my multi tool in my pocket and my Spanish dictionary on hand just incase I needed to do some quick negotiating.

We hiked up the beach as far as possible before coming into view of the outcropping that reportedly hid the thieves from view. We left the beach immediately and marched into the dense jungle habitat. Just ahead of us was endless jungle terrain and in our rear view mirrors the cooling waters of the Caribbean were beginning to fade from view.

The sound of the pounding surf in the distance muted the jungles tell tale signs of critters moving about the vast expanse. This dulled sense of hearing coupled with my concern of bandits in the area forced me to keep an extra vigilant eye as we made our way through the heavy foliage.

By now I was starting to become a little more hardened to international travel and I was less likely to let the threat of a boogie man in the bushes spoil my experience. Still I kept a watchful eye as we passed by the back side of the "lugar peligroso."

Just passed the "lugar peligroso" my fascination with the jungle began to distract me. Before long I found myself immersed in another world. I nearly forgot all about the bandits back on the beach. Each step seemed to force a new creature to slither or scurry across my path and the flora and fauna alone were enough to hold my attention for hours.

After awhile however the trip began to get a little more repetitive and I started to comb my mind for some productive ways to pass the time. I decided this

would be a great opportunity to expand my Spanish vocabulary. I took out the Spanish dictionary and studied one page at a time.

After I thought that I had memorized the contents of a given page I would give the dictionary to Heather and she would quiz me. This went on until my mind was saturated and my belly was rumbling.

We found a spot in the shade where a fallen tree provided the perfect bench for a rest. After a quick survey for deadly slithery things we sat down for a quick boost of energy. Heather had packed some peanut butter and jelly sandwiches which were always good for a quick carbo boost and some other quick snacks. We each scarffed down a banana and had some water before Heather retrieved the trail mix.

I could see her grappling with the trail mix bag as I opened my multi tool and handed it to her. Shortly after she cut through the plastic I felt a familiar burning sensation on the back of my thigh. It did not take me long to figure out that I had once again encroached upon the domain of the fire ants. I jumped off the log, brushed myself off and declared our snack break complete. Heather threw the multi tool into the lunch bag along with my Spanish book and we made a hasty exit.

Our goal was to stay in the jungle long enough to get well past the "lugar peligroso" and the enterprising young vagabonds who called it home. When we were in the clear we were going to cut back down to the beach and find a safe spot for some lunch and a bit of snorkeling.

About the time we thought it was safe to cut back down to the beach we noticed a large branch bent over the faint trail in front of us.

Without thought we unwittingly bent down with our packs and began to slowly crawl under the branch. We were attacked from all sides before we even have a chance to react. Before I could figure out what had happened I heard Heather screaming as she shed her pack and ran.

I felt one and then two of them jump on my back. I remember contemplating for a brief second whether or not to give my pack up and run or stay and fight. I chose a combination of the two. As I shed my pack I could see Heather was out of harms way and I turned to face my attackers. I remember noticing the filthy teeth of the first one as he charged directly at me. I was amazed at the length of this animals teeth as he nashed them in my direction. Before I knew it

I was surrounded by a hoard of the little bastards. The ring leader kept me at bay while the rest of the filthy monkeys ransacked our packs.

The first treasure they claimed was the sack with our food that Heather flung into the air as she made her departure. It did not take long for one of the little shits to grab it and scurry up a tree with the entire thing. Meanwhile the rest of them seemed to be fighting over who got to steal what out of the remaining bags. They proceeded to tear through our discarded packs like cartoon Tasmanian devils

At this point I had seen enough. I was not about to be fleeced by a band of two foot tall pseudo primates with un-evolved brains. I was going to make a stand and I was going to do it now.

I knew it would be a battle to establish dominance. A sorting out of alpha males if you will. I rushed the ring leader to let him know I was the biggest dog in the pack. I thought he would turn and run but he called my bluff. He stood strong while his colleagues continued to have their way with my only worldly possessions.

My attempt to establish dominance seemed to backfire. If anything it made him more aggressive. I found that I was the one backing up as he charged me with every tooth in his head fully exposed. I hated being bullied by these little hooligans and I just wanted to bull rush the whole pack of diminutive demons and reclaim what was mine. Fortunately I remembered that damn rabies shot that I took a pass before doing anything drastic.

It was now clear that I would have to fight this battle with my superior intellect not my superior size. As I formulated my plan I set my sights on the first offender who was now perched in a tree over head just beyond my reach. He was hooting and hollering like he had just hit the lottery. Taunting me really……as he went through the contents of my bag, sniffing each item one by one.

First to be discarded after close examination was my multi tool……stupid monkey……it was probably the best thing in the whole bag. Next down was the Spanish book and that would be the last thing he would give up.

As the little felon carefully opened the zipper on the plastic bag and removed the peanut butter and jelly sandwich he glared sarcastically in my direction. My blood was beginning to boil. I didn't want to hurt the little bastards but my journal was in one of those bags they were destroying and the whole thing had gone on long enough.

I looked down and saw one of my swim fins sticking out of my tussled pack. Eureka, the perfect monkey swatter. Only problem was I couldn't get close enough to it with all the gnashing teeth. This is where my comparatively enormous, tool using brain came into play. I broke off a branch and used it to hook the swim fin from a safe distance. I pulled it into reach and picked it up. Once secured, I had not one but two tools at my disposal and it didn't take me long to mount a counteroffensive.

Using the fin as more of a shield than a weapon I blocked my way into stick range. I used the stick to reclaim the tattered pack with the other fin. I drug it away from the frenzied fur balls as they focused their attention on the remaining pack. Heather was now some distance away and I gave her the pack to keep at her feet along with a fin and some specific instructions to swat the hell out of anything that came within reach.

Then I went in for the second pack which proved to be a little more difficult. This was their only remaining treasure and they seemed a bit more reluctant to part with it. They now sent more soldiers to aid the ring leader and I soon found myself surrounded. Pretty convinced I was going to get bitten anyway I rushed the bag while flailing the fin wildly. I was not bluffing this time and anybody with their teeth out was going to get a taste of my scuba gear.

I latched onto the bag and backed away from the angry hoard. I retrieved the discarded multi-tool and Spanish book and made my way back to Heather. As I did the monkeys were making such a ruckus I was sure they were going to draw the attention of the real bandits. Hell for all I knew at this point they could have been working together.

We put our packs on frontwards snapped a few photos for evidence and started out of the jungle. The monkeys however were not through with us yet. They followed us almost the entire way out of the jungle making charges periodically only to be met with the angry end of my size ten swim fin.

At first I was quite impressed with myself for retrieving our gear. But as the hike back lingered on I realized this was the second time we had been chased out of the jungle by animals a quarter of our size. Not only were these animals smaller than us but they did not have the intelligence to disregard their own feces……..and that did not sit well.

Then I remembered why we went into the jungle in the first place. I wanted to see some monkeys……………I guess we both got what we wanted in the end.

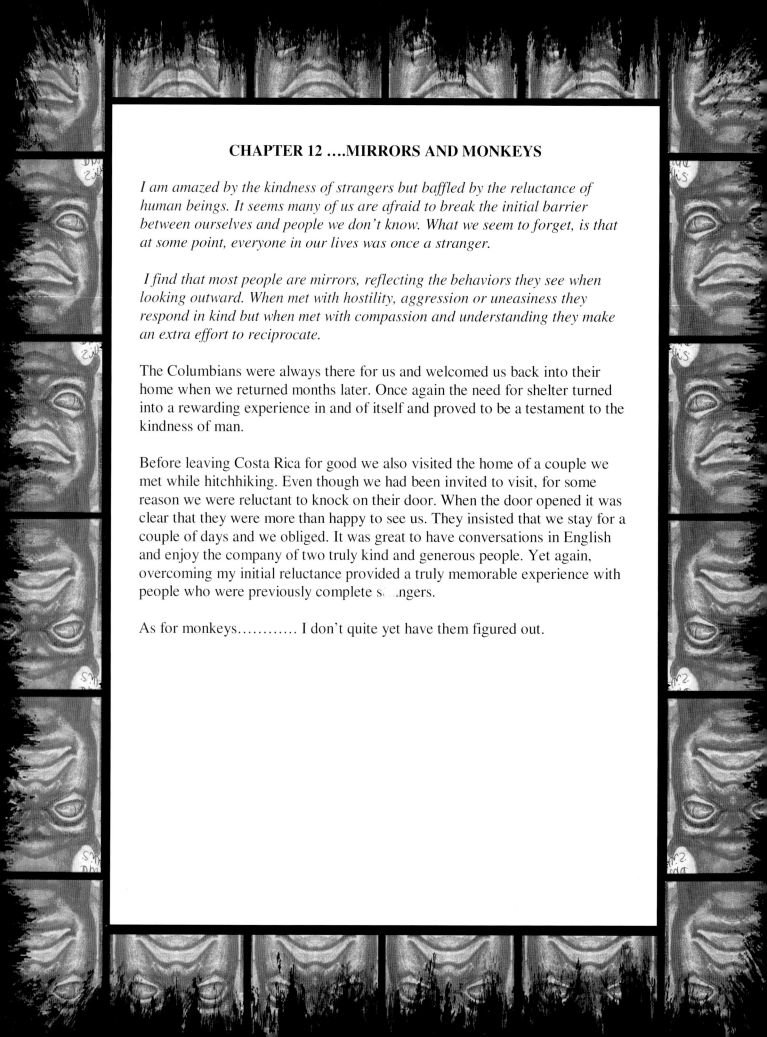

CHAPTER 12 ....MIRRORS AND MONKEYS

I am amazed by the kindness of strangers but baffled by the reluctance of human beings. It seems many of us are afraid to break the initial barrier between ourselves and people we don't know. What we seem to forget, is that at some point, everyone in our lives was once a stranger.

I find that most people are mirrors, reflecting the behaviors they see when looking outward. When met with hostility, aggression or uneasiness they respond in kind but when met with compassion and understanding they make an extra effort to reciprocate.

The Columbians were always there for us and welcomed us back into their home when we returned months later. Once again the need for shelter turned into a rewarding experience in and of itself and proved to be a testament to the kindness of man.

Before leaving Costa Rica for good we also visited the home of a couple we met while hitchhiking. Even though we had been invited to visit, for some reason we were reluctant to knock on their door. When the door opened it was clear that they were more than happy to see us. They insisted that we stay for a couple of days and we obliged. It was great to have conversations in English and enjoy the company of two truly kind and generous people. Yet again, overcoming my initial reluctance provided a truly memorable experience with people who were previously complete strangers.

As for monkeys............ I don't quite yet have them figured out.

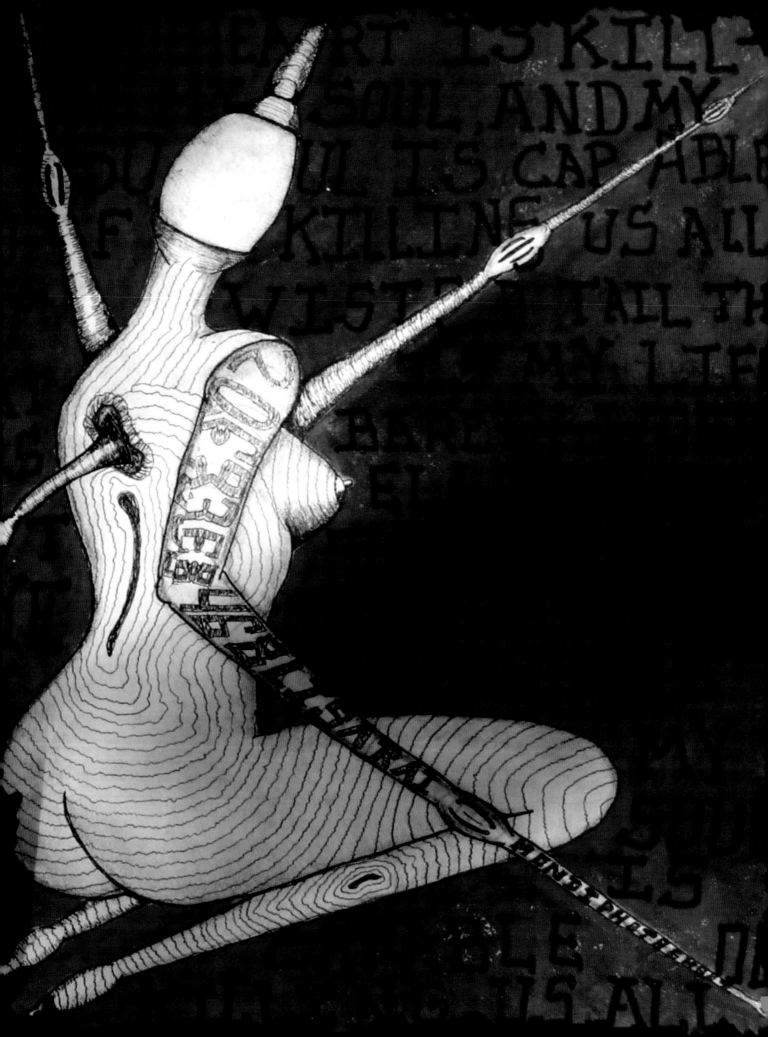

Today in Antigua my mind is a little better a long way from healed but

To Panajachel in the morning for one night and day.

it is better than day. Next Costa Rica I hope jungle mad is not quite Even time longer my wounds seems open than wider almost sur cision. So I see how much pain bring. At least the distracted my mind few al

it was yes er

stop where the ness so bad heals it to even with gical pre wait to each day will Dengue fever ness for a days. But as ways it was

a temporary reprieve.

CHAPTER 13.......A DANGEROUS PASSAGE TO PANAMA

After returning from our second unsuccessful monkey safari we spent some time exploring the rest of the Caribbean side of Costa Rica before plotting a course for Panama.

Tired of traveling the standard bus routes I thought it would be nice to explore some other options. One morning we bumped into a talkative local woman on our way to the beach who offered some advice. She said the local canoe carver had visited Panama many times and may be able to help us.

When we finally found the gruff old man he seemed to be in quite a hurry.......and not all that anxious to aid us in our quest for Panama. He spoke in quick curt Spanish sentences and I was only able to pick up every third word or so.

After asking him to repeat himself several times his impatience began to escalate. I thought it best to change the topic to more casual conversation. I asked him if he enjoyed Panama when he visited, I enquired about his handmade canoes and spent quite some time discussing his family and children.

As the old man seemed to warm up a little I took out my journal and began to write down his frenzied directions.

As near as I could tell we were to walk about a mile out of town to a very sharp corner in the road at precisely 7:00am. We were to wait there between 7:00am and 8:00am for a farmer who often transported the locals to a neighboring village on his daily rounds. In the neighboring village the farmer could put us in touch with a man named Manuel that could take us to a different village where we could secure a driver for a nominal fee.

The whole thing seemed a little convoluted but still better than another bus ride so I wrote the directions down carefully. As I enquired a bit more about the specific island I wanted to visit I could feel the old mans patience expiring once again. He said the driver we hired would know all about it.

The next morning we loaded our packs and did as directed. After some brief dialogue with the farmer we got in the back of his truck and headed off down the road. After winding through a half dozen banana plantations we reached a small gravel parking lot with some outbuildings. Here we caught a ride with Manuel who transported us to the closest official city.

The city was a little shady but the driver seemed to be pretty good spirited and he had air conditioning so we were quite pleased. I assumed he was going to drive us to the border but instead he took us to a bus stop just outside of town. He said he was unable to drive us on this particular day but he assured us the bus would take us where we wanted to go. We had jumped through a lot of hoops to avoid the bus that ran right through our village but now it seemed that we were going to be relegated to the oven on wheels once again.

The bus ride was not nearly as beautiful as our previous cross country trips and we began to wonder what we had gotten ourselves into as we passed one unsavory town after another.

As the bus started to slow down we were praying that it wasn't going to stop in this particular city. When it finally rolled to a motionless halt the driver signaled for us to get off. As we departed I asked him about getting to the island. He shook his head abruptly without answering and motioned aggressively for us to disembark.

We were in a place that seemed to have trouble written all over it. It was clearly not a tourist border crossing and we stuck out of the hostile environment like a sore thumb.

The town was absolutely filthy and the second we stepped off the bus people started grabbing at our bodies and our packs. They were yelling, come with me, get a room, get a taxi, get some drugs and anything else they thought might get me to part with a few green backs. For us the scene was chaos, but the locals seemed to go unmolested.

Looking around the town gave me an immediate unsettling feeling. I knew we were going to have problems here. As I scanned the town for a safe haven I felt an aggressive tug on my backpack. A particularly untrustworthy looking gentleman was insisting on taking my bag. As I refused he became more and more aggressive. Eventually I had to reclaim my pack by force.

After a brief survey of the area I realized we didn't know which way the border was. We desperately needed some directions but I did not want to advertise the fact that we were lost. I did not see a single place in the entire town that looked inviting so we reluctantly targeted an open air restaurant just across the street.

As we walked towards the restaurant I noticed three things, first everyone was leering at us. The stares weren't stares of curiosity they were more like glares of resentment. I also noticed that as we passed people on the street rather than respecting our personal space they seemed to be getting uncomfortably close as they sneered into our faces. My final observation was that we were being followed by the guy from the bus.

I knew every move we made was being watched closely and I knew it was important that no one got the idea that we were going to be easy prey. Each time someone leaned in to sneer at me I leaned in a little myself and sneered back. When we reached the restaurant and sat down I casually threw our packs on the floor trying to give the impression that there was nothing in them of value.

I went to the counter and ordered a Coke. When the woman returned with my drink I asked her which way the border was and how far we were from it. She did not seem eager to help as she pointed up the road. As we finished our transaction I noticed the man from the bus was now also standing near the counter.

We slowly finished our Cokes hoping he would leave, but of course he did not. He waited until we got up and then followed us out into the street. Once outside the restaurant, he said he would take us to the border. My alarm bells were going off and I was quite firm when I told him we did not need nor want any help. This did not deter him as he followed us up the street.

After a fairly short walk out of town we could see what looked like a border crossing station just up the road. When we reached the building it was covered with warning signs in multiple languages. Each sign bore the same unmistakable message. I don't remember the exact words but the point was unforgettable.

IF YOU ATTEMPT PASSAGE WITH COUNTERFEIT OR ALTERED TRAVEL DOCUMENTS OF ANY KIND YOU WILL BE PROSECUTED TO THE FULL EXTENT OF THE PANAMANINAN LAW WHICH WILL INCLUDE AT A MINIMUM A MULTI YEAR PRISON SENTENCE.

Even though we had legitimate passports and our research indicated that we did not need to pre purchase a visa we were still a little nervous. The number of signs posted and the general demeanor of the people at the border office gave us a very uneasy feeling. Corruption ran rampant in these kinds of places and something just didn't smell right.

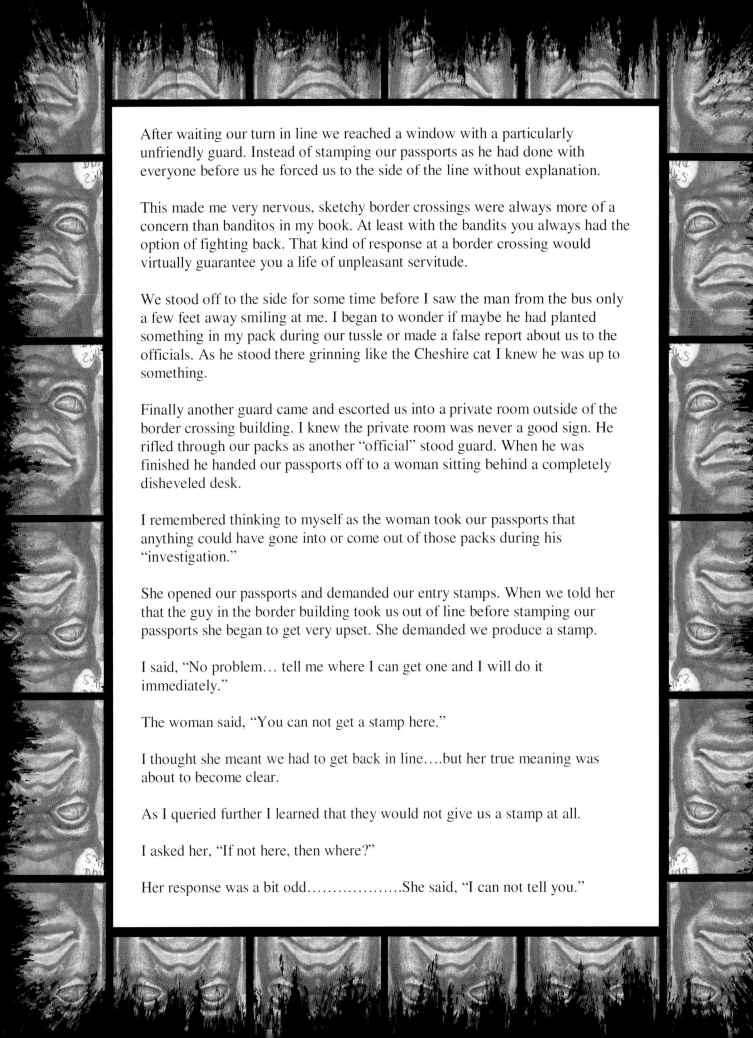

After waiting our turn in line we reached a window with a particularly unfriendly guard. Instead of stamping our passports as he had done with everyone before us he forced us to the side of the line without explanation.

This made me very nervous, sketchy border crossings were always more of a concern than banditos in my book. At least with the bandits you always had the option of fighting back. That kind of response at a border crossing would virtually guarantee you a life of unpleasant servitude.

We stood off to the side for some time before I saw the man from the bus only a few feet away smiling at me. I began to wonder if maybe he had planted something in my pack during our tussle or made a false report about us to the officials. As he stood there grinning like the Cheshire cat I knew he was up to something.

Finally another guard came and escorted us into a private room outside of the border crossing building. I knew the private room was never a good sign. He rifled through our packs as another "official" stood guard. When he was finished he handed our passports off to a woman sitting behind a completely disheveled desk.

I remembered thinking to myself as the woman took our passports that anything could have gone into or come out of those packs during his "investigation."

She opened our passports and demanded our entry stamps. When we told her that the guy in the border building took us out of line before stamping our passports she began to get very upset. She demanded we produce a stamp.

I said, "No problem… tell me where I can get one and I will do it immediately."

The woman said, "You can not get a stamp here."

I thought she meant we had to get back in line….but her true meaning was about to become clear.

As I queried further I learned that they would not give us a stamp at all.

I asked her, "If not here, then where?"

Her response was a bit odd……………….She said, "I can not tell you."

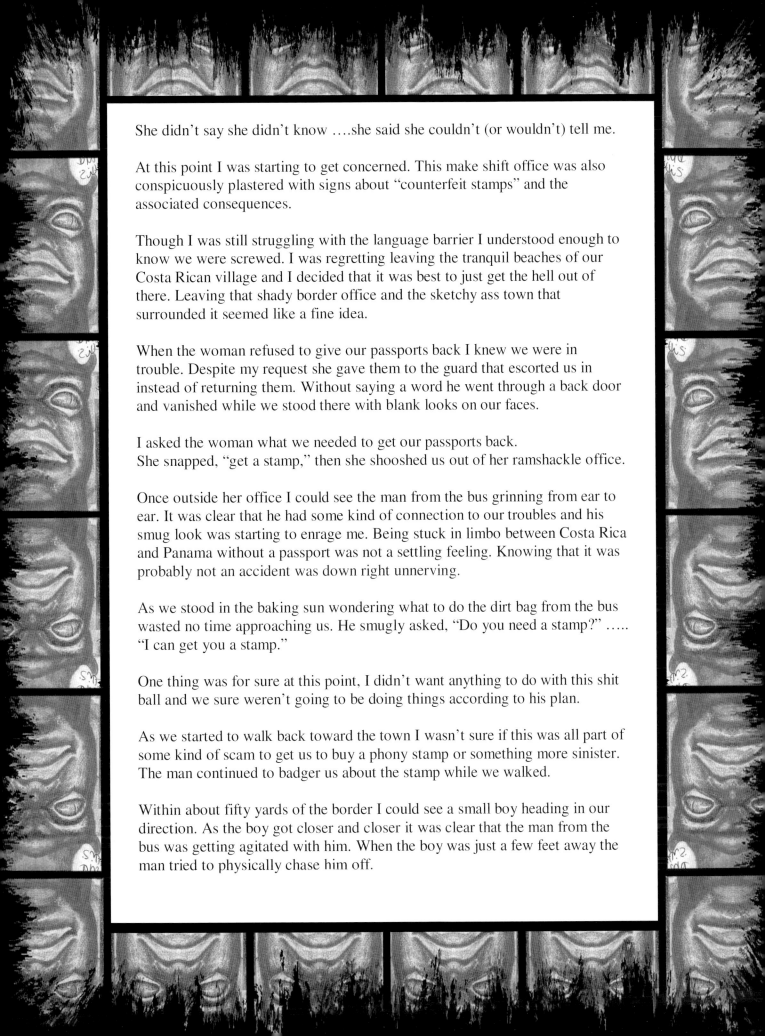

She didn't say she didn't know ….she said she couldn't (or wouldn't) tell me.

At this point I was starting to get concerned. This make shift office was also conspicuously plastered with signs about "counterfeit stamps" and the associated consequences.

Though I was still struggling with the language barrier I understood enough to know we were screwed. I was regretting leaving the tranquil beaches of our Costa Rican village and I decided that it was best to just get the hell out of there. Leaving that shady border office and the sketchy ass town that surrounded it seemed like a fine idea.

When the woman refused to give our passports back I knew we were in trouble. Despite my request she gave them to the guard that escorted us in instead of returning them. Without saying a word he went through a back door and vanished while we stood there with blank looks on our faces.

I asked the woman what we needed to get our passports back.
She snapped, "get a stamp," then she shooshed us out of her ramshackle office.

Once outside her office I could see the man from the bus grinning from ear to ear. It was clear that he had some kind of connection to our troubles and his smug look was starting to enrage me. Being stuck in limbo between Costa Rica and Panama without a passport was not a settling feeling. Knowing that it was probably not an accident was down right unnerving.

As we stood in the baking sun wondering what to do the dirt bag from the bus wasted no time approaching us. He smugly asked, "Do you need a stamp?" …..
"I can get you a stamp."

One thing was for sure at this point, I didn't want anything to do with this shit ball and we sure weren't going to be doing things according to his plan.

As we started to walk back toward the town I wasn't sure if this was all part of some kind of scam to get us to buy a phony stamp or something more sinister. The man continued to badger us about the stamp while we walked.

Within about fifty yards of the border I could see a small boy heading in our direction. As the boy got closer and closer it was clear that the man from the bus was getting agitated with him. When the boy was just a few feet away the man tried to physically chase him off.

It was clear that the boy and the man were not allies which made the kid alright with me. As the boy began to speak I stepped forward and separated him and the man with my arm. In English the boy said "Mister, do you need a stamp…..six dollars American?"

It soon became clear that those were the only English words the kid knew. I asked him a bunch of questions in English and he kept nodding as though he understood, but when I probed further I knew he was just going through the motions. None the less I liked my chances with this kid better than the other guy whom I was truly starting to loathe.

I asked the boy some questions in Spanish to get a sense of his character and build a little rapport…..all the while the other man was interrupting and trying to disrupt our dialogue. After some casual chat I asked the boy if the stamp he was going to get for me would cause me trouble with the officials. He seemed quite sincere when he said that he did this all the time and could guarantee me an official stamp.

I was pretty sure that "guarantee" didn't exactly mean he was going to serve time for me if I got thrown in prison but I didn't really have a lot of choices. As I reached into my pocket to pay the boy the man started insisting that the stamp the boy was going to get would not be official. If I wanted an official stamp I would have to get it from him.

I gave the boy twelve dollars US and told him to bring me two official stamps. I half expected I would never see him again, but at least I had the other guy off my back.

After about twenty minutes or so the young man retuned with two small red stamps. I asked him again if he was sure that it was OK to use these stamps……he assured me it was, but that did not ease my mind much.

As I returned to the little outbuilding by the border I now feared those warning signs in a way that was not apparent to me earlier. They were really more about illegal stamps than anything else and I just couldn't quite put the pieces together. I couldn't figure out if this was all some sort of scam to extort a measly twelve dollars out of me or if the real surprise was about to become clear when I tried to use my ill be gotten stamps.

With one stamp in my pocket and one in my hand I told Heather to stand by as I nervously approached the woman. She took the stamp from my hand and studied it for what seemed like hours. She then motioned toward Heather and asked for the other stamp. When I told her we only had one she seemed quite skeptical. She picked up the phone and said something in Spanish I did not understand.

A few minutes later a man returned with our passports. The woman handed him the stamp and he left with passports in tow. When he returned with my passport stamped for entry into Panama I gave him the second stamp.

Once we both had our stamped passports in hand we were relieved that we only lost twelve dollars in the transaction and we were anxious to get the hell out of there. As we passed the guard station we could see that the crossing was for foot traffic only. It was an old tattered foot bridge littered with massive holes. It looked like something straight out of an Indiana Jones movie. You could clearly see the river over a hundred feet below as you focused on avoiding the massive holes and tattered boards.

About halfway across I looked back to see I was once again being followed by the man from the bus. As we neared the end of the bridge he approached me and demanded money......thirty five US dollars to be exact. When I asked him why he thought I owed him money, he said "it was for safe passage across the border."

My patience had expired and in a slur of English and Spanish profanities I told him I was not going to pay him a dime. He responded with a threat. He said we had a long way left to travel and it would not be safe for us because he knew many other people along the way and they were very dangerous men. With anger building inside me I told him that perhaps it was those men that were in danger, not me....and then I took my pack off and dropped it on the ground.

I was done with the threats and extortion and I was no longer in the mood to be bullied. I think this man could tell by the look in my eyes that he was now the one in danger. I began to raise my voice louder and louder as I stepped toward him spewing obscenities.

He raised his hands in a submissive gesture and backed away. I felt bad about making a scene but also felt it was necessary to send a message. I was given a very wide berth as I walked the last few yards of the bridge and people were no longer glaring at me.

When we reached the other side we were officially in Panama. There were a bunch of cars parked haphazardly at the end of the bridge but nothing resembling a taxi in sight. It soon became clear that these private vehicles were there to win the business of people crossing the border.

I knew they had just witnessed my tirade on the bridge so I was very cordial in making my introductions. We soon agreed upon a price and the driver set off into Panama. I asked about the island and like everyone before him he said the next guy would know all about it.

After a short ride the car came to a stop and the driver motioned for us to get out, before I could ask any questions he said, "Don't worry…. one price." He then called another man over to the car where once again we were handed off like packages as we changed vehicles. The new driver was very friendly and said that he would take us to a marina where we could charter a boat to our island. After driving for some time we reached the outskirts of another rough and tumble town. This one however was bustling and you could see families out and about doing their daily business. It definitely had a much better feel than our previous stop.

Even though the driver and the city seemed a bit nicer I was still a bit nervous when he took us to a deserted alley and ordered us out of the car. He told us to wait for his brother who would soon be there to pick us up. In about ten minutes time two very dark skinned men in their thirties approached the alley on rickety bicycles. They gestured for us to get on and though we found it a little strange we obliged. As we sat on their seats they stood up and peddled. They took us down a long pathway much to narrow for cars and after a mile or so of peddling we could see a marina in the distance.

The marina itself was pretty well organized but the surroundings were a bit less put together. All along the river were homes made from scraps of tin, cardboard and tar paper. Many of them were without windows or doors and debris littered the banks. After about an hour wait our boat finally departed. The atmosphere in this part of Panama was a lot different from that of Costa Rica and the boat ride down the river provided some real insight into the way of life outside of Panamas bigger cities.

After a pretty long boat ride we arrived at another marina. Once off the boat we got directions to our next mode of transport. We walked through a nice little neighborhood on our way to a much smaller marina. Here we met up with a man that said he knew all about the little island we sought and would be glad to take us. We were a little surprised to see that his boat was actually a hollowed out log but we were more than happy to climb aboard.

The waves splashed over the sides of the log canoe as we headed out into the open water. Soon we could see the tiny island in the distance and we knew our long journey was coming to an end.

Once we hit land again our luck began to improve.

We secured the best accommodations on the island. For about twelve dollars a night we stayed in a rustic but wonderful cabana literally built "on the water." Our twelve bucks also got us a home cooked dinner each night and a handmade hammock that swung gently in the island breeze.

Our long and eclectic trip was definitely well worth it. We spent several wonderful days exploring the island, snorkeling for conch shells and playing dominoes with the locals.

In the end the final destination was great but the journey is what made the experience special.

CHAPTER 14 ....THE SWING OF A BIG STICK

In my travels I have found that it is the people I meet that make a place special not the beauty of my surroundings. I have met the most genuine of people and made the best of friends in places that offer very little in the way of luxury or pleasures for the eye.

The people I have met on lifes' grand journey have not all come from strange lands and exotic places. They have not all been great scholars or inspiring teachers. In fact, they have not all meant me well. None the less each of them has possessed a very valuable gift. They have all experienced a life very different than my own and they have all had something from which I could learn.

Not only have I realized that life is about people not things but I have also gained a great respect for the trials it has placed in my path. I have discovered that the destinations I once found so important often pale in comparison to the journeys required to reach them.

In my travels I have been to all seven continents and I have touched the corners of our planet. I have journeyed from North of the Arctic Circle to the Southern reaches of Antarctica. I have experienced the heights of Mount Everest and the depths of the worlds' oceans. I have traveled by everything from elephants and dog sleds to bamboo rafts.

Still I would have to say one of my more memorable trips was the journey between Costa Rica and Panama. I was handed off like a baton in a relay race at least a half dozen times but in the end the people who said they would get me to my destination did just that.

Perhaps not everyone had my best interest in mind but from that I learned two things. Sometimes extreme behavior requires an extreme response…….and sometimes you have to trust your instincts.

I believe kindness and reason elicit far more cooperation than aggression and confrontation but sometimes the swing of a big stick simply can not be avoided.

PANAMA

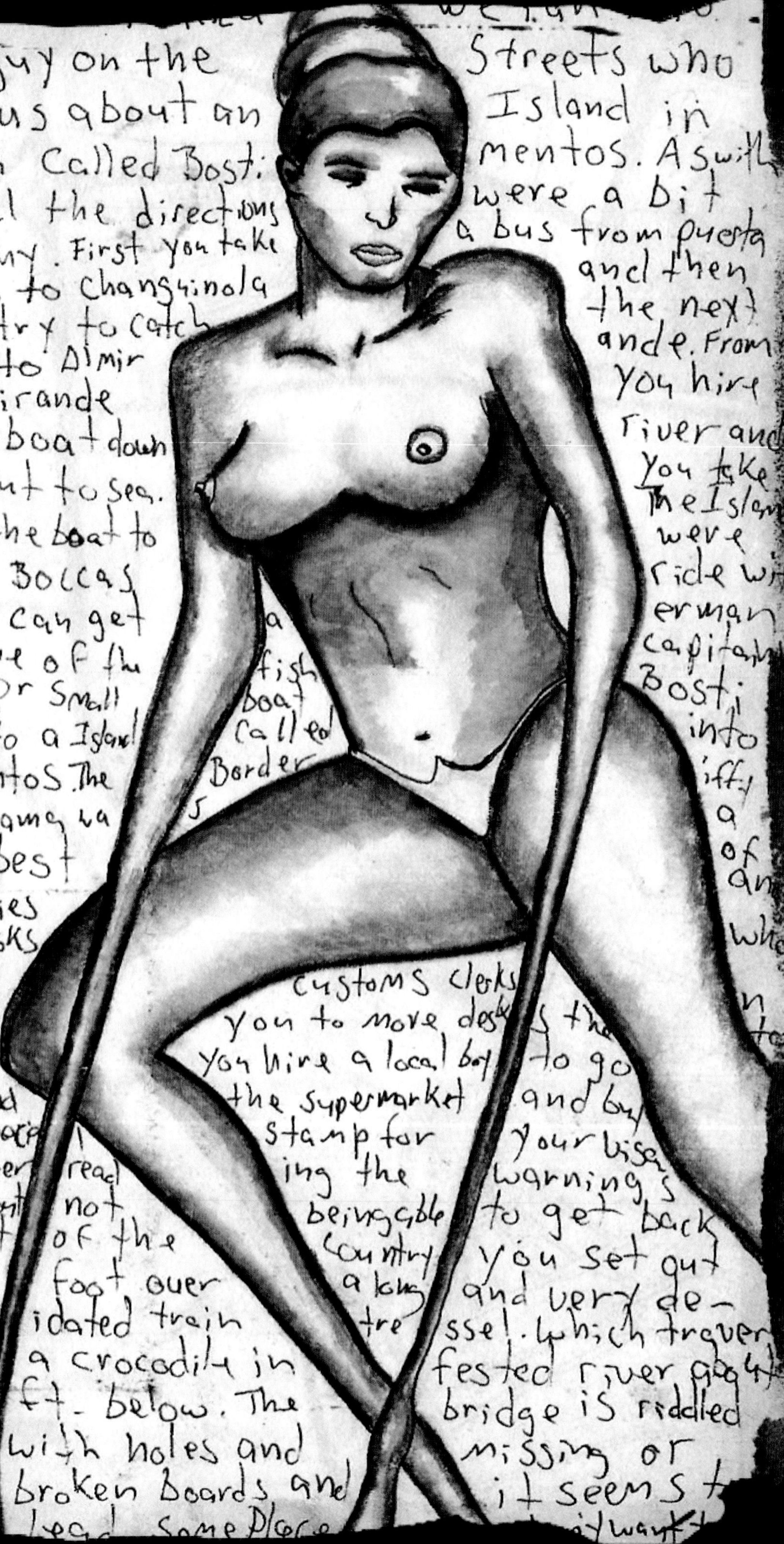

a guy on the
told us about an
Panama called Bost.
all travel the directions
sketchy. First you take
Ueijo to changuinola
you try to catch
van to Almir
Almirande
a boat down
out to sea.
the boat to
of Boccas
you can get
one of the
or small
to a Island
mentos. The
Panama va
at best
series
desks

streets who
Island in
mentos. A swift
were a bit
a bus from puerta
and then
the next
ande. From
you hire
river and
you take
the Islan
were
ride wit
erman
capita
Bost.
into
iffy
a
of
an
whe
n to

a
fish
boat
called
Border

Send
a space
After read
about not
out of the
on
lap
ses
30

customs clerks
you to move desk the
you hire a local boy to go
the supermarket and buy
stamp for
ing the
being able
country
a long
tre

foot over
idated train
a crocodile in
ft. below. The
with holes and
broken boards and
lead some place

your visa
warning
to get back
you set out
and very de-
ssel. which traver
fested river righ
bridge is riddled
missing or
it seems t

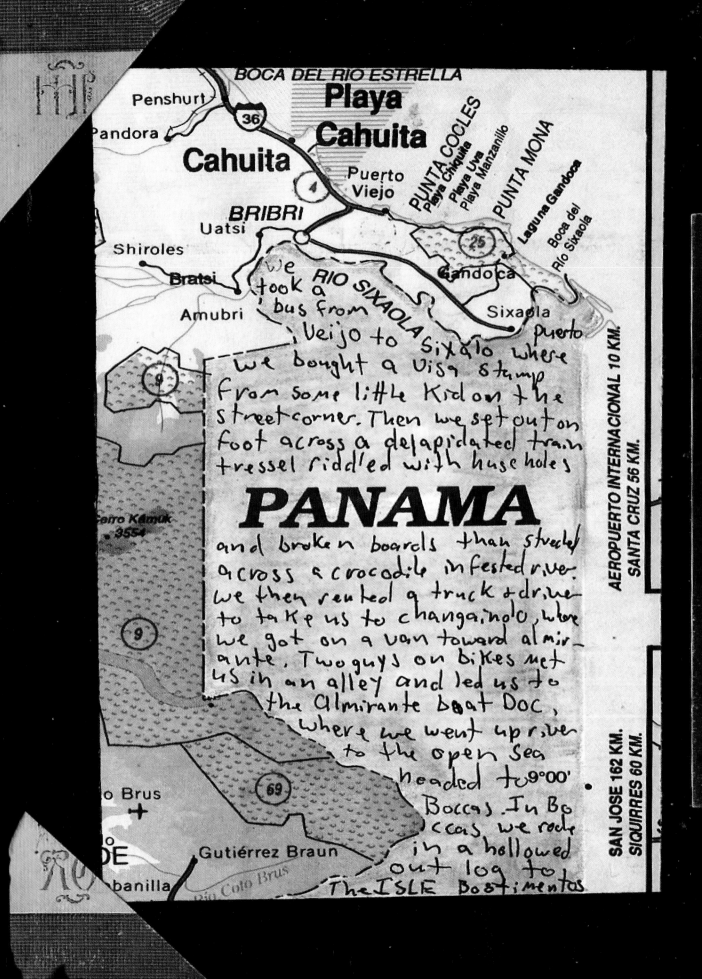

BOCA DEL RIO ESTRELLA

Penshurt

Pandora

Playa

Cahuita

36

Cahuita

Puerto
Viejo

PUNTA COCLES
Playa Chiquita
Playa Uva
Playa Manzanillo

PUNTA MONA

4

BRIBRI

Uatsi

Laguna Gandoca

Boca del
Río Sixaola

Shiroles

25

Bratsi

We took a bus from Veijo to Sixola where

RIO SIXAOLA

Gandoca

Amubri

Sixaola

Puerto

we bought a visa stamp from some little kid on the streetcorner. Then we set out on foot across a delapidated train tressel riddled with huge holes

Cerro Kámuk
3554

PANAMA

and broken boards than steaded across a crocodile infested river. We then rented a truck & drive to take us to changainolo, where we got on a van toward almirante. Two guys on bikes met us in an alley and led us to the almirante boat Doc, where we went upriver to the open Sea headed to 9°00' Boccas. In Boccas we rode in a hollowed out log to The ISLE Bastimentos

9

69

o Brus

Gutiérrez Braun

ROE

banilla

Río Coto Brus

THE TREE
OF LIFE

III

Find this door
and you are
one step closer

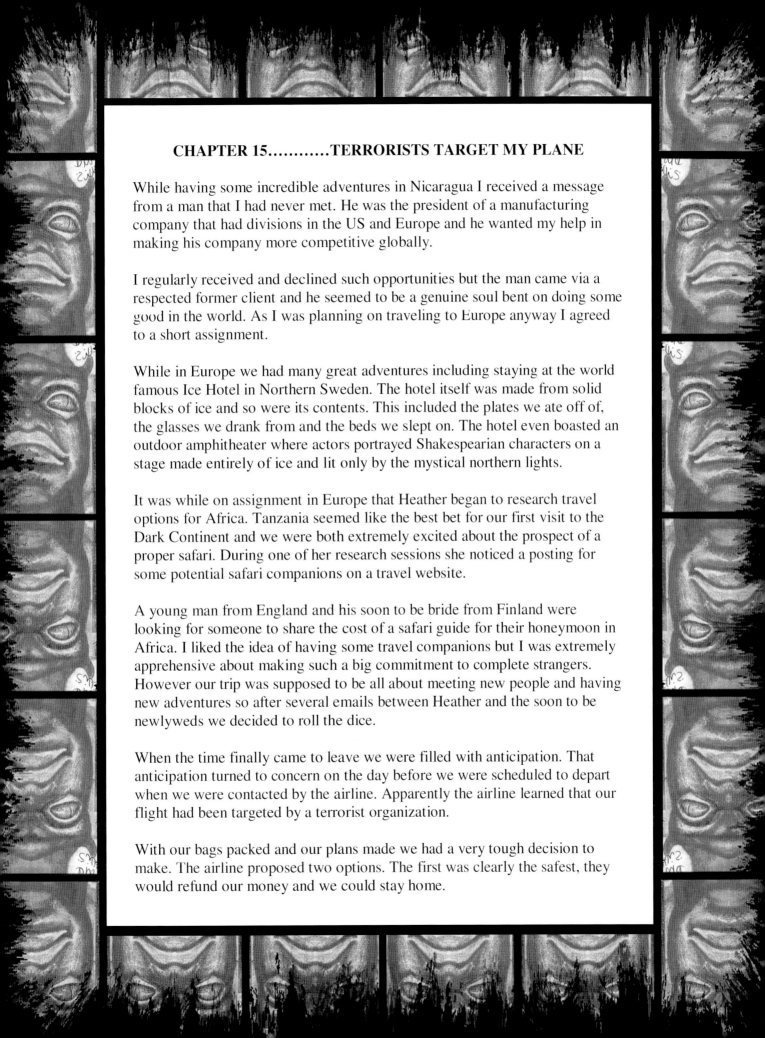

CHAPTER 15...........TERRORISTS TARGET MY PLANE

While having some incredible adventures in Nicaragua I received a message from a man that I had never met. He was the president of a manufacturing company that had divisions in the US and Europe and he wanted my help in making his company more competitive globally.

I regularly received and declined such opportunities but the man came via a respected former client and he seemed to be a genuine soul bent on doing some good in the world. As I was planning on traveling to Europe anyway I agreed to a short assignment.

While in Europe we had many great adventures including staying at the world famous Ice Hotel in Northern Sweden. The hotel itself was made from solid blocks of ice and so were its contents. This included the plates we ate off of, the glasses we drank from and the beds we slept on. The hotel even boasted an outdoor amphitheater where actors portrayed Shakespearian characters on a stage made entirely of ice and lit only by the mystical northern lights.

It was while on assignment in Europe that Heather began to research travel options for Africa. Tanzania seemed like the best bet for our first visit to the Dark Continent and we were both extremely excited about the prospect of a proper safari. During one of her research sessions she noticed a posting for some potential safari companions on a travel website.

A young man from England and his soon to be bride from Finland were looking for someone to share the cost of a safari guide for their honeymoon in Africa. I liked the idea of having some travel companions but I was extremely apprehensive about making such a big commitment to complete strangers. However our trip was supposed to be all about meeting new people and having new adventures so after several emails between Heather and the soon to be newlyweds we decided to roll the dice.

When the time finally came to leave we were filled with anticipation. That anticipation turned to concern on the day before we were scheduled to depart when we were contacted by the airline. Apparently the airline learned that our flight had been targeted by a terrorist organization.

With our bags packed and our plans made we had a very tough decision to make. The airline proposed two options. The first was clearly the safest, they would refund our money and we could stay home.

The second option was a bit more risky but it would allow us to continue our trip. The airline would fly us "safely" into Uganda where an unmarked plane would be waiting to transport us to Kenya. From Kenya we would be responsible for finding our own ground transportation to the border and on into Tanzania.

It was the night before we planned to fly out and we had little time to weigh our options. We tried desperately to contact Joe and Hannah to see if they still wanted to continue with the plan, but we did not have a phone number for them and they weren't responding to email. We decided to evaluate the risks and study our options over dinner.

We had some real concerns to consider. Our flight was to leave from London and hostilities between the British and certain terror groups in the Middle East were almost as high as they were in the States. On top of this we were not sure how well the "unmarked" plane trick was really going to work. Additionally we knew that Uganda had a history of instability.

We wanted to get some advice, but this was not the kind of thing a lot of people had experience with. Anyone that was not an experienced traveler would of course advise against it and we didn't know anyone that had experience traveling in Africa.

We knew there were several US government sites that advised travelers on the safety of foreign destinations. We also knew that if we took those sites literally we would never make it past Canada. Every place that we had been previously was flagged with one travel advisory or another and we didn't find the site to be of that much help.

With nowhere to turn for advice we just had to weigh our options. To tell you the truth it probably would have been an easy decision if not for our commitment to the young honeymooners. All of our research had been on Tanzania not Kenya and Uganda. In fact we chose Tanzania because we felt it was generally safer than Kenya and definitely a better bet than Uganda.

In weighing our risks we were primarily concerned about two things. The first was obviously being blown out of the sky. The second was being blown off the road somewhere between Kenya and Tanzania.

We felt like the risk of getting into Uganda was minimal. It was a different flight number and different destination........ The likelihood of being targeted

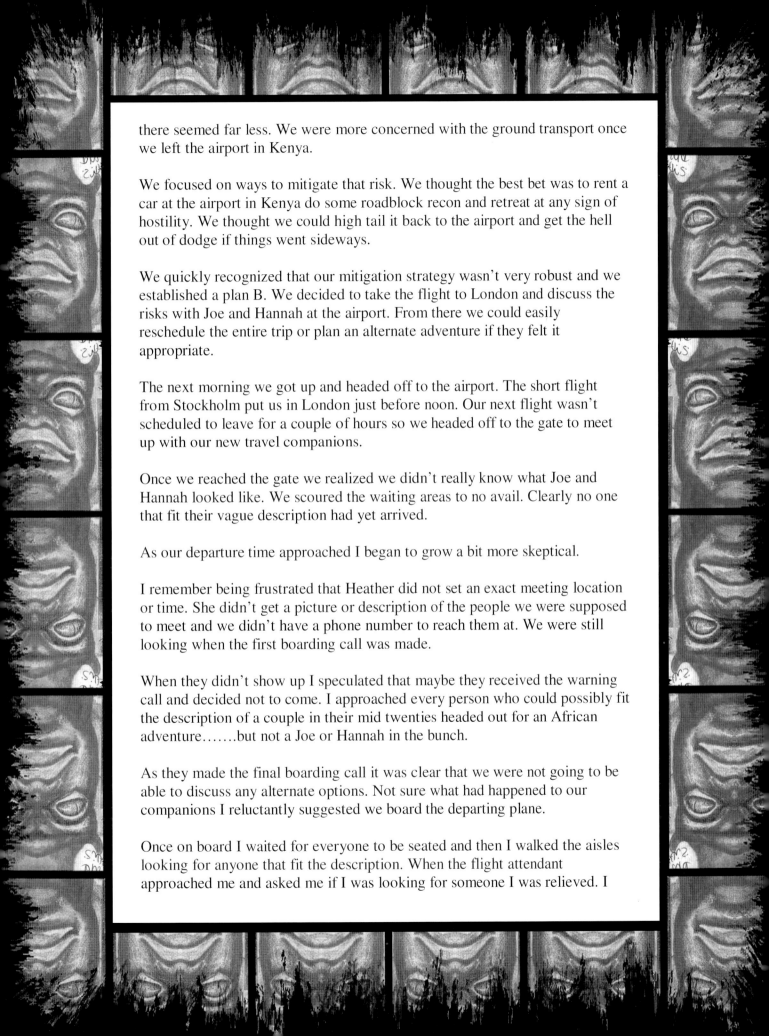

there seemed far less. We were more concerned with the ground transport once we left the airport in Kenya.

We focused on ways to mitigate that risk. We thought the best bet was to rent a car at the airport in Kenya do some roadblock recon and retreat at any sign of hostility. We thought we could high tail it back to the airport and get the hell out of dodge if things went sideways.

We quickly recognized that our mitigation strategy wasn't very robust and we established a plan B. We decided to take the flight to London and discuss the risks with Joe and Hannah at the airport. From there we could easily reschedule the entire trip or plan an alternate adventure if they felt it appropriate.

The next morning we got up and headed off to the airport. The short flight from Stockholm put us in London just before noon. Our next flight wasn't scheduled to leave for a couple of hours so we headed off to the gate to meet up with our new travel companions.

Once we reached the gate we realized we didn't really know what Joe and Hannah looked like. We scoured the waiting areas to no avail. Clearly no one that fit their vague description had yet arrived.

As our departure time approached I began to grow a bit more skeptical.

I remember being frustrated that Heather did not set an exact meeting location or time. She didn't get a picture or description of the people we were supposed to meet and we didn't have a phone number to reach them at. We were still looking when the first boarding call was made.

When they didn't show up I speculated that maybe they received the warning call and decided not to come. I approached every person who could possibly fit the description of a couple in their mid twenties headed out for an African adventure…….but not a Joe or Hannah in the bunch.

As they made the final boarding call it was clear that we were not going to be able to discuss any alternate options. Not sure what had happened to our companions I reluctantly suggested we board the departing plane.

Once on board I waited for everyone to be seated and then I walked the aisles looking for anyone that fit the description. When the flight attendant approached me and asked me if I was looking for someone I was relieved. I replied, "Yes, we were supposed to be taking this trip with some friends but I haven't seen them and I am afraid they missed the flight."

"No problem" she responded, "Give me their last name and I will check the boarding registry."

I felt like an idiot when I realized I did not know the last name of the people I just described as friends. To avoid looking like a complete moron I did some quick thinking and then proclaimed that we had just met them.......and I could not remember their last name.

The flight attendant gave me a suspicious look and then said, "Well what do they look like?"

I looked back at Heather and shook my head.

Now I knew I was going to look like a moron and a stalker.

The flight attendant then said, "Just give me their description and I will look for them as I make my rounds."

Why I was so embarrassed to say we met them on the internet I don't know. I guess I assumed only pedophiles and desperate shut ins "met friends on the internet." Or maybe I was still pissed that we arranged this whole trip around traveling with two people whose last name and phone number we had neglected to secure. Or maybe it was the fact that if we had bothered to establish a meeting place and time I wouldn't be in this awkward situation.

In any case I was forced to say.....UHHHHHH....... I don't know what they look like......UHHHHHH.....never mind.

It was clear that I just secured the distinction of being the most suspicious guy on the plane. I returned to my seat in disgust and went to sleep.

When I awoke I was in better spirits and we started to discuss our plan. Without Joe and Hannah on board we would have to bare the entire cost of the guide, but that wasn't really my concern. I was more concerned about our overland journey. I was determined that we would rent our own car and maintain control of our itinerary. Somehow, this simple detail gave me the illusion of control with regards to the whole messed up situation.

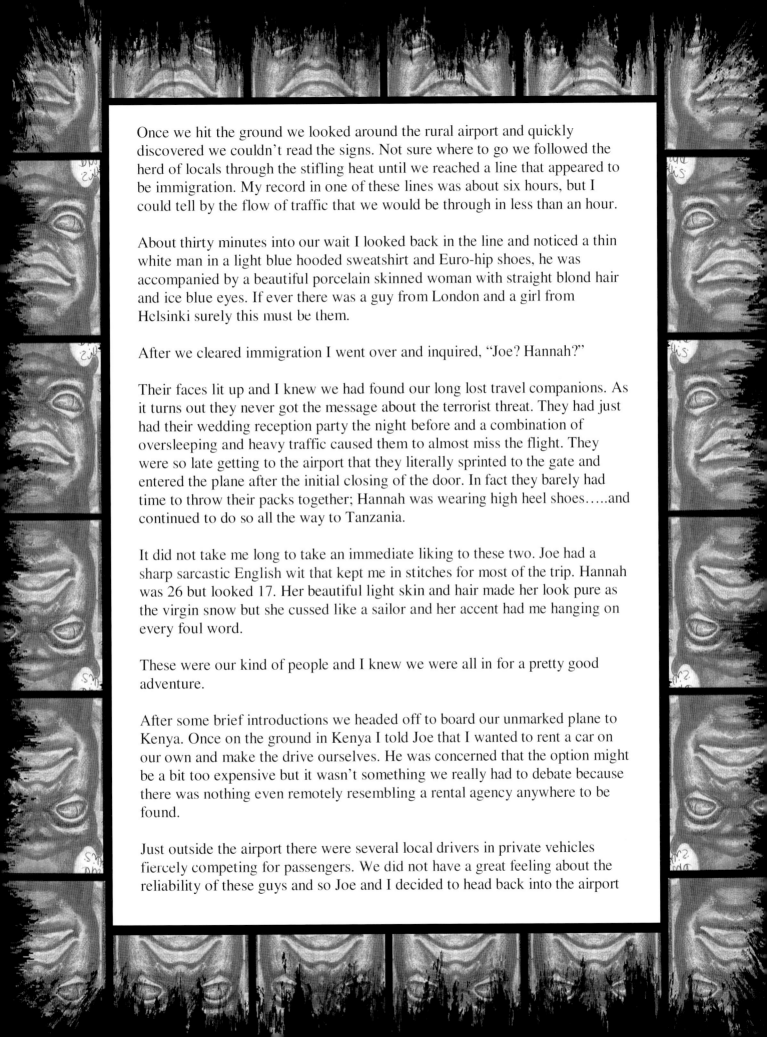

Once we hit the ground we looked around the rural airport and quickly discovered we couldn't read the signs. Not sure where to go we followed the herd of locals through the stifling heat until we reached a line that appeared to be immigration. My record in one of these lines was about six hours, but I could tell by the flow of traffic that we would be through in less than an hour.

About thirty minutes into our wait I looked back in the line and noticed a thin white man in a light blue hooded sweatshirt and Euro-hip shoes, he was accompanied by a beautiful porcelain skinned woman with straight blond hair and ice blue eyes. If ever there was a guy from London and a girl from Helsinki surely this must be them.

After we cleared immigration I went over and inquired, "Joe? Hannah?"

Their faces lit up and I knew we had found our long lost travel companions. As it turns out they never got the message about the terrorist threat. They had just had their wedding reception party the night before and a combination of oversleeping and heavy traffic caused them to almost miss the flight. They were so late getting to the airport that they literally sprinted to the gate and entered the plane after the initial closing of the door. In fact they barely had time to throw their packs together; Hannah was wearing high heel shoes…..and continued to do so all the way to Tanzania.

It did not take me long to take an immediate liking to these two. Joe had a sharp sarcastic English wit that kept me in stitches for most of the trip. Hannah was 26 but looked 17. Her beautiful light skin and hair made her look pure as the virgin snow but she cussed like a sailor and her accent had me hanging on every foul word.

These were our kind of people and I knew we were all in for a pretty good adventure.

After some brief introductions we headed off to board our unmarked plane to Kenya. Once on the ground in Kenya I told Joe that I wanted to rent a car on our own and make the drive ourselves. He was concerned that the option might be a bit too expensive but it wasn't something we really had to debate because there was nothing even remotely resembling a rental agency anywhere to be found.

Just outside the airport there were several local drivers in private vehicles fiercely competing for passengers. We did not have a great feeling about the reliability of these guys and so Joe and I decided to head back into the airport

to try and find a more sanctioned mode of transportation. Once inside we found a makeshift office that served as a booking agency for cross country drivers and other assorted services. The girls stayed with the bags and Joe and I went in to negotiate.

Once we came to agreement on price we emerged to share our tales of victory with the awaiting ladies. We proudly shared the final price and Hannah immediately said, "Good job boys, I think you got stitched up quite nicely."

I thought she was congratulating us for shrewdly sealing the deal but as it turns out "getting stitched up" is British for "getting screwed." I had no idea how right she was.

While we were waiting for our driver to arrive we approached one of the guys on the street to inquire about price. Sure enough he was about half the price. But at least we had secured more reliable transportation…….or so we thought.

As we were standing there talking to the man on the street our driver arrived and motioned for us to get into his car. Before we could move an inch a heated argument broke out between the two men. We could not understand a word, but it was pretty clear that it wasn't all greetings and salutations. The screaming match seemed to go on forever.

Feeling guilty for starting the rift we pulled out our vouchers and tried to explain to the man on the street that we had already paid the other driver. That just seemed to anger him more.

We had only been in Kenya for 20 minutes and already we were drawing attention to ourselves…...this was not the low profile I had in mind. After some more harsh words between the men the first man conceded and we got into the dilapidated vehicle of the second angry man. Hannah gave us the "I told you so" look and we got underway.

The ride gave us a great chance to get to know each other and it soon became apparent that Hannah was not going to hold our poor negotiating skills against us. We had a great time talking and taking in the scenery for a couple of hours before our tranquility was shattered.

Out of nowhere we heard a huge thud underneath the van followed by a terrible grinding sound and a trail of sparks. The driver hit the brakes and within a few hundred feet the van sparked to a stop. We piled out of the van

and followed the driver underneath to assess the damage. What I saw was definitely not good news. The drive shaft was severed into two pieces.

With Swahili books in hand we grabbed our packs and hit the tar. A couple miles up the road we found a farming compound and a man with a tractor. I knew it was not very likely that the van was going to be operational anytime soon so I assumed the driver would call for a back up vehicle. Nothing could have been further from the truth.

As we waited at the farming complex for the tractor driver to drag the hobbled van back an older man with skin as black as the night sky came up and gave me a tap on the arm. In English he said "It is not safe for you here, if someone with skin like mine asks you to follow them do not do it........and keep a watch on your women too," he then turned and slowly meandered off.

I appreciated and respected the warning. I kept a close eye on our surroundings as we waited for the tractor to return with the van in tow. Now that he had retrieved the van I expected that we would be calling in the replacement vehicle.......but once again no such luck.

Two of the men from the farm crawled under the van and began to smash it unmercifully with large metal hammers. The driver claimed they were fixing it but it seemed more like the final death blows to me.

After quite a bit of vigorous smashing the deafening banging subsided and the two men emerged from the underside of the truck. One of them left shortly thereafter only to return sometime later with a rusty torch and a small bottle of welding gas. I could not believe that their plan was to try and weld the severed driveshaft together.

Did they truly intend to send us away with only a big metal band aid preventing us from being stranded in the middle of the Kenyan backlands? Surely it would only be a matter of time before our stranded van would be overrun with ravenous lions.

But alas that was exactly their plan. After another hour or so of banging and welding sparks they proclaimed the job finished. We gave the men a couple of dollars and we were underway once again. The misshapen drive shaft thumped against the bottom of the van like a bowling ball in a clothes dryer but somehow it held together. We all held our breath as we inched toward Tanzania.

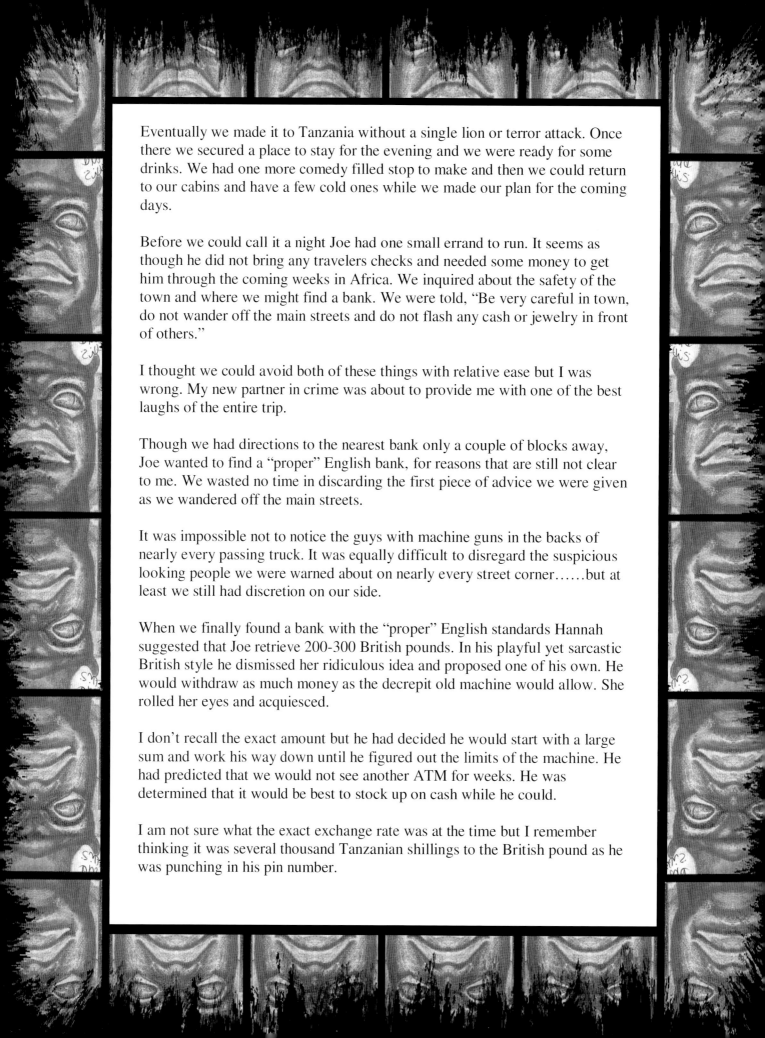

Eventually we made it to Tanzania without a single lion or terror attack. Once there we secured a place to stay for the evening and we were ready for some drinks. We had one more comedy filled stop to make and then we could return to our cabins and have a few cold ones while we made our plan for the coming days.

Before we could call it a night Joe had one small errand to run. It seems as though he did not bring any travelers checks and needed some money to get him through the coming weeks in Africa. We inquired about the safety of the town and where we might find a bank. We were told, "Be very careful in town, do not wander off the main streets and do not flash any cash or jewelry in front of others."

I thought we could avoid both of these things with relative ease but I was wrong. My new partner in crime was about to provide me with one of the best laughs of the entire trip.

Though we had directions to the nearest bank only a couple of blocks away, Joe wanted to find a "proper" English bank, for reasons that are still not clear to me. We wasted no time in discarding the first piece of advice we were given as we wandered off the main streets.

It was impossible not to notice the guys with machine guns in the backs of nearly every passing truck. It was equally difficult to disregard the suspicious looking people we were warned about on nearly every street corner……but at least we still had discretion on our side.

When we finally found a bank with the "proper" English standards Hannah suggested that Joe retrieve 200-300 British pounds. In his playful yet sarcastic British style he dismissed her ridiculous idea and proposed one of his own. He would withdraw as much money as the decrepit old machine would allow. She rolled her eyes and acquiesced.

I don't recall the exact amount but he had decided he would start with a large sum and work his way down until he figured out the limits of the machine. He had predicted that we would not see another ATM for weeks. He was determined that it would be best to stock up on cash while he could.

I am not sure what the exact exchange rate was at the time but I remember thinking it was several thousand Tanzanian shillings to the British pound as he was punching in his pin number.

He was about to put in the final digit when a truck load of machine gun toting Africans pulled in behind us. Hannah told him to wait for them to leave but he insisted that he would just quickly grab the cash and stick it in his money belt before anyone noticed what he was doing.

Don't get me wrong, Joe was an extremely bright guy but he could be a bit cavalier at times, especially when being given directions from his day old bride. As he typed in the amount he decided to start in the thousands of pounds range and work his way down until the machine accepted his request.

Much to his surprise the machine granted his very first request. At first he was quite pleased with the result. The machine spit out a wad of money and he quickly scooped it up and tucked it into his money belt. Before he could zip the belt out came another wad......... and then another. Much to his horror Joe was literally becoming a Tanzanian millionaire right before our eyes. The machine just kept spitting out wad after wad and it was clear that we weren't going to be heeding the second piece of advice we were given either. Avoiding flashing cash in this situation was like trying to dodge raindrops.....it just wasn't going to happen.

As the men with the machine guns started to get out of their truck Joe was frantically cramming literally millions of shillings into every open orifice he could find. He crammed his front pockets full and then his back. Once he crammed his sweatshirt pockets full he began pawning huge handfuls of cash off to his scowling wife......all the while jabbering away in a hilarious English tirade.

He had money crammed down his pants, he was sticking huge handfuls into his shirt and the machine just wouldn't stop dispensing. He was cursing the machine and having a tiff with his impatient wife that was so hilarious I almost wet my pants with laughter. I just couldn't believe how much money one machine could hold and that it would dispense it to a single customer but it just kept coming.

As we walked back to our cabins Hannah was eager to get off the back streets and she was rushing Joe along. All I can remember from the hilarious argument is him saying he was so stuffed full of bloody cash that he felt like the bloody scarecrow from the Wizard of Oz.........and that he would like to see her run down the bloody street with two million shillings sticking out of her bloody knickers.

It was at this very moment that I knew it was going to be an unforgettable trip. Somehow the first day in a new country never failed to disappoint.

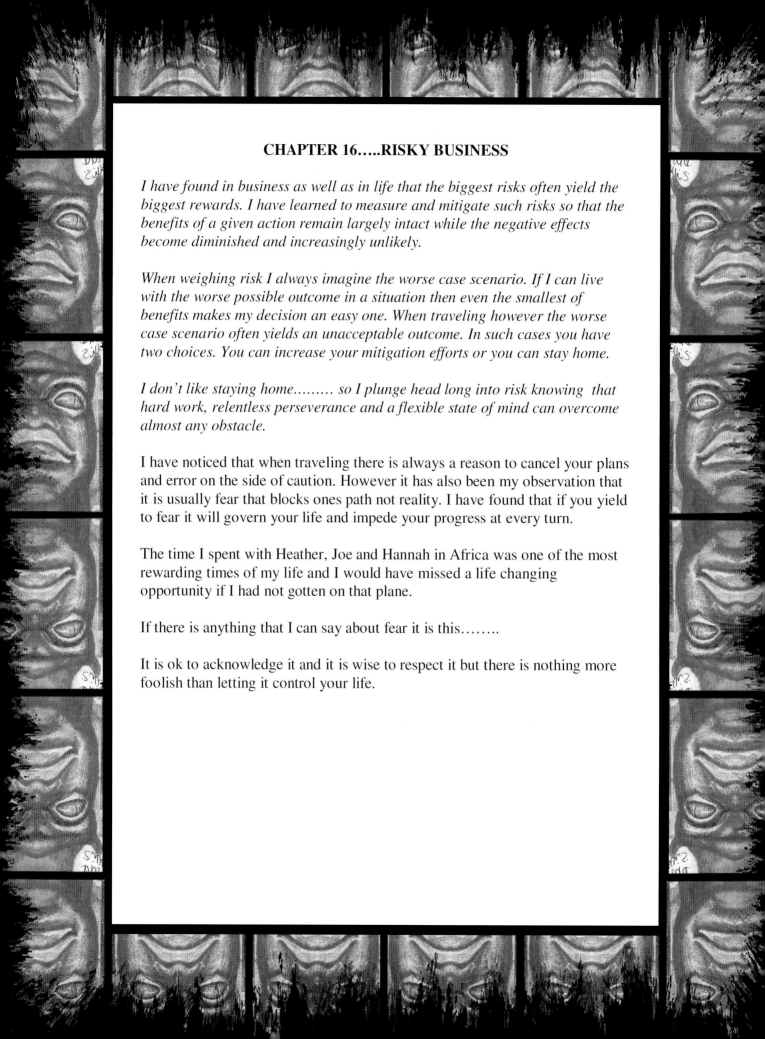

CHAPTER 16.....RISKY BUSINESS

I have found in business as well as in life that the biggest risks often yield the biggest rewards. I have learned to measure and mitigate such risks so that the benefits of a given action remain largely intact while the negative effects become diminished and increasingly unlikely.

When weighing risk I always imagine the worse case scenario. If I can live with the worse possible outcome in a situation then even the smallest of benefits makes my decision an easy one. When traveling however the worse case scenario often yields an unacceptable outcome. In such cases you have two choices. You can increase your mitigation efforts or you can stay home.

I don't like staying home......... so I plunge head long into risk knowing that hard work, relentless perseverance and a flexible state of mind can overcome almost any obstacle.

I have noticed that when traveling there is always a reason to cancel your plans and error on the side of caution. However it has also been my observation that it is usually fear that blocks ones path not reality. I have found that if you yield to fear it will govern your life and impede your progress at every turn.

The time I spent with Heather, Joe and Hannah in Africa was one of the most rewarding times of my life and I would have missed a life changing opportunity if I had not gotten on that plane.

If there is anything that I can say about fear it is this........

It is ok to acknowledge it and it is wise to respect it but there is nothing more foolish than letting it control your life.

TERRORISTS

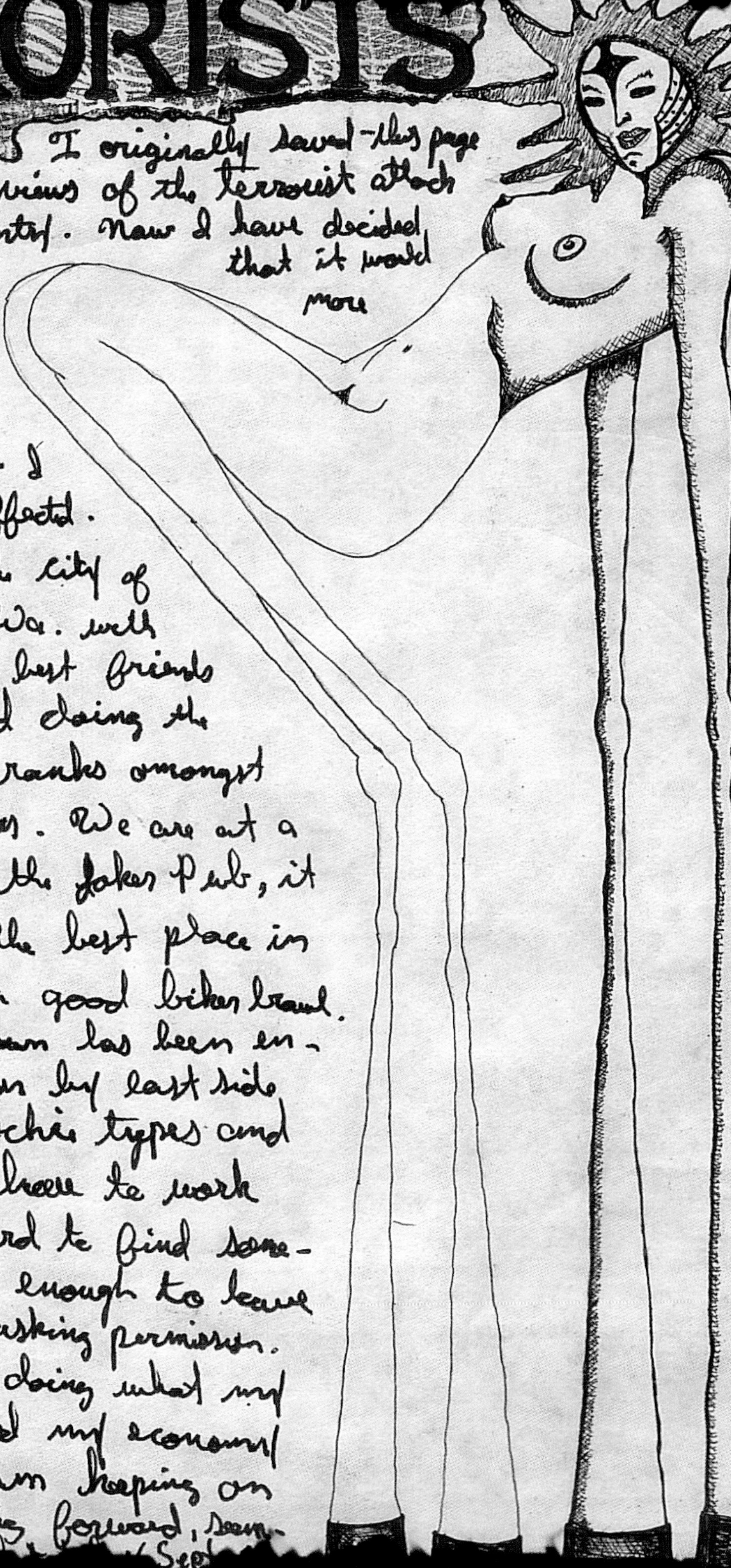

I originally saved this page to write my views of the terrorist attack on my country. Now I have decided that it would for the time be far more appropriate to write about how I am not affected. I am in the city of Issaquah Wa. with two of my best friends in the world doing the thing that ranks amongst my favorites. We are at a place called the Lakes Pub, it was once the best place in town for a good biker brawl. Now this town has been encroached upon by east side Microsoft techie types and you would have to work awfull hard to find some-one brave enough to leave without asking permission. But I am doing what my country and my economy needs, I am keeping on and moving forward, seem-ingly ... Sept

TERRORISTS ATTACKED ME TODAY

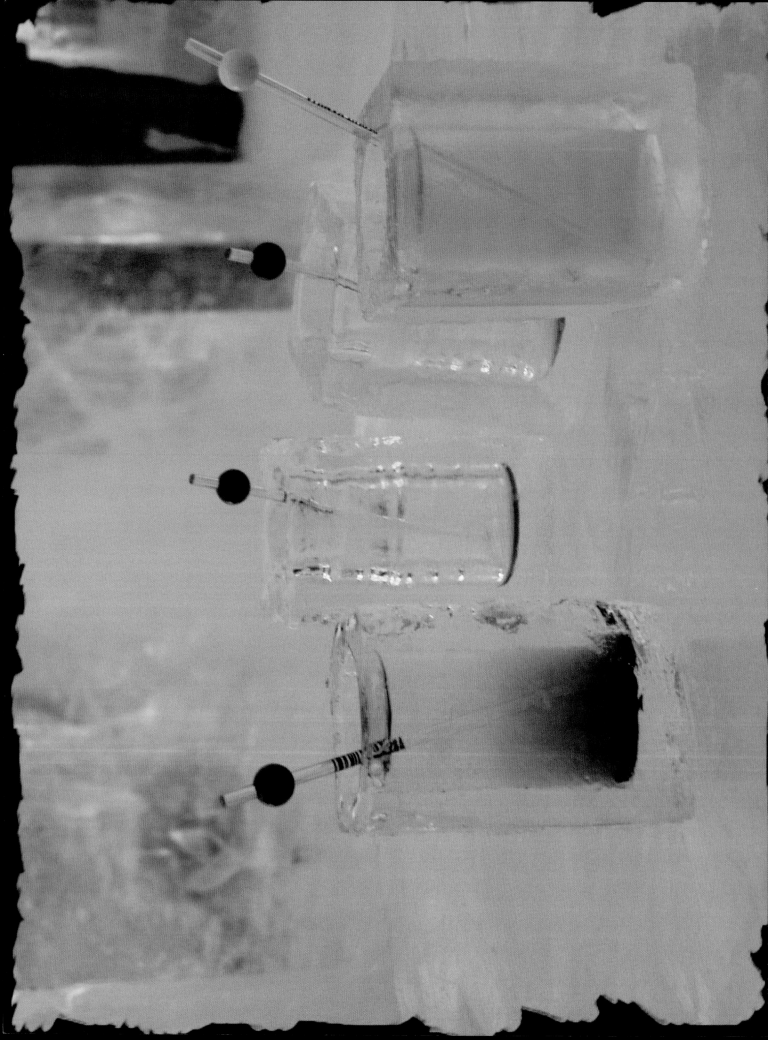

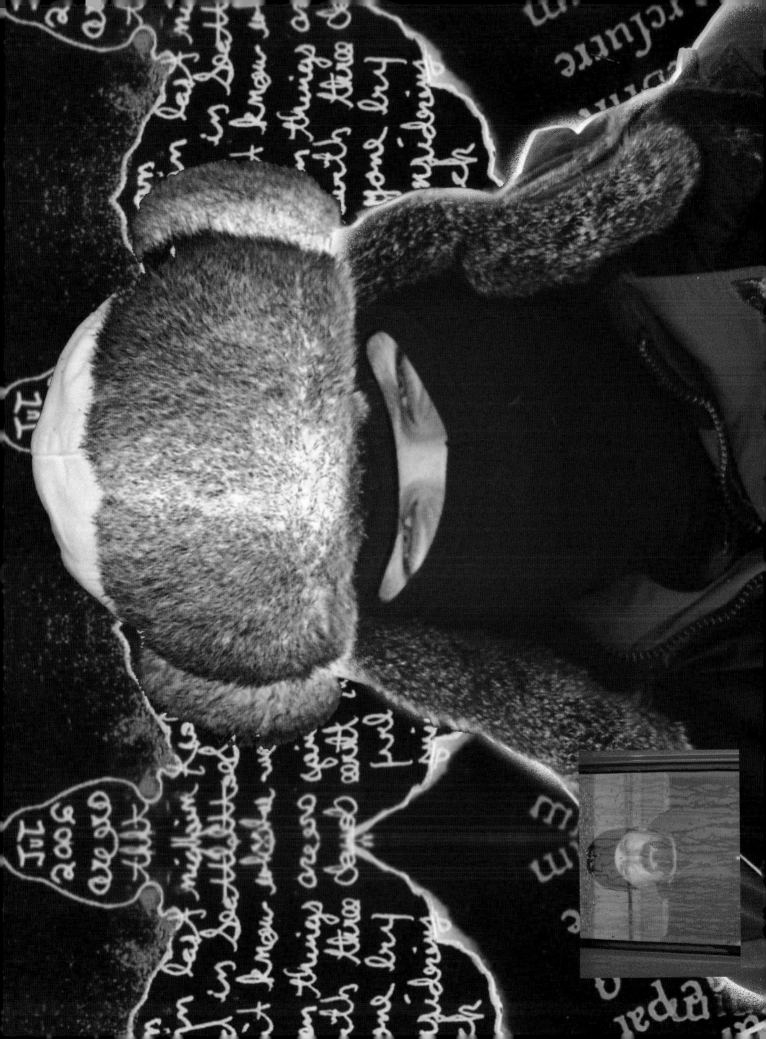

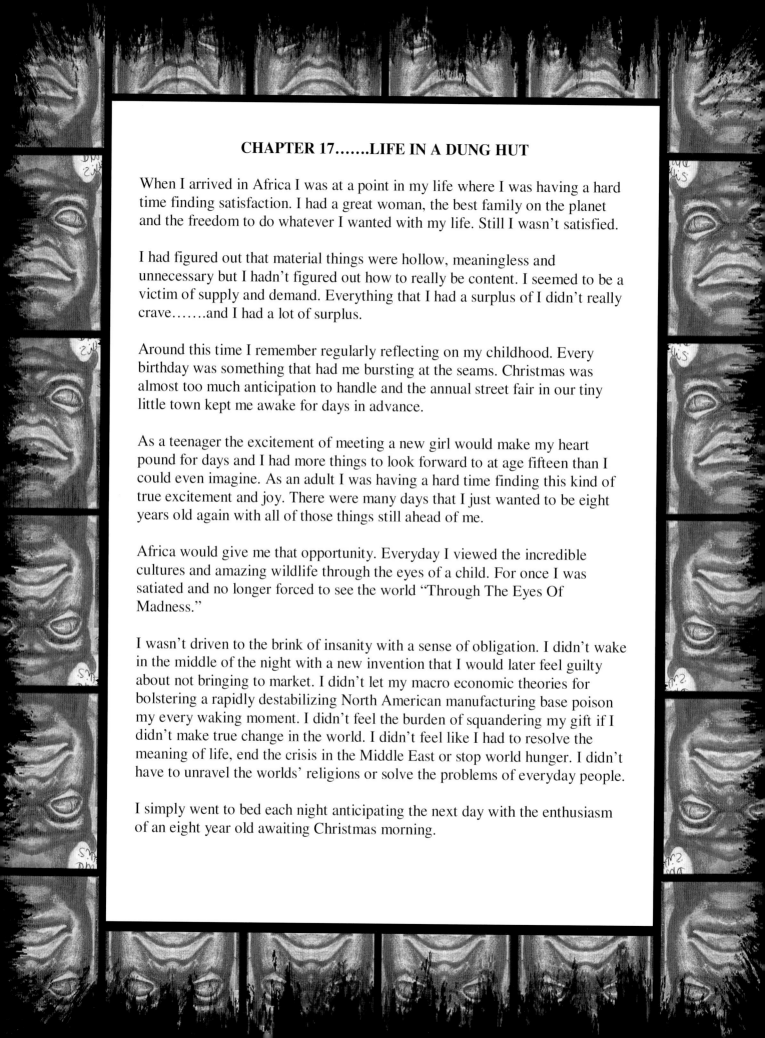

CHAPTER 17.......LIFE IN A DUNG HUT

When I arrived in Africa I was at a point in my life where I was having a hard time finding satisfaction. I had a great woman, the best family on the planet and the freedom to do whatever I wanted with my life. Still I wasn't satisfied.

I had figured out that material things were hollow, meaningless and unnecessary but I hadn't figured out how to really be content. I seemed to be a victim of supply and demand. Everything that I had a surplus of I didn't really crave.......and I had a lot of surplus.

Around this time I remember regularly reflecting on my childhood. Every birthday was something that had me bursting at the seams. Christmas was almost too much anticipation to handle and the annual street fair in our tiny little town kept me awake for days in advance.

As a teenager the excitement of meeting a new girl would make my heart pound for days and I had more things to look forward to at age fifteen than I could even imagine. As an adult I was having a hard time finding this kind of true excitement and joy. There were many days that I just wanted to be eight years old again with all of those things still ahead of me.

Africa would give me that opportunity. Everyday I viewed the incredible cultures and amazing wildlife through the eyes of a child. For once I was satiated and no longer forced to see the world "Through The Eyes Of Madness."

I wasn't driven to the brink of insanity with a sense of obligation. I didn't wake in the middle of the night with a new invention that I would later feel guilty about not bringing to market. I didn't let my macro economic theories for bolstering a rapidly destabilizing North American manufacturing base poison my every waking moment. I didn't feel the burden of squandering my gift if I didn't make true change in the world. I didn't feel like I had to resolve the meaning of life, end the crisis in the Middle East or stop world hunger. I didn't have to unravel the worlds' religions or solve the problems of everyday people.

I simply went to bed each night anticipating the next day with the enthusiasm of an eight year old awaiting Christmas morning.

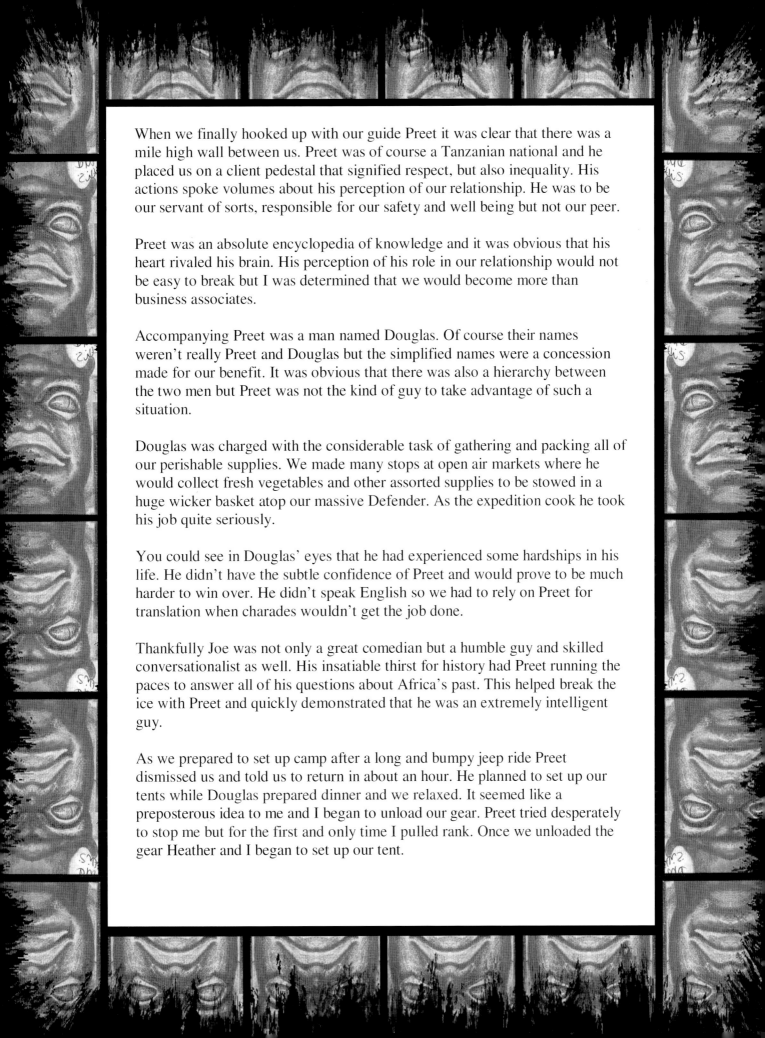

When we finally hooked up with our guide Preet it was clear that there was a mile high wall between us. Preet was of course a Tanzanian national and he placed us on a client pedestal that signified respect, but also inequality. His actions spoke volumes about his perception of our relationship. He was to be our servant of sorts, responsible for our safety and well being but not our peer.

Preet was an absolute encyclopedia of knowledge and it was obvious that his heart rivaled his brain. His perception of his role in our relationship would not be easy to break but I was determined that we would become more than business associates.

Accompanying Preet was a man named Douglas. Of course their names weren't really Preet and Douglas but the simplified names were a concession made for our benefit. It was obvious that there was also a hierarchy between the two men but Preet was not the kind of guy to take advantage of such a situation.

Douglas was charged with the considerable task of gathering and packing all of our perishable supplies. We made many stops at open air markets where he would collect fresh vegetables and other assorted supplies to be stowed in a huge wicker basket atop our massive Defender. As the expedition cook he took his job quite seriously.

You could see in Douglas' eyes that he had experienced some hardships in his life. He didn't have the subtle confidence of Preet and would prove to be much harder to win over. He didn't speak English so we had to rely on Preet for translation when charades wouldn't get the job done.

Thankfully Joe was not only a great comedian but a humble guy and skilled conversationalist as well. His insatiable thirst for history had Preet running the paces to answer all of his questions about Africa's past. This helped break the ice with Preet and quickly demonstrated that he was an extremely intelligent guy.

As we prepared to set up camp after a long and bumpy jeep ride Preet dismissed us and told us to return in about an hour. He planned to set up our tents while Douglas prepared dinner and we relaxed. It seemed like a preposterous idea to me and I began to unload our gear. Preet tried desperately to stop me but for the first and only time I pulled rank. Once we unloaded the gear Heather and I began to set up our tent.

Joe and Hannah tried to follow suit but their playful bickering soon turned into a hysterical wrestling match with their tent. Preet and I shared a good laugh and decided not to spoil the show by helping. Preet then erected a tiny tent for him and Douglas to share and then we all went over to help with the dinner. At first Douglas also refused our help but we insisted and made short work of the prep. Unlike Preet he actually seemed more put off than grateful that we had invaded his domain and we were careful not to overstep.

While we waited for him to put the finishing touches on dinner we enjoyed some Tusk…..a local African beer that Joe and I acquired during one of Douglas' supply stops. We could tell that Preet was still a little nervous around us but we got to know him a little better as we began to plan our coming adventures.

When dinner came Preet and Douglas served us and then promptly excused their selves. They huddled over a pan near the fire and began to eat dinner on their own…..as if they were not welcome at our table.

We called them over and laid down the ground rules. We were going to be together for a considerable amount of time and we wanted to be sure everyone enjoyed themselves, including Preet and Douglas. While we were together we would behave like family, we would work together, we would play together and we would eat together.

They seemed a bit apprehensive but joined us for dinner anyway. During dinner we wanted them to feel welcome so we poked fun at them in much the same way we poked fun at each other. They seemed to appreciate this brand of humor and even gave a few barbs back. It was clear they were starting to let their walls down a little.

After dinner we helped with the clean up and they knew better than to protest. When our chores were done Preet moved the food inside the Defender and then drove it away from our campsite. We learned that keeping the food that attracted animals at a safe distance was an important ritual when sleeping in a canvas tent.

When Preet returned we discussed our plan for the next few days. Though we were all very excited to see some animals we were also fascinated with the Masai village we passed earlier in the day. We told Preet that we would love to spend some time with the Masai people. Our ultimate goal was to find a tribe that had little to no contact with the modern world and learn how life without modern conveniences really worked.

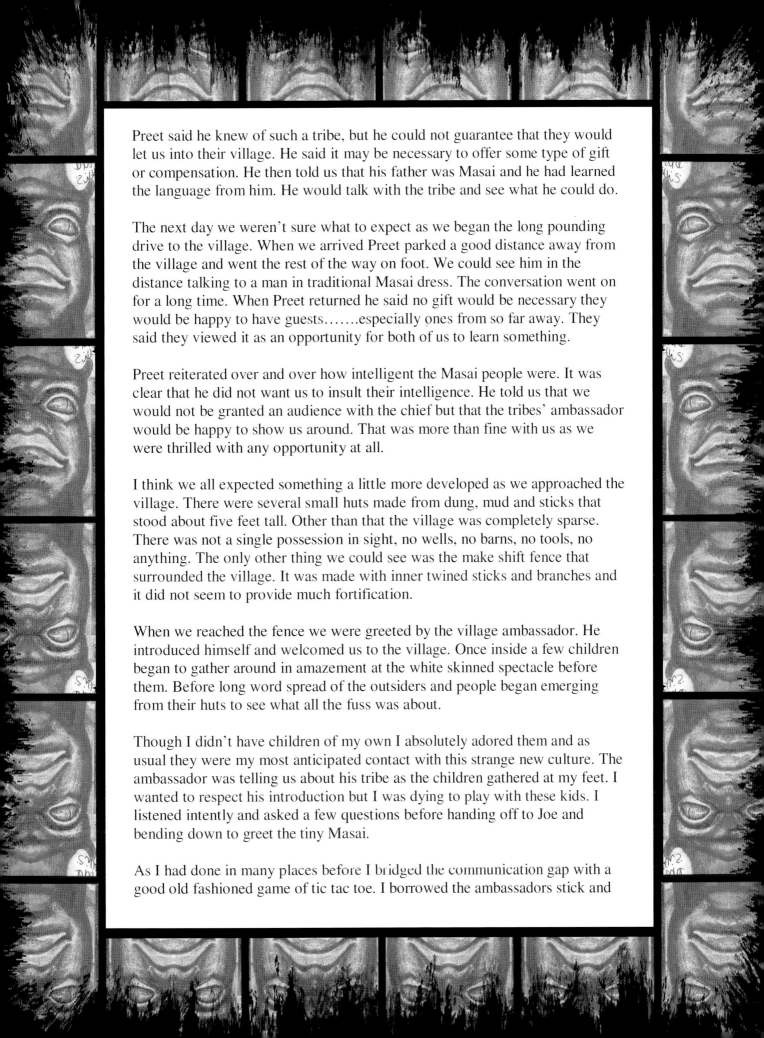

Preet said he knew of such a tribe, but he could not guarantee that they would let us into their village. He said it may be necessary to offer some type of gift or compensation. He then told us that his father was Masai and he had learned the language from him. He would talk with the tribe and see what he could do.

The next day we weren't sure what to expect as we began the long pounding drive to the village. When we arrived Preet parked a good distance away from the village and went the rest of the way on foot. We could see him in the distance talking to a man in traditional Masai dress. The conversation went on for a long time. When Preet returned he said no gift would be necessary they would be happy to have guests…….especially ones from so far away. They said they viewed it as an opportunity for both of us to learn something.

Preet reiterated over and over how intelligent the Masai people were. It was clear that he did not want us to insult their intelligence. He told us that we would not be granted an audience with the chief but that the tribes' ambassador would be happy to show us around. That was more than fine with us as we were thrilled with any opportunity at all.

I think we all expected something a little more developed as we approached the village. There were several small huts made from dung, mud and sticks that stood about five feet tall. Other than that the village was completely sparse. There was not a single possession in sight, no wells, no barns, no tools, no anything. The only other thing we could see was the make shift fence that surrounded the village. It was made with inner twined sticks and branches and it did not seem to provide much fortification.

When we reached the fence we were greeted by the village ambassador. He introduced himself and welcomed us to the village. Once inside a few children began to gather around in amazement at the white skinned spectacle before them. Before long word spread of the outsiders and people began emerging from their huts to see what all the fuss was about.

Though I didn't have children of my own I absolutely adored them and as usual they were my most anticipated contact with this strange new culture. The ambassador was telling us about his tribe as the children gathered at my feet. I wanted to respect his introduction but I was dying to play with these kids. I listened intently and asked a few questions before handing off to Joe and bending down to greet the tiny Masai.

As I had done in many places before I bridged the communication gap with a good old fashioned game of tic tac toe. I borrowed the ambassadors stick and began to scratch in the sand. At first the children did not understand the game. I used charades and gestures to explain the rules and they began to catch on. As their enthusiasm began to escalate the ambassador could not help but join in on the fun. He quickly figured out the strategy and challenged me to a game.

I let him win twice in a row thinking he had no idea. He quickly turned to Preet and said that I did not have to let him win…..he wanted a fair match. He immediately picked up the basic strategy and was able to play to at least a draw nearly every time. It seemed to please him that the children were rooting for me instead of him and he was very jovial as we played game after game.

Wanting to trade knowledge I asked if he knew any games that he could teach me…..he hesitated a little and I did not want to put him on the spot so I changed the question. I asked him if he could teach me to count to ten in Masai. As near as I could tell a portion of the Masai language was nonverbal and the numbers were communicated exclusively through sign.

Through Preet he asked me if I knew how to sign the number "1."

I remember thinking that this was going to be easier than I thought. I held up a single finger and said the English word for one. The children seemed to get quite a kick out of my abysmal failure and laughter erupted amongst the masses.

I quickly learned that one finger wasn't one and two wasn't two. The ambassador had the patience of a saint and he taught me sign after sign. After mimicking the sign I repeated the words back to him in English and then waited for the next sign. Every so often I would go back to the beginning of the list and repeat what I had already learned so that I did not forget.

Shortly into our lesson the ambassador turned to Preet and began to have a very lengthy conversation. When they were finally finished Preet turned to me and said he thinks you are very intelligent. I asked Preet why he thought this……was it because I had learned to count to ten quickly?

I was stunned at his answer………The ambassador gave such an eloquent description of the inner workings of the human mind that I could not believe I was talking to a man that lived in a dung hut. He explained in great detail that it was my style of learning that he was impressed with. He was surprised to see that I used repetition to increase my retention and he was intrigued by the fact that I kept repeating things back to him. He said that this is how an intelligent man acknowledges his understanding of new ideas and signals for more information.

It was pretty ironic that a few minutes earlier we were both standing there assuming that the other was not so bright. Preet was right; their simple way of life did not mean these people were not intelligent. As the ambassador and I began to discuss all things philosophical, Heather and Hannah wandered off to visit with the women of the tribe.

It still makes me emotional today when I think about Heathers' experience during our time with the Masai. I do not have a single photo of her without tears rolling down her face. She was so happy there and so deeply moved that tears filled her eyes constantly as she laughed and played with the children and women of the tribe.

It made me so happy to see her moved in that way that I had a hard time not tearing up myself. As I looked up I saw her dancing with the women of the tribe and just letting go. She was truly living in the moment and I was proud of her. After some time she returned with an elderly woman leading her by the arm. The ancient woman had a devious smile on her face and I could tell that she was up to something.

The women of the tribe were plotting against the men and needed our help to bring their plan to life. She explained to Preet that they loved to see the men of the tribe dance. According to her the men had recently become stubborn and refused to dance......... this is where we came in.

Apparently it was a tribal custom that they could not refuse a request to dance if it came from a guest. Because the ambassador had invited us into the village the unsuspecting men would have no choice but to dance if we made such a request.

I loved the idea but did not want to upset the men.....after all, they were carrying spears and clubs. I thought it would be wise to clear the idea with the ambassador.

The ambassadors' priority was looking after us and he was excluded from the obligation to dance. Therefore he thought it was a marvelous idea.

We made the request and the men begrudgingly sprung into action. The women were clearly delighted. Their tired faces filled with a glow as they watched their men perform.

With all the commotion the chief could not help but to emerge from his hut and investigate his previously peaceful domain. Once outside it was not hard for him to see the excitement in the air. The children were scampering around, amazed with their strange new guests, the women were ecstatic that their men were dancing and the men had even given in to the spirit of things and seemed to be enjoying their duties.

The chief came over and the ambassador introduced us. Through the sound of the dancing we had very little opportunity for conversation. After things settled down a bit we got the opportunity to ask each other all kinds of things about our respective worlds. We talked for awhile and then he invited all of us back to his hut for some more visiting.

I could tell that Preet was nervous about this proposition; he knew it would be very offensive if we declined. However he also knew that the conditions in the hut would be less than comfortable and he didn't really know if we were up to the task. Knowing that the chief was watching closely to see our responses Preet skillfully asked if we would like to join the chief and his family in their hut. We could tell by his delicate posturing that we would be in for an ordeal but we didn't care.

Of course we were honored by the offer and jumped at the chance. Inside the tiny hut Preets' reluctance soon became clear. The tiny dung hut was well under five feet on the inside making it impossible to stand up. The floor plan was barely large enough to accommodate a single sleeping area and the only remaining room was taken up by a smoldering caldron of cows' blood. The heat outside was incredible, but inside the temperature was approaching unbearable. The dung and mud made the chance of a breeze minimal and the fire added an extra intensity to the cramped quarters.

The chief motioned for us to take a seat on the edge of the dirt bed and we all squeezed together in the darkened corner. The chief, Preet and the ambassador squatted by the fire and we sat directly across from them. As our eyes adjusted to the lack of light we could see several people lying on the bed behind us. The tiny bed was not large enough for two people to lie side by side. With us sitting on the edge it was even smaller. Through the darkness we could faintly make out three bodies stacked on top of each other like bricks and mortar.

Only the glow of the coals lit the aromatic room and the flies were as thick as mud. The Masai had become so accustomed to the flies that were drawn by the cattle and the dung that they did not even brush them away from their faces.

The problem was so bad that many of the children were afflicted with blindness because the flies would land directly on their eyeballs and lay eggs.

With the three people on the bed, the chief, Preet and the ambassador crouching by the fire plus the four of us we had managed to cram ten people into a darkened room that would not comfortably accommodate one. The extra bodies not only added to the heat but contributed to the claustrophobic conditions as well.

All that aside I think the most significant assault on the senses had to be the flies. Because we had so graciously been invited into the chiefs' home none of us wanted to be disrespectful with regards to these maggot breeding pests. I must confess however it was difficult not to run from the room while clawing at my fly encrusted cranium.

As the flies swarmed our faces we all struggled not to swat them away. We all assumed that it might somehow be construed as a rude gesture. My technique was to subtlety attempt to blow them off my own face……it was not effective.

All that I could hope for is that it would be a short visit. I assumed that my colleagues shared that sentiment. I loved visiting with the chief and I could have done it for days, but the great outdoors seemed like a much better venue for lengthy conversation.

Just when I was sure that we were all of like mind, Joe began to ask the chief about every single aspect of African history for the last four hundred years or so. His quest for historical knowledge somehow seemed to dull his senses to the unbearable conditions around him. Like a cyborg he asked question after question and then waited for it to be translated into Masai. Each response had to then be given back in Masai and translated back into English at a mind numbing pace.

As I was trying to decide between killing Joe and committing suicide I noticed his curly locks whisping back and forth. The bastard was sitting closest to the door and the breeze was not only soaking him in a cooling bliss but it was also keeping the flies off his face.

Before I was forced to break off a dung soaked stick and stab my new friend through the heart Preet came to our rescue. He suggested that the chief take us outside and tell us all about his new school.

I thought to myself……..Ah……. Preet……. you brilliant man……I knew I liked you for a reason.

Once outside the chief introduced us to the tribes' teacher. It was getting late and class was finished for the day but the teacher asked if we would like to see the school. I was expecting some sort of adobe like building with rough hewn desks and a dilapidated blackboard. When we reached the school I was surprised at how far off the mark I was.

The school was nothing more than a bunch of crooked sticks stuck in the ground. There were no desks or seats of any kind, no black board, no pencils, no pens, nothing even resembling a school at all. The only hint of an educational environment was all of the children who had followed us from the village.

In the front of the stick room was a discarded piece of wall board about two feet wide and three feet high. It had been found by one of the cattle tenders and salvaged for future use. This piece of debris was their chalkboard.

Somehow they also managed to come into possession of a single piece of chalk. Their teacher guarded this chalk with an iron hand. He had been rationing the thing out for two years by the time we visited. Each day a select handful of kids would be granted permission to write a single word on the scrap wall board in an effort to preserve the chalk.

Because we were guests, the schools star pupil was allowed to write a second word for the day on this board to showcase her talents. We took it as quite an honor.

When we finally left the village we were determined to find some proper school supplies and return with them to the stick school house. We asked the village chief if there was anything else that we could bring back for him.

His request was quite simple. He had heard that there was a machine that could make a picture of a man. He believed that in the strange place called Arusha one might be able to find such a machine. He wanted us to find the machine and return with it to make a picture of him and his new bride.

He had been watching us take pictures the entire time we were there but he did not put together that our camera was the machine he had heard stories about. I took his photo and we said our goodbyes…………………………………………
…………….We could not wait to return as the village faded from our view.

CHAPTER 18......A BETTER PLACE

When I first started to travel my immediate instinct was to improve the people and places I encountered. I knew that I could teach the simple people of the world the things that made my life so great and together we could create a better place for them.

Somewhere along the way I realized that I was the simple one and the world was teaching me a better way of life. I had all that life could offer and yet somehow people living in dung huts with no water to drink managed to find the contentment that had eluded me for much of my adult life.

I am passionate about helping the world...... but it's the definition of "a better place" that gives me pause.

I was on a beach near the border of Belize having a beer and chatting with a congenial local lady when for no reason the woman became enraged and started yelling at me. I quickly reviewed our conversation in my mind for potentially offensive dialogue.........but there was none to be found.

My offense at it seems was that I had left a three dollar tip at the beachside bar. At first I thought the lady was offended that I had not tipped enough. That was not the case. Her argument was as follows:

First....... By paying so much for the beer in the first place, tourists such as myself were encouraging the local shop owners to raise prices.

Secondly........ The locals did not leave tips but were starting to be shunned by shopkeepers who expected them. The local shop owners were making more off the tourists and their tips once a month (when the cruise ships came to a near by port) than they were off the locals during the rest of the month. Tourists would come in for a few days time and then they would leave. In that time they would artificially inflate the economy and leave the locals unable to afford the escalated prices they left in their wake. Many shopkeepers were closing their doors for most of the month. They made more money in three days off the tourists than they did slaving over the locals in the other twenty seven days of the month.

Thirdly ....She wanted her son to become a school teacher and he had long since planned on doing so. But since the cruise ships started coming to town the boys' uncle was making five dollars in tips every time he dropped a family off in the village. In just a couple of days work he was making more than a school teacher did in a month.

To make matters worse, now her son had lost interest in academics and wanted to drop out of school to start driving a cab. What the hell did I expect her to do with a village full of cab drivers and bartenders?

The tirade was unexpected and all her complaints weren't necessarily my fault but she made some good points.

All over the world I have watched the best intentions of outsiders destroy the people they were trying to help. In many cases charitable organizations have raised millions of dollars only to achieve consequences far worse than escalated prices and an abundance of cab drivers.

I am not sure what the perfect balance is but I do know that our eagerness to help must be tempered with an understanding of the long term effects of our efforts.

When I left the Masai village, I wondered if providing my new friends with modern school supplies was really the right way to help. They had been getting along fine with the same piece of chalk for the last two years and probably with less than that for hundreds of years before. What ripples in the pond would I create by giving them something they didn't ask for?

As I contemplated, I was pretty sure "that doing nothing," never solved any problems.

Then again they didn't describe one piece of chalk as a "problem"……..that was my choice of words.

Deciding I couldn't advocate "doing nothing"……I did what I thought was best.

I bought the school supplies.

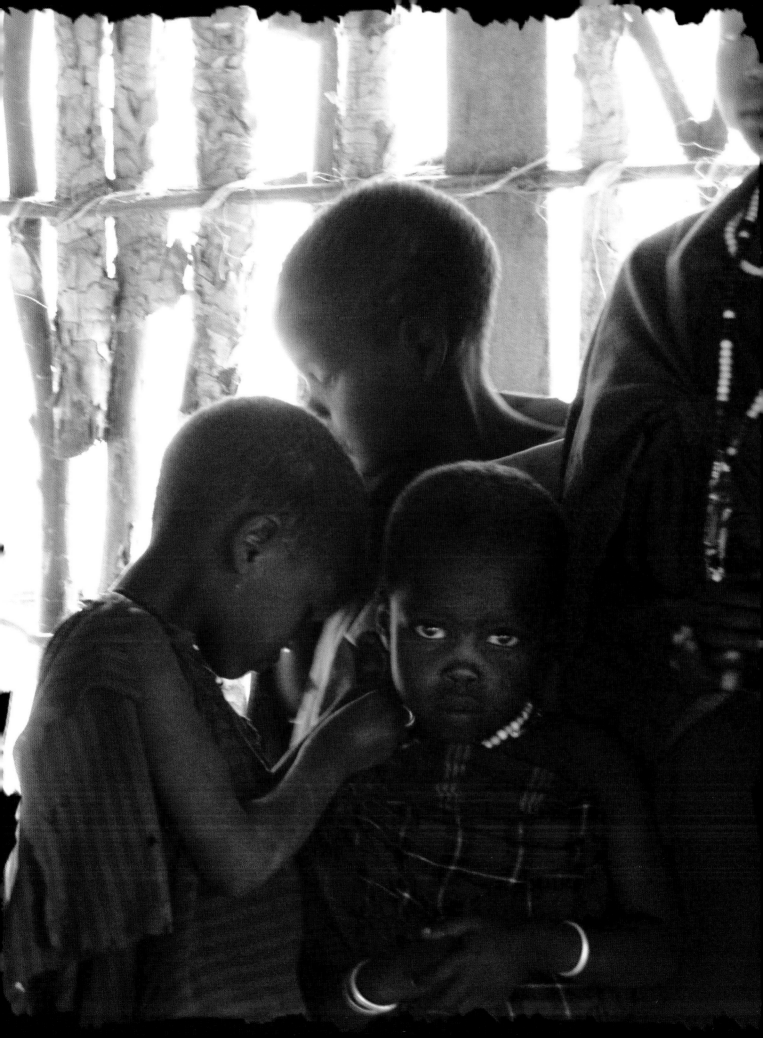

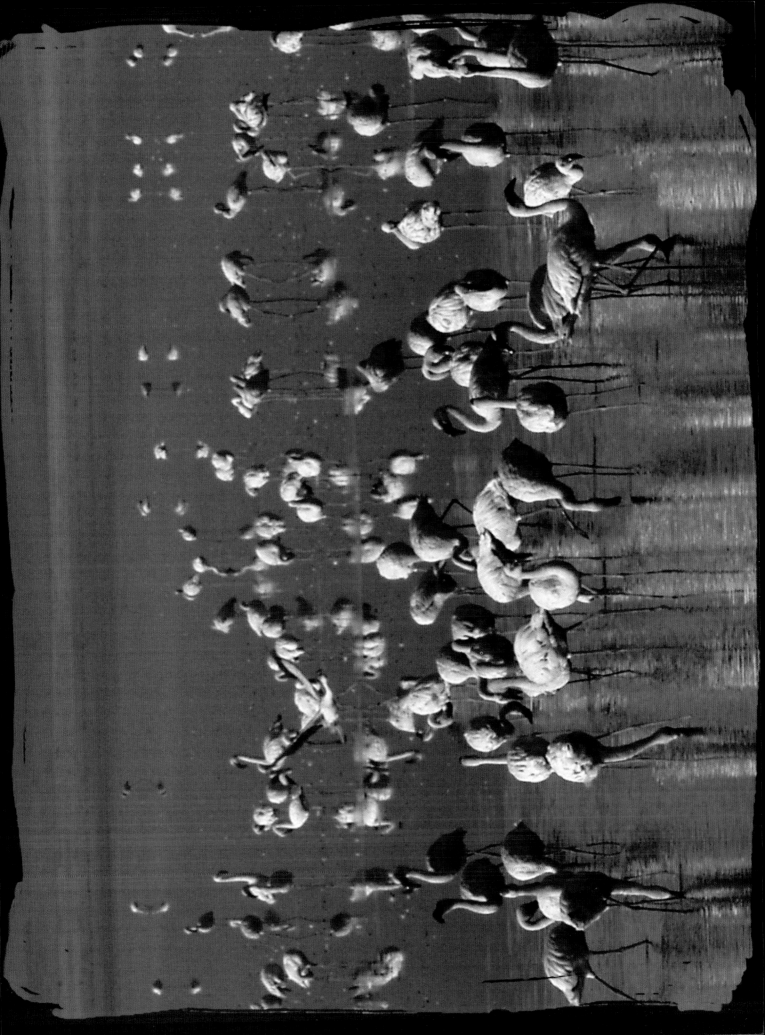

CHAPTER 19.....A BOY AND A LION

Shortly after leaving the Masai tribe I noticed a solitary young man leaning against a tree a couple of miles from the village. His appearance was quite different from any of the natives we had encountered and I assumed he must be from a new tribe. The thing that immediately drew my attention was his stark white face paint. He was painted with thick white stripes that criss crossed his entire face. I also noticed that unlike the Masai, who were adorned with bright red wraps, this boy was without color in his sparse wardrobe.

When I asked Preet which tribe the boy came from he said the young man was Masai. It made no sense to me that he looked so different from every other Masai I had seen. When I enquired further Preet told me that the young man had been ostracized from the tribe. From Preets' choice of words I assumed that the boy must have committed some type of criminal offense or infraction. When Preet told me the real story it was clear to me that we needed to turn around and go back so that I could meet this fascinating young man.

When we got near the boy I could see that he was in his early teens. The others stayed in the Defender as I approached the young man. Preet spoke a few words to him in Masai and it seemed to calm his nerves. As I got closer it was clear that we had a mutual fascination and apprehension about our encounter. I greeted the young man and then presented my camera for his examination. Though he had no idea what it was I still gestured to acquire his acceptance before snapping a shot. Of course he did not protest and I took the photo.

As I had done many times before with people unfamiliar with the magical ways of a camera I turned it around and let him see his image on the back. He smiled with pride and readily posed for a couple more shots. As we examined the shots together a second boy emerged from the bushes. He was dressed and painted in the same fashion but appeared to be a little younger. The boys seemed to like the attention and I was very disappointed to have run out of film for my instant camera. I wanted nothing more than to give the curious duo a photo of themselves right there on the spot.

After some mutual admiration and a little charades the boys and I parted company. Back in the Defender I had a million questions for Preet. Unfortunately Preets' normal speaking voice was so quiet that it was barely audible. With the banging of the truck, Preets accent, the language issues and the distance between the front and back seats it was nearly impossible to have a conversation while driving......but I simply could not wait.

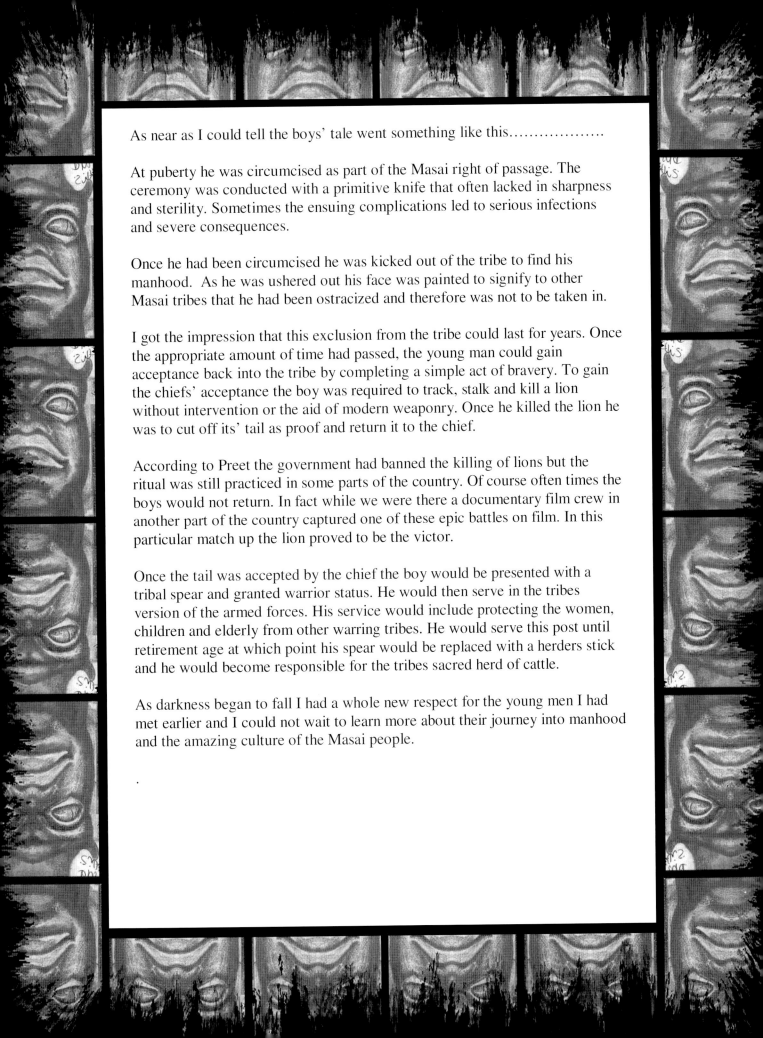

As near as I could tell the boys' tale went something like this……………….

At puberty he was circumcised as part of the Masai right of passage. The ceremony was conducted with a primitive knife that often lacked in sharpness and sterility. Sometimes the ensuing complications led to serious infections and severe consequences.

Once he had been circumcised he was kicked out of the tribe to find his manhood. As he was ushered out his face was painted to signify to other Masai tribes that he had been ostracized and therefore was not to be taken in.

I got the impression that this exclusion from the tribe could last for years. Once the appropriate amount of time had passed, the young man could gain acceptance back into the tribe by completing a simple act of bravery. To gain the chiefs' acceptance the boy was required to track, stalk and kill a lion without intervention or the aid of modern weaponry. Once he killed the lion he was to cut off its' tail as proof and return it to the chief.

According to Preet the government had banned the killing of lions but the ritual was still practiced in some parts of the country. Of course often times the boys would not return. In fact while we were there a documentary film crew in another part of the country captured one of these epic battles on film. In this particular match up the lion proved to be the victor.

Once the tail was accepted by the chief the boy would be presented with a tribal spear and granted warrior status. He would then serve in the tribes version of the armed forces. His service would include protecting the women, children and elderly from other warring tribes. He would serve this post until retirement age at which point his spear would be replaced with a herders stick and he would become responsible for the tribes sacred herd of cattle.

As darkness began to fall I had a whole new respect for the young men I had met earlier and I could not wait to learn more about their journey into manhood and the amazing culture of the Masai people.

.

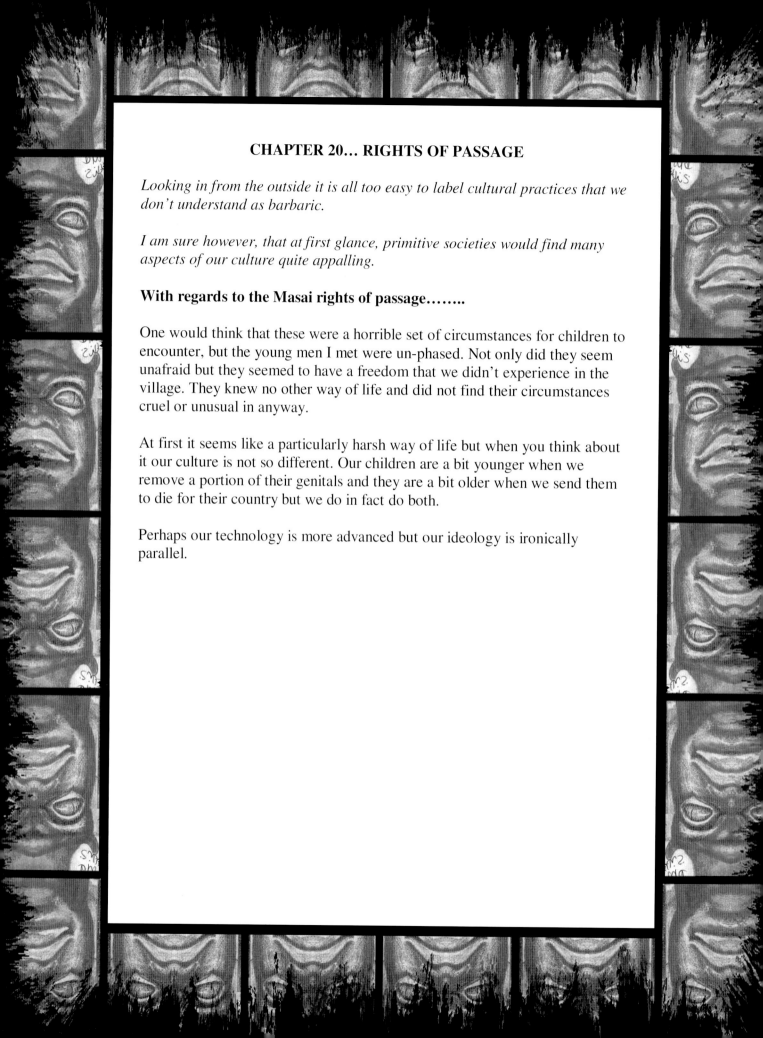

CHAPTER 20... RIGHTS OF PASSAGE

Looking in from the outside it is all too easy to label cultural practices that we don't understand as barbaric.

I am sure however, that at first glance, primitive societies would find many aspects of our culture quite appalling.

With regards to the Masai rights of passage……..

One would think that these were a horrible set of circumstances for children to encounter, but the young men I met were un-phased. Not only did they seem unafraid but they seemed to have a freedom that we didn't experience in the village. They knew no other way of life and did not find their circumstances cruel or unusual in anyway.

At first it seems like a particularly harsh way of life but when you think about it our culture is not so different. Our children are a bit younger when we remove a portion of their genitals and they are a bit older when we send them to die for their country but we do in fact do both.

Perhaps our technology is more advanced but our ideology is ironically parallel.

The Serengetti is clearly one of the most beautiful places on earth.
While trekking through the great planes I really took time to
realize just how   lucky I was to have
so many big   beautiful animals
at my door step   Serengetti
means the   endless
plane   us
the   lan
guage of. Sleeping out   swa
dogs sniffing around you   feli
praying by for a late night   for food and Zebras
just cant begin to apprec   snack is something you
07-04-03   iate.

The Serengetti is clearly one of the most beautiful places on earth.
While trekking through the great planes I really took time to
realize just how   lucky I was to have
so many big   beautiful animals
at my door step   Serengetti
means the   endless
plane   us
the   lan
guage of. Sleeping out   swa
dogs sniffing around you   feli
praying by for a late night   for food and Zebras
just cant begin to apprec   snack is something you
07-04-03   iate.

The Serengetti is clearly one of the most beautiful places on earth.
While trekking through the great planes I really took time to
realize just how   lucky I was to have
so many big   beautiful animals
at my door step   Serengetti
means the   endless
plane   us
the   lan
guage of. Sleeping out   swa
dogs sniffing around you   feli
praying by for a late night   for food and Zebras
just cant begin to apprec   snack is something you
07-04-03   iate.

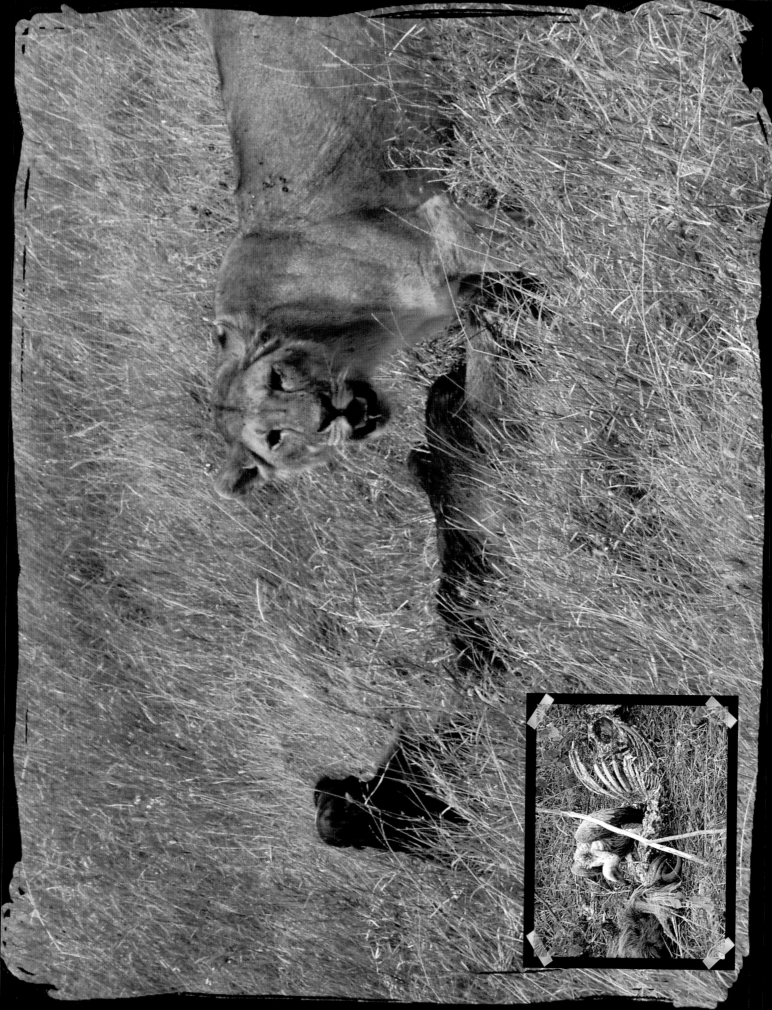

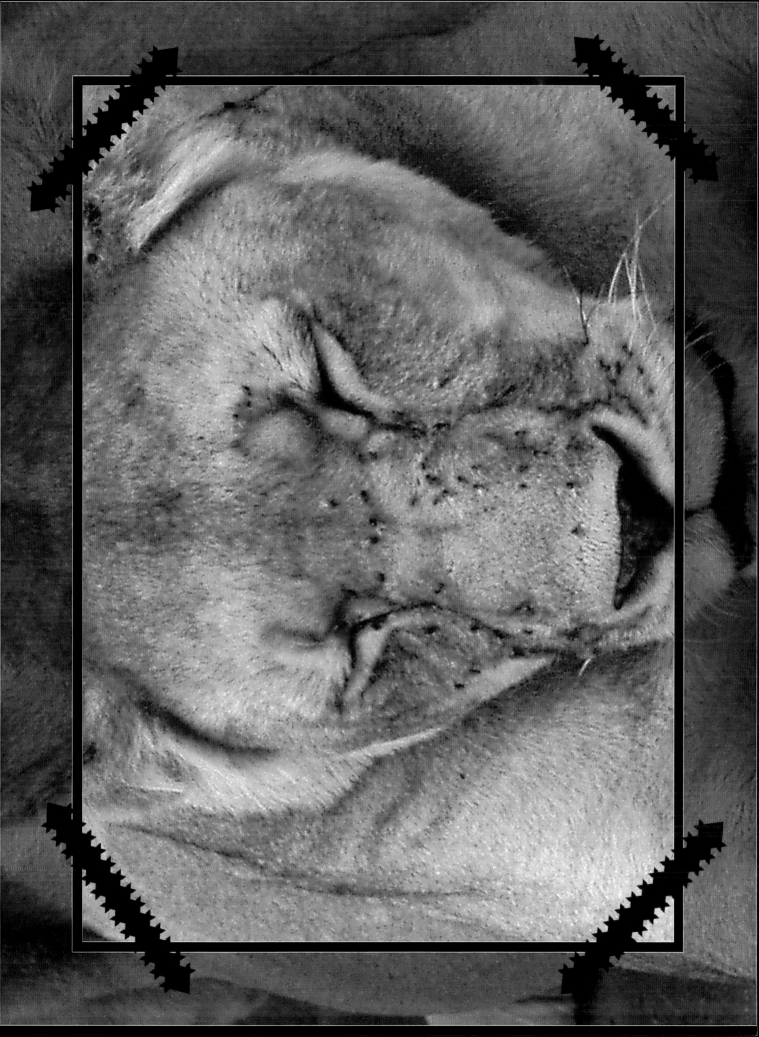

Uganda,
Kenya,
Tanzania
and the
Island of
Zanzibar.

Today we are recovering after a week
long safari in the Ngorangoro Crater,
the Serengetti, Lake Manyara and
Tarangire. We are in a mountain Village
outside of Arusha, Tanzania. We
are the only people in the en'
and it is truly heaven on
earth. In the morning we ta
a walking
Safari. 07-0

CHAPTER 21.........STALKING BIG PREY IN AFRICA

I am often asked.............of all the places I have traveled which place is my favorite. At first this was a difficult question to answer. So many places hold a special significance for me for so many different reasons.

There have been places that house people with wisdom and knowledge that has changed my life. There have been places where the architecture and history have filled me with awe and emotion. There have been places where the natural landscapes have left me unable to speak. There have been places where churches and temples have inspired me to look beyond our worlds' boundaries and there have been places that have taught me more about myself than I thought possible.

Of all these places I would have to say that Africa moved something inside me like no other. Words can not describe the feeling I had when I saw my first wild elephant. Text can not explain my insignificance when that elephant roared with a mock charge that shook the very ground at my feet. Pictures can not communicate my stark realization that I was just another animal as lions feasted on a wildebeest twice my size. I definitely can not translate the shame I felt for my petty complaints as I walked amongst people without food and water who somehow managed to find happiness.

Everyday in Africa provided a special experience and many of them came far away from the wild animals I had gone there to see.

One such experience would come in an area where the lion populations were particularly dense and the surrounding landscapes provided little if any barrier between us and Gods other creatures. In this place our tents provided sanctuary from bugs and mosquitoes but little else. We found it necessary to pair ourselves with the only known predator of the lion....................the Masai.

We hired a young warrior to patrol our camp at night as we slumbered under the stars. In the long history of the Masai people hunting lions, the apex predators had come to recognize their scent as something to fear. The mere odor of a Masai warrior was enough to give all but the hungriest of lions incentive to avoid our camp. I on the other hand gave off the scent of a delicious snack. I was pleased to have the aromatic young man patrolling my sleeping quarters.

On our first night in this location we could hear lions less than fifty feet or so from where our tents were pitched. We knew when we went to sleep we would be separated from them by only a small mound of thickets and some thin canvas walls.

While we had our dinner by fire light we were surprised that the lions didn't roar as we expected. They made low nasally snorts that could be clearly heard as they devoured their evening meal. The sound was distinctive and a little unnerving.

After dinner we enjoyed the typical Tusk or two by the fireside before heading off to bed. I remember having a particularly difficult time sleeping in this location. Contrary to what I expected, the nights were very cold and the thin summer sleeping bags I brought just didn't do the trick.

Our tent site only complicated my insomnia. It provided good visibility for our Masai patrolman and a favorable juxtaposition to the protective thickets but the trade off was a particularly hard and rocky foundation. To top it all off, I had forgotten my favorite pillow in Sweden and the damn Tusk was forcing me to get up every ten minutes to pee. Add in the fact that we were being circled by man eating lions and regularly assaulted by wild boars trying to burrow their way into our tent for a midnight snack and the sleep was less than sound.

Much like in a teenage horror flick when the brave football player goes down to the basement to "investigate"…………..something bad always seemed to happen to Heather while I was sleeping. While in Africa she made no bones about waking me up to accompany her to the bathroom whenever nature called. Normally I was happy to do so; however my spurts of sleep on this particular night were so sporadic that I think she felt guilty about waking me.

When I awoke to the sound of her scream I was not all that alarmed…….I could tell that it was more of a startled scream than anything else. I jumped up and stuck my head out to see what ill fate had befallen her this time. As I looked around the tent I could see a zebra bouncing off into the darkness. Apparently as she crouched to use the bathroom the two managed to startle each other and in its bid to escape it nearly trampled her. She was a little embarrassed and a little awed but not all that frightened so we went back to sleep.

We returned to our slumber in a spot that was purposely chosen for its access to clean drinking water. The massive water tower that had been erected here provided one of the only sources of drinkable water for miles. The locals would travel great distances to this otherwise barren site to retrieve water from the fifty foot tower.

About an hour or so before dawn one of the locals came to this same spot to retrieve some water for himself. Though I didn't know it at the time this local was not human but rather a massive bull elephant.

Elephants can smell water from miles away and this enormous bloke had come to satiate his midnight craving for some nice clean drinking water. Frustrated that he could not get to the water, the intelligent giant simply decided to bring the water to him. With a single push from his massive head he toppled the mammoth tower and its huge reservoir of water, once again interrupting my illusive slumber.

The tower had probably been there for years but for some reason the rogue elephant chose this night to wander into our camp and rudely awaken me yet again. After the dust settled I tossed and turned for awhile longer before conceding.

Grumpy and still half asleep I grabbed my camera and abruptly left the tent. I was relieved to see that Douglas had beaten me awake and started a fire. I was surprised to see however that he was nowhere to be found.

As I put a pot of water on the fire I realized that it was probably our tentless Masai friend that kept the fire going through the night not Douglas. While I was waiting for the water to boil my attitude improved and I was actually quite happy to be up and alone. It was incredible having all of Africa to myself and I knew I would probably get some great pictures as the sun peeked its head over the plains.

When my water reached a boil I pulled up to the fires edge and made some coffee. As I sat drinking my coffee in the morning light and taking in my surroundings I felt truly at peace with myself and the world around me.

Sitting alone with the gentle sounds of morning in the background I had a real moment of clarity. I realized I had beaten the system…………………………..

I wasn't answering to an alarm clock.
I wasn't shouldered with massive fiscal responsibilities.
I didn't have countless others for which to bare responsibility.
I didn't have the daunting schedule of a successful executive.
I didn't have the prying eyes and public limitations of a celebrity.

I didn't have the 24hr duties of a parent.
I held life in my hand and I was finally free.

Feeling satisfied inside I surveyed my surroundings for the first photo of the morning. As I did I saw something that filled me with equal parts intrigue and excitement. About seventy five yards behind our Defender, I could see our keen night watchman. As I studied him something caught his attention.

His head snapped to attention and his expression hardened as he raised his spear. The truck was obstructing my view and I couldn't tell what had his eyes so fixated. I wanted to move into a better position but I was afraid to frighten off his prey. At first I thought that maybe he had spotted some type of game animal and was about to make it his breakfast.

Moments later I realized this was most likely not the case. I remembered Preet telling me that the Masai made cows their only significant source of nutrients because they believed that the Gods had placed them on earth solely for their benefit.

I became even more intrigued as I watched the scene unfold. As the young warrior moved in my direction he quickly ducked behind a tree for cover. As I strained my eyes to see what he was looking at my heart began to race but I remained absolutely motionless. I did not want the Masai man to see me and alter his course of action in any way.

As he emerged from behind the tree I could see intensity in his eyes. I knew it was not a small animal in his sights. His face was filled with focus but not an ounce of fear could be detected.

When he ducked behind another tree for cover I could not stand not knowing what he was stalking. I could only assume that it was a lion based on his intensity and obvious caution. His head darted out for an instant from behind the tree and then he briskly and silently approached his next point of cover. My anticipation thickened as he moved ever closer to his target.

Once he was within range he raised his spear and made a final charge. About twenty feet from the truck he stopped dead in his tracks. With his spear still hoisted above his head he began to walk forward ever so slowly. As he got closer and closer to the truck I could see his intensity diminish until eventually he lowered his spear.

When we met up with this hunter the night before, it was dark. But now the morning light presented a foe he did not really know how to combat. He stood for some time and examined it with the curiosity of a child. His head tilted from side to side like a dog encountering his own reflection for the very first time. As he studied his opponent he noticed me looking on with amazement.

When he realized what he had just done he was obviously embarrassed. He looked over at my smiling face and returned a sheepish grin. Before I could snap a single frame he pointed to the truck, proudly pounded his chest and planted the butt end of his spear in the ground as he raised his shield.

There before him was something he had never seen before. On the side of our Defender was a painting of a Masai warrior with his spear planted and his shield raised. Now that it was clear that this was not a warring tribesman trying to ambush him his combination of embarrassment and pride made for an interesting expression.

Of course he was embarrassed for stalking a painting but he was also proud when he realized that the painting immortalized him and his tribe.

He stood with a smile on his face and we shared a laugh at his expense. I clicked a picture or two and then went over to talk to him. By now I had mastered a few words of Swahili but they were meaningless to the Masai. Nonetheless we had a lot to talk about.

First things first, we had to get over the newness of the magical image capturing camera. Unlike some of the other Masai warriors who could be a little intimidating this young man was filled with curiosity and he was dying to examine the apparatus.

I was surprised to see that he was not fascinated with his own image. More than anything he wanted to use the mystical device on me. It seemed almost as if he wanted to wield its incredible power to trap me inside the tiny box. I immediately showed him how to look through the viewfinder but no matter how hard I tried, I just could not convince him to close one eye. Shot after shot and attempt after attempt he captured nothing more than sky and earth.

I thought using the digital screen on the back of the camera would surely solve this problem but I was wrong. Fortunately, he had endless patience for the task. After literally twenty or so attempts he got one blurry shot of the top of my head. The photo clearly showed my eyeballs and it was enough for him to thrust his hands in the air for victory.

I have included the photo at the end of this chapter and it remains one of my all time favorites.

Now that the photo taking was out of the way we could get on to more serious matters. I introduced myself and we butchered each others names for awhile before moving on to charades. It did not take long for my new pal to show me the damage caused by the elephant during the night. It was the perfect topic for charades.

He led me over to the demolished wooden tower and acted out the scene with academy award winning prowess. First he raised his bicep to his face and then he thrust the rest of his arm into the air while trumpeting out the sound of an elephant. He then lowered his arm between his waist and knees and clenched his fist to simulate the infamous third leg of the male African Elephant. Now he lowered his head in the direction of the tower and extended his neck to show me how the elephant toppled the tower with a single thrust. He raised his hand high in the air and puffed up his chest to show that the elephant was not only massive but strong.

I charaded out a few questions to determine if the elephant was angry or crazed and my counterpart responded by showing me that the elephant simply wanted a drink. With that mystery solved I could move on to the topic that really fascinated me. The Masai right of passage and the lion hunt.

I acted out my best lion imitation and threw in a couple of roars for authenticity. I then signaled to the man and raised an imaginary spear. I acted out the stalking I had seen him do earlier and then repeated the lion impression. He immediately caught on and began to show me how to hunt a lion. It was pretty clear that the shield was the secret to the whole thing, not the spear as I had imagined.

As the lion advanced, the hunter would hold his shield above his head. When the lion raised his front feet to pounce, the shield was used to block the attack. With a single motion the hunter would thrust his spear beneath the raised shield and pierce the lions' chest. If he was lucky he would get the lion directly in the heart dropping it with a single blow. If not, the hunter would step back and deliver as many blows as needed to finish the job.

With this well taught lesson in hand I was almost ready to hunt one of the beasts on my own. With just a couple more questions I would be ready to do battle in the event of an impromptu attack. Forgetting that some of the Masai

language was communicated through hand gestures I fired up the old charades machine once again and went at it.

My goal was to ascertain the number of men required for such a hunt. Did one warrior face a lion alone or did he have an ally in the battle? I reflected back on the two young boys I had seen earlier and wondered if they would rely on each other when they encountered their first lion.

Our communications up to this point were going swimmingly and I had almost forgotten that we spoke two different languages. I had no idea that I was about to soil our rapport as I asked my next question.

I pointed to the young warrior and raised a single finger as I motioned toward an imaginary lion. I then raised two fingers pointed to an imaginary second warrior and signaled to the other side of the invisible lion. My new friend got a very cross look on his face, shook his head abruptly, scolded me a bit and then acted out a scene of two men fighting a lion together.

I thought to myself……….Yep that is exactly what I just said. I repeated my scene to confirm that I had it right. The once jovial Masai was now becoming irritated. He shook his head and reenacted the scene yet again.

I was desperate to figure out what part I was getting wrong so I went through my routine a couple more times. I thought maybe my colleague was insulted at the implication that it took two men to fight one lion, but every time he acted out the scene he clearly depicted two men as well.

Just when I thought all was lost, once again, Preet came to my rescue. Apparently he had been amusing himself for some time by watching my attempts to communicate to the agitated young Masai when he decided to come over and see what kind of trouble I had gotten myself into.

I explained to Preet that everything was going well up to the point when I tried to figure out how many men it took to kill a lion. I told him I thought that my new friend was becoming agitated with me……..he agreed.

As I began to charade out my inquiry once again Preet cracked the riddle. Something about the way I was signaling two men attacking the lion emulated a Masai sign for retreating in fear or running away. The warrior was quite indignant over the fact that I kept insisting he was afraid of lions. Once Preet explained the faux pas to the young man we all had a good laugh at my expense.

Preet snapped a couple pictures of us together and we parted ways after taking a vow of silence about each others indiscretions. I would not tell his fellow tribesman that I saw him stalking an inanimate object and he would not tell my sleeping friends that I was to dumb to figure out how many men it took to hunt a lion.

It was the perfect arrangement.

CHAPTER 22......DYING WITH A BRAVE HEART

Being older and wiser doesn't mean we make less mistakes ....it means we are better at admitting the ones we do make.

A truly evolving human being constantly stretches their own envelope until they find themselves in new challenges and unfamiliar circumstances. This means not always having the answers to lifes' riddles.

Not always having the answers means not always being right and not always being right means that sometimes we fail. How we deal with these failures is what distinguishes the evolving from the obsolete.

Being able to laugh at ourselves when we do foolish things means we are able to acknowledge that those things were foolish, this in turn proves that we are not.

I don't know why I assumed that less developed cultures meant a less developed sense of humor. The Masai loved to play jokes and tease one another and they seemed to be able to have a good laugh at their own expense.

I remember trying to teach the ambassador how to invert his hands and make a teeter totter with his middle fingers. The children and other tribe members laughed hysterically at his tangled hands, but no one was more amused at his bungled attempts than the ambassador himself.

Some good old fashion ribbing is what broke the ice with Preet and let us start treating each other as equals and eventually friends. This somehow seemed to level the playing field and endeared us to one another.

He reciprocated by feeding me all sorts of bogus facts and ridiculous information about the African way of life, only to let me off the hook later, after taking the bait.

I think my favorite Preet wisdom was his advice to me regarding a lion attack. We were often less than a few feet away from wild lions and I wanted to know what to do in the event that one of them turned toward us for an attack.

Preet immediately stood up and his expression became very serious. In a stern voice he told me to make myself appear as large as possible by standing up and raising my hands above my head. He said that I should replicate the natural behaviors of a predator and stare the lion directly in the eyes while making a fierce face and roaring as loud as possible. He then demonstrated the technique.

When I asked him if the lion would retreat because he thought that I was a larger and stronger predator his answer was quite on point. He said……………………………….

"Of course not, but you will die with bravery in your heart."

After the laughter subsided I said seriously Preet, what do you do? Then he gave me the real answer. If a lion attacks you ……you are going to die, what you chose to do with your last breaths is up to you.

Well man. much to go ... off is a ...
continent I wrote this first sentence in Sweden, and I drew the picture
is Spain. Now I am in a small village outside of Arusha Africa. Below
is a partial list of the seventy some animals I saw on safari. - Masai giraff
zebra - Africa Elephants - WaterDuck (Antelope) Eland (Antelope) - Wart hog - imp
Red+Yellow Barbet (bird) - Tawny Eagle - Saddle bill stork - Hornbill - Guinea Fo
Red necked spowfowl - Red oxpecker (giraffe bird) lilac breasted Rata - Ostrich
Olive baboon - Blue monkey - yellow billed stork - pelican pink back - Heron
Hippo pontamus - white pelican - Egyptian goose - Sacred Ibis - Wildabeast
Malibu Stork - African buffalo - Ground Hornbill - African Fish Eagle
DikDik - Long crested - Eagle - black faced Vervet - Bush Buck
ugur buzzard - Francolin - Rock Hyrex -
Mongoose - Grey headed King Fisher
lati beast - Vulture - Topi (Antelope)
Lion - Superb Starling - lovebirds
Hyena - Black Backed Jackal
Servul (cat)
Leopard

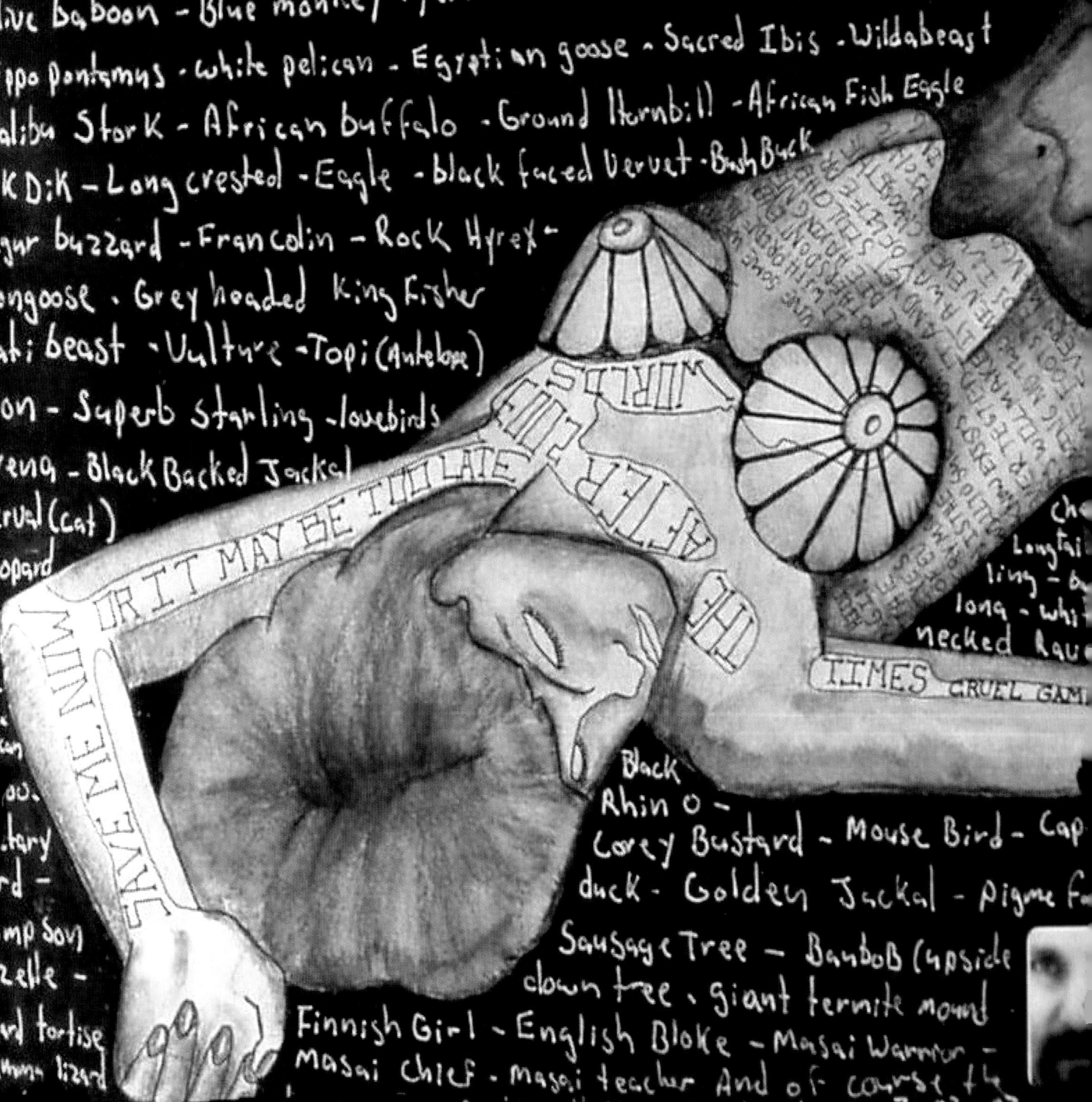

SAVE ME NOW OR IT MAY BE TOO LATE
THE AFTER LIFE
WORLDS
TIMES
CRUEL GAM

rican
oo.
tary
ird -
omp Son
azelle -
opard tortise
gama lizard

Ch
Longtai
ling -
long - whi
necked Rav

Black Rhino - Corey Bustard - Mouse Bird - Cap
duck - Golden Jackal - Pigme F
Sausage Tree - BaoBoB (upside down tree - giant termite mound
Finnish Girl - English Bloke - Masai Warrior -
Masai Chief - Masai teacher And of course the

is supposed to snow... ever. Now
ago and here I am. From Nice again to every
...ss and travel on to France but that was days
other country I have been to, this is next to
Germany, the place I feel least like being. And
Yet still here I am. I know that
there is something here

people
not going
the surface
oddly enough
the realist pe-
ple here seem
to be the cab dr-
vers. This is an anc-
ient city, with some
of the most moving arch-
itecture I have seen. But it
clearly hides something beneath its surface. Something that I am destined to unearth. I do
not want to leave this city with that
ling that it was solely a place for me to k-
time while waiting for the next city. I h-
not yet been to a country that has fa-
to crack. A city that has not provided
single story or anidote for my book. I kno-
such a story exists here. If only
I could crack the shell on the
surface and truly connect with
one single human being, who

23

An awesome head painter in Kentucky

Some of my journals

NOZZLE
UTIONED FOR
FIRING)

...the eagles are playing on the radio - the suns rays are peeking through the clouds and all seems quite well. Hangin out with a dive instructor living here in Kendwa, and a co[uple of] local blokes. As per usual I am not trying to [do anything] I am waiting for a local artist named Moses to [get back] from Nungwiso I can have him do a painting [in my] journal. I have tried to catch up to him every day for the last week...

[left margin] ...al /Sha...ced me I would do picture for him so I suppose I should go and apply my-lf, but as for now I am talking to a Swede who has been Tanzania for fifteen years or so. And I still have full beer to contend with, not to men-tion more eagles on the radio.

The swedish guy is a boat captain who takes people out on dive and sailing chapter excursions. That's what I love about traveling the world very one you meet has a story to tell. Always somet-ing to talk about and not the same old shit over end ver. I don't think I can ever go home again. And even more importantly, I don't think I want to.

July eleven 03

[bottom] ...e are discussing the difficulties of Swahili. The sounds are asically the same. I find it a much easier language than say wedish, which has only a few different letters and pronunciations. The Swahili words are pronounced pretty much like they are written, and the sounds are about the same his little village just got electricity and now the beers cold as spain, which seems fo...

[right margin] ...a Swiss uple of ...t anyth... get back in my every day for the last week... som-how way's s to mis him. Tod is abso-utely per-ect. The tempera-t is just... and the b is blown through the beech ba I am taki time to a reciate exa how good to really is So it is a time for o more nice co beer and th may be anoth look for m But as I a learning can't be

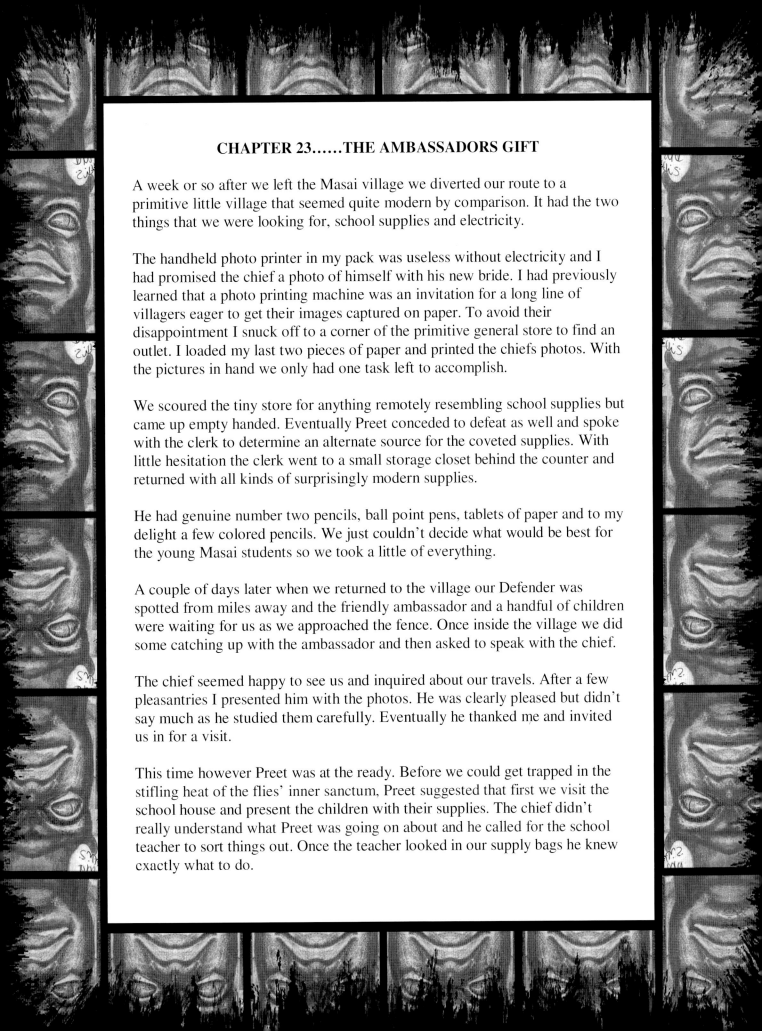

CHAPTER 23......THE AMBASSADORS GIFT

A week or so after we left the Masai village we diverted our route to a primitive little village that seemed quite modern by comparison. It had the two things that we were looking for, school supplies and electricity.

The handheld photo printer in my pack was useless without electricity and I had promised the chief a photo of himself with his new bride. I had previously learned that a photo printing machine was an invitation for a long line of villagers eager to get their images captured on paper. To avoid their disappointment I snuck off to a corner of the primitive general store to find an outlet. I loaded my last two pieces of paper and printed the chiefs photos. With the pictures in hand we only had one task left to accomplish.

We scoured the tiny store for anything remotely resembling school supplies but came up empty handed. Eventually Preet conceded to defeat as well and spoke with the clerk to determine an alternate source for the coveted supplies. With little hesitation the clerk went to a small storage closet behind the counter and returned with all kinds of surprisingly modern supplies.

He had genuine number two pencils, ball point pens, tablets of paper and to my delight a few colored pencils. We just couldn't decide what would be best for the young Masai students so we took a little of everything.

A couple of days later when we returned to the village our Defender was spotted from miles away and the friendly ambassador and a handful of children were waiting for us as we approached the fence. Once inside the village we did some catching up with the ambassador and then asked to speak with the chief.

The chief seemed happy to see us and inquired about our travels. After a few pleasantries I presented him with the photos. He was clearly pleased but didn't say much as he studied them carefully. Eventually he thanked me and invited us in for a visit.

This time however Preet was at the ready. Before we could get trapped in the stifling heat of the flies' inner sanctum, Preet suggested that first we visit the school house and present the children with their supplies. The chief didn't really understand what Preet was going on about and he called for the school teacher to sort things out. Once the teacher looked in our supply bags he knew exactly what to do.

He assembled the children and marched them out to the "crooked stick" school house. Once all the children were accounted for he told us that our last visit inspired the children to learn a new song. There was an aura of excitement in the air and we could tell that the children were eager to perform. We knew that this was intended to be a gift from them, to us, and we listened intently as their glowing faces belted out the beautiful sonata.

We thanked them several times and then told them that we too had a gift to share. I think they expected a song in return but they were equally pleased when we exposed the school supplies. All four of us got down on our hands and knees and organized the supplies into evenly divided kits. Each one contained a "clickable" ball point pen, a pencil, a tablet and a few colored pencils.

At first the scene was chaos as the children rushed to get their supplies but within seconds the teacher sternly organized the children into four lines, one in front of each of us. The first little boy in my line was a happy little fellow that I spent a lot of time with on our first visit. He just glowed from the inside and I truly adored him.

I handed him a tablet with a light blue cover adorned with some writing and graphics. It was clear that the little guy did not know what to do with it but he loved it none the less. He studied the cover intently and flipped through the blank pages several times. He held the tablet high above his head showing it to the world.

When he was done I handed him the next surprise…..the clickable ink pen. When I showed him how to click the stylus in and out, he did not care if the pen did one more single thing. He clicked it repetitively as many times as his tiny thumb would allow before stopping for a break.

Next was the item that I was particularly excited about………..the colored pencils. I just could not wait to do some drawing with these little guys and give them a way to release their creative energy. I handed the brightly colored pencils to my little muse and waited anxiously for him to make his first scratches in the tablet.

To my horror he did not waste any time attempting to eat the brightly colored treats. I immediately retrieved the chewed pencils from the confused lads' mouth and used them to draw a picture in his tablet. The other kids quickly gathered around and I demonstrated the different characteristics of each "non edible" writing implement.

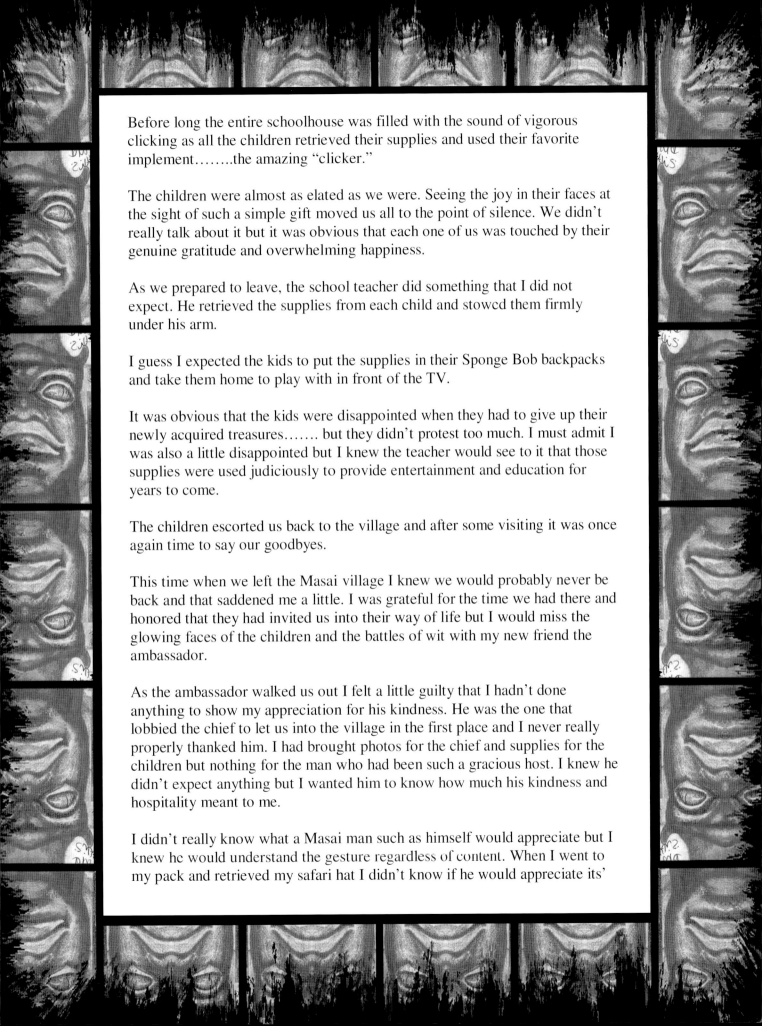

Before long the entire schoolhouse was filled with the sound of vigorous clicking as all the children retrieved their supplies and used their favorite implement……..the amazing "clicker."

The children were almost as elated as we were. Seeing the joy in their faces at the sight of such a simple gift moved us all to the point of silence. We didn't really talk about it but it was obvious that each one of us was touched by their genuine gratitude and overwhelming happiness.

As we prepared to leave, the school teacher did something that I did not expect. He retrieved the supplies from each child and stowed them firmly under his arm.

I guess I expected the kids to put the supplies in their Sponge Bob backpacks and take them home to play with in front of the TV.

It was obvious that the kids were disappointed when they had to give up their newly acquired treasures……. but they didn't protest too much. I must admit I was also a little disappointed but I knew the teacher would see to it that those supplies were used judiciously to provide entertainment and education for years to come.

The children escorted us back to the village and after some visiting it was once again time to say our goodbyes.

This time when we left the Masai village I knew we would probably never be back and that saddened me a little. I was grateful for the time we had there and honored that they had invited us into their way of life but I would miss the glowing faces of the children and the battles of wit with my new friend the ambassador.

As the ambassador walked us out I felt a little guilty that I hadn't done anything to show my appreciation for his kindness. He was the one that lobbied the chief to let us into the village in the first place and I never really properly thanked him. I had brought photos for the chief and supplies for the children but nothing for the man who had been such a gracious host. I knew he didn't expect anything but I wanted him to know how much his kindness and hospitality meant to me.

I didn't really know what a Masai man such as himself would appreciate but I knew he would understand the gesture regardless of content. When I went to my pack and retrieved my safari hat I didn't know if he would appreciate its'

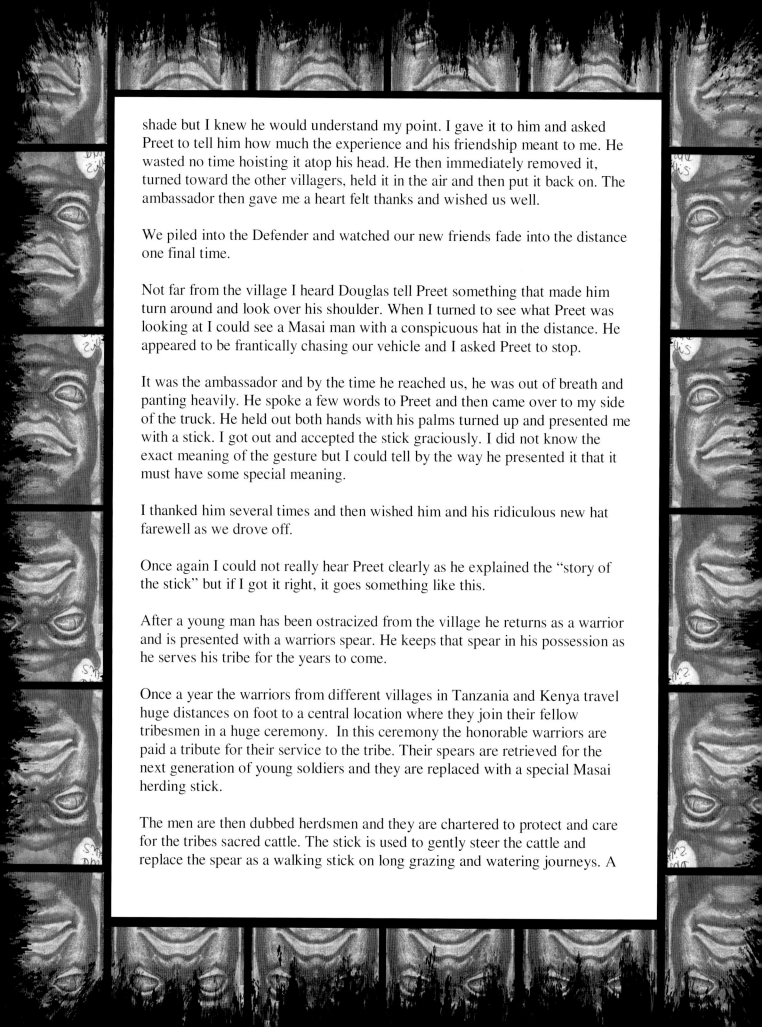

shade but I knew he would understand my point. I gave it to him and asked Preet to tell him how much the experience and his friendship meant to me. He wasted no time hoisting it atop his head. He then immediately removed it, turned toward the other villagers, held it in the air and then put it back on. The ambassador then gave me a heart felt thanks and wished us well.

We piled into the Defender and watched our new friends fade into the distance one final time.

Not far from the village I heard Douglas tell Preet something that made him turn around and look over his shoulder. When I turned to see what Preet was looking at I could see a Masai man with a conspicuous hat in the distance. He appeared to be frantically chasing our vehicle and I asked Preet to stop.

It was the ambassador and by the time he reached us, he was out of breath and panting heavily. He spoke a few words to Preet and then came over to my side of the truck. He held out both hands with his palms turned up and presented me with a stick. I got out and accepted the stick graciously. I did not know the exact meaning of the gesture but I could tell by the way he presented it that it must have some special meaning.

I thanked him several times and then wished him and his ridiculous new hat farewell as we drove off.

Once again I could not really hear Preet clearly as he explained the "story of the stick" but if I got it right, it goes something like this.

After a young man has been ostracized from the village he returns as a warrior and is presented with a warriors spear. He keeps that spear in his possession as he serves his tribe for the years to come.

Once a year the warriors from different villages in Tanzania and Kenya travel huge distances on foot to a central location where they join their fellow tribesmen in a huge ceremony. In this ceremony the honorable warriors are paid a tribute for their service to the tribe. Their spears are retrieved for the next generation of young soldiers and they are replaced with a special Masai herding stick.

The men are then dubbed herdsmen and they are chartered to protect and care for the tribes sacred cattle. The stick is used to gently steer the cattle and replace the spear as a walking stick on long grazing and watering journeys. A

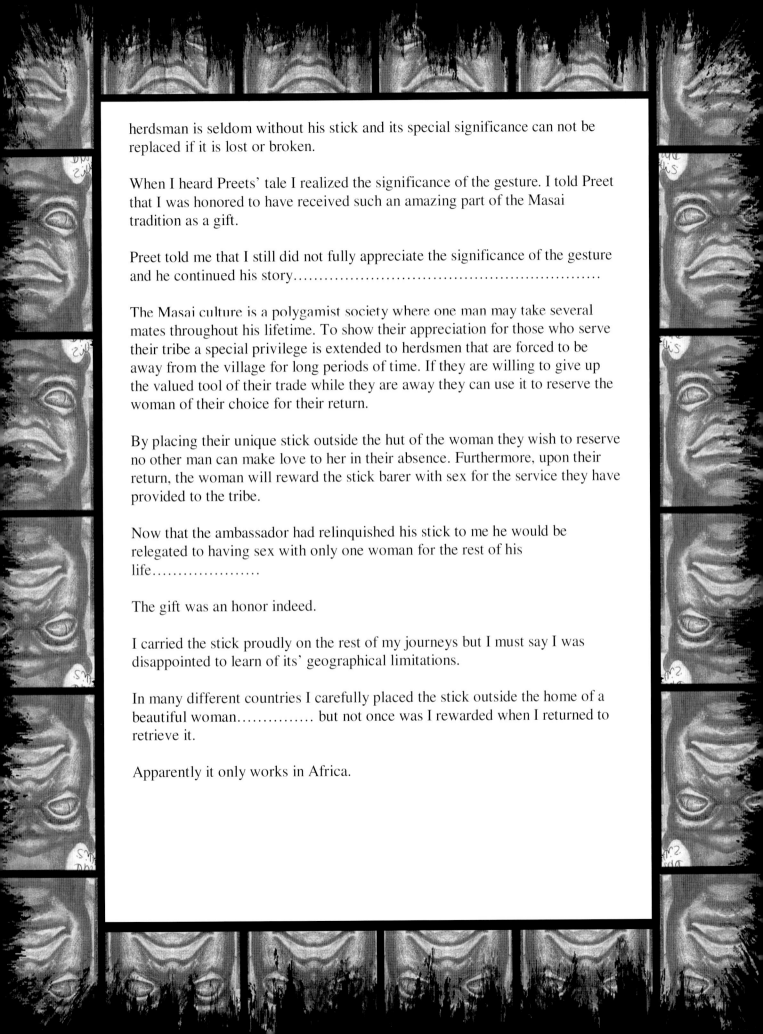

herdsman is seldom without his stick and its special significance can not be replaced if it is lost or broken.

When I heard Preets' tale I realized the significance of the gesture. I told Preet that I was honored to have received such an amazing part of the Masai tradition as a gift.

Preet told me that I still did not fully appreciate the significance of the gesture and he continued his story……………………………………………………

The Masai culture is a polygamist society where one man may take several mates throughout his lifetime. To show their appreciation for those who serve their tribe a special privilege is extended to herdsmen that are forced to be away from the village for long periods of time. If they are willing to give up the valued tool of their trade while they are away they can use it to reserve the woman of their choice for their return.

By placing their unique stick outside the hut of the woman they wish to reserve no other man can make love to her in their absence. Furthermore, upon their return, the woman will reward the stick barer with sex for the service they have provided to the tribe.

Now that the ambassador had relinquished his stick to me he would be relegated to having sex with only one woman for the rest of his life…………………

The gift was an honor indeed.

I carried the stick proudly on the rest of my journeys but I must say I was disappointed to learn of its' geographical limitations.

In many different countries I carefully placed the stick outside the home of a beautiful woman…………… but not once was I rewarded when I returned to retrieve it.

Apparently it only works in Africa.

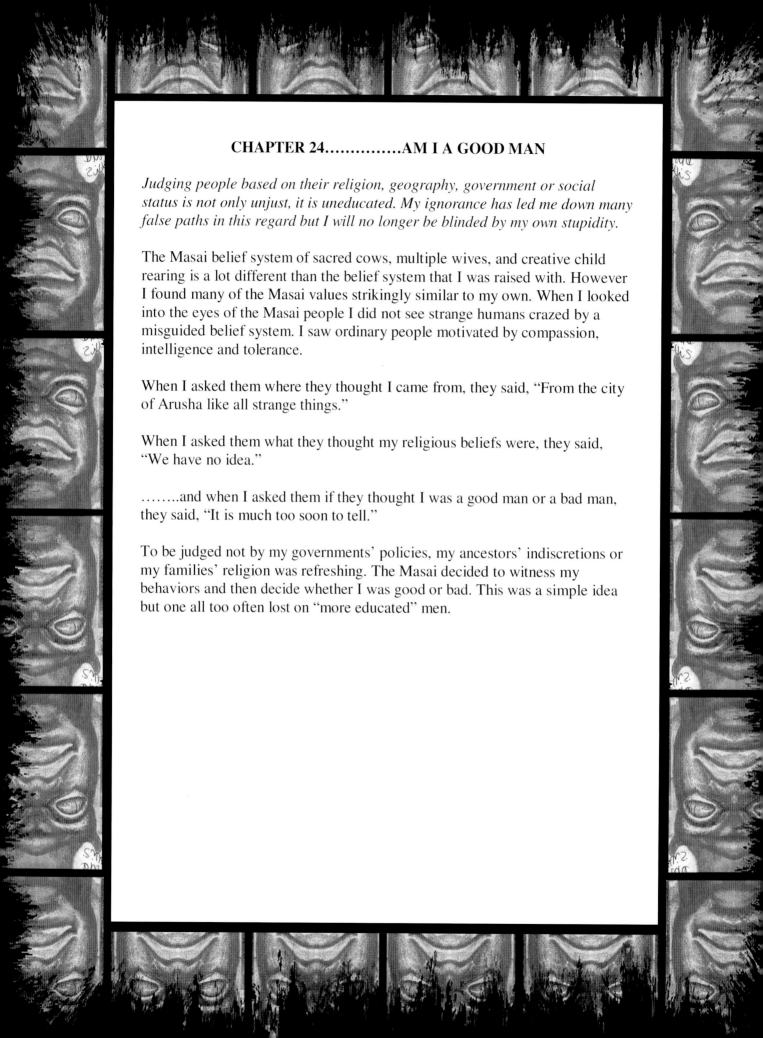

CHAPTER 24...............AM I A GOOD MAN

Judging people based on their religion, geography, government or social status is not only unjust, it is uneducated. My ignorance has led me down many false paths in this regard but I will no longer be blinded by my own stupidity.

The Masai belief system of sacred cows, multiple wives, and creative child rearing is a lot different than the belief system that I was raised with. However I found many of the Masai values strikingly similar to my own. When I looked into the eyes of the Masai people I did not see strange humans crazed by a misguided belief system. I saw ordinary people motivated by compassion, intelligence and tolerance.

When I asked them where they thought I came from, they said, "From the city of Arusha like all strange things."

When I asked them what they thought my religious beliefs were, they said, "We have no idea."

……..and when I asked them if they thought I was a good man or a bad man, they said, "It is much too soon to tell."

To be judged not by my governments' policies, my ancestors' indiscretions or my families' religion was refreshing. The Masai decided to witness my behaviors and then decide whether I was good or bad. This was a simple idea but one all too often lost on "more educated" men.

The Spiral of life leads to an inevatable ending. No matter which path you attempt to choose the spiral eventually carries you to choose the spiral eventually carries you choose the manner in which you choose the manner in which others who have travelled the road are determined by the keepers of time your destination is the same as

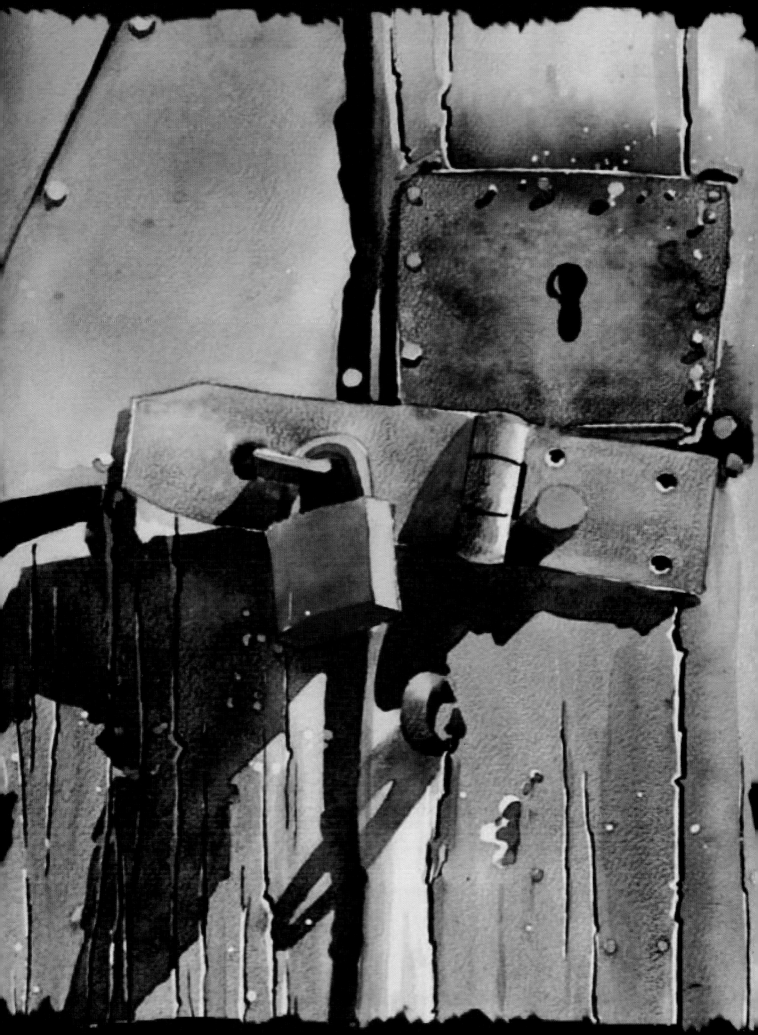

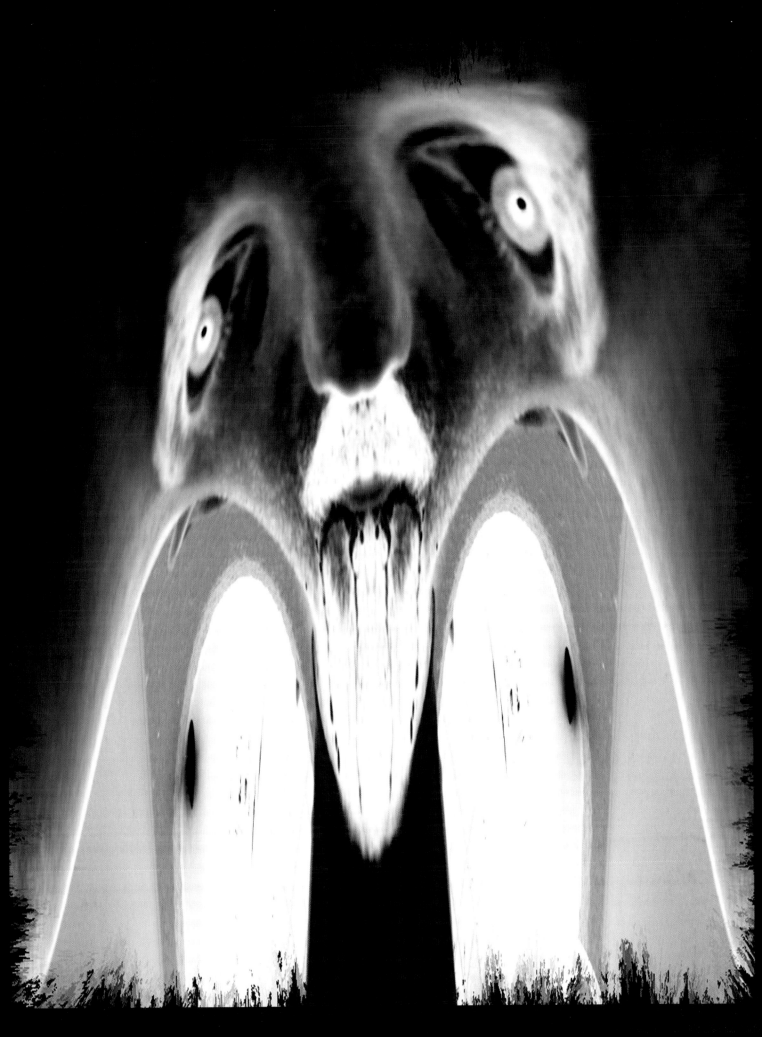

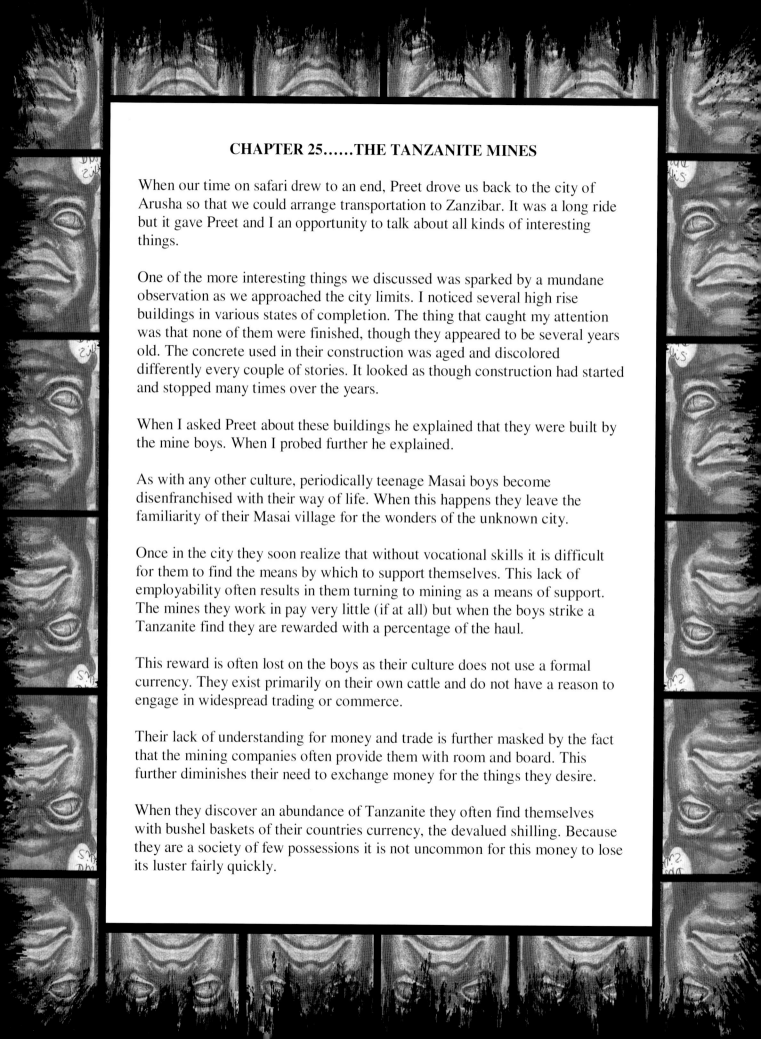

CHAPTER 25......THE TANZANITE MINES

When our time on safari drew to an end, Preet drove us back to the city of
Arusha so that we could arrange transportation to Zanzibar. It was a long ride
but it gave Preet and I an opportunity to talk about all kinds of interesting
things.

One of the more interesting things we discussed was sparked by a mundane
observation as we approached the city limits. I noticed several high rise
buildings in various states of completion. The thing that caught my attention
was that none of them were finished, though they appeared to be several years
old. The concrete used in their construction was aged and discolored
differently every couple of stories. It looked as though construction had started
and stopped many times over the years.

When I asked Preet about these buildings he explained that they were built by
the mine boys. When I probed further he explained.

As with any other culture, periodically teenage Masai boys become
disenfranchised with their way of life. When this happens they leave the
familiarity of their Masai village for the wonders of the unknown city.

Once in the city they soon realize that without vocational skills it is difficult
for them to find the means by which to support themselves. This lack of
employability often results in them turning to mining as a means of support.
The mines they work in pay very little (if at all) but when the boys strike a
Tanzanite find they are rewarded with a percentage of the haul.

This reward is often lost on the boys as their culture does not use a formal
currency. They exist primarily on their own cattle and do not have a reason to
engage in widespread trading or commerce.

Their lack of understanding for money and trade is further masked by the fact
that the mining companies often provide them with room and board. This
further diminishes their need to exchange money for the things they desire.

When they discover an abundance of Tanzanite they often find themselves
with bushel baskets of their countries currency, the devalued shilling. Because
they are a society of few possessions it is not uncommon for this money to lose
its luster fairly quickly.

One of the things that seemed to bring them some satisfaction was to use the money to build huge concrete skyscrapers. They looked to their village way of life for inspiration in their building efforts. In their tribes the chief always built his hut on the highest plot of land so he could overlook the village. Therefore, it has become a symbol of respect and honor in their culture to have the highest building in the village.

The mine boys start the basic structure for their buildings by going straight up as far as their money will take them. They intend to complete their buildings when they score another find. However it is not uncommon that one of their fellow miners will strike it rich before they hit Tanzanite a second time. When this happens the second mine boy then builds his building a few stories higher with the same idea in mind.

By the looks of the multi colored concrete this has apparently been the case for quite some time. Several young men are obviously competing to have the tallest building in town and finishing the buildings seems unimportant.

When I asked Preet what they intended to do with the buildings when they were finished he explained that the point wasn't to finish the buildings the point was to make your building taller than your competitors building. I could not grasp why people would waste their earnings in this way so Preet told me a story to help me better comprehend their true lack of understanding for the idea of "money."

Preet said he was just outside of town one day waiting for Douglas when he noticed a confrontation between one of the mine boys and an elderly Arab man. He was too far away to hear their conversation but he could clearly see they were arguing about something that seemed pretty important. After the confrontation Preet enquired around town and got an explanation for the strange scene.

Apparently a young mine boy had just made his first big find. Not satisfied with the competition for the towns' largest building he did some asking around. When he asked local merchants what people with lots of money used it for he learned that they bought fancy things and stayed in nice hotels. With little use for fancy things the young man checked into a nice hotel to experience the amazing luxury that the merchants described.

In the finest hotel in town he found many things that were new to him but the one that captured his attention most was of course the television. With satellite channels from around the world the boy could learn about other cultures, distant lands and the true meaning of wealth and commerce.

He began to click through the channels feverishly until a beautiful woman caught his eye. As he watched, more and more beautiful women appeared. Unbeknownst to him, he had discovered the amazing glory of music television. In video after video he saw young rap stars surrounded by gorgeous women. It did not take him long to figure out that these young men had a lot of money, a lot of nice cars and most importantly, a lot of nice women.

He knew he already had the money part covered and quickly deduced that all he needed were some nice cars and the beautiful women would be soon to follow. This is where Preet began to witness the strange transaction between the boy and an elderly man with a Mercedes.

The boy was being driven by a friend in a disheveled pickup truck when he spotted the man in the Mercedes. The boy instructed the driver of the truck to block the road and he jumped out to speak with the driver of the car. The boy gestured for the man to get out of the car but the man dismissed him with impatience.

The persistent boy continued to badger the man. He was determined that because the man had something he wanted and he had "money," the man was obligated to give him the car. However, to the boy's dismay the man repeatedly refused. Eventually the boy threw back the tarp of the pickup truck and started to set bushel basket after bushel basket on the ground next to the Mercedes. Eventually, the shocked driver stuck his hand out of the car window and handed the keys to the jubilant boy.

Once out of his car the man looked at the baskets and began to assess how he was going to transport such a large sum of currency without a car. As he studied the baskets on the ground the young man sat down in the Mercedes and motioned to the former owner. The man then leaned into the car window and explained the basic operation of the vehicle.

With his lesson complete the boy put the car in reverse and promptly plowed it into a large tree behind him. The man went to the window, scolded the boy and gave him some more instruction. The boy then put the car into drive, floored the accelerator and smashed into a tree on the other side of the street.

The man watched in shock as the boy freed the smoking car and then weaved his way down the dirt road and out of sight.

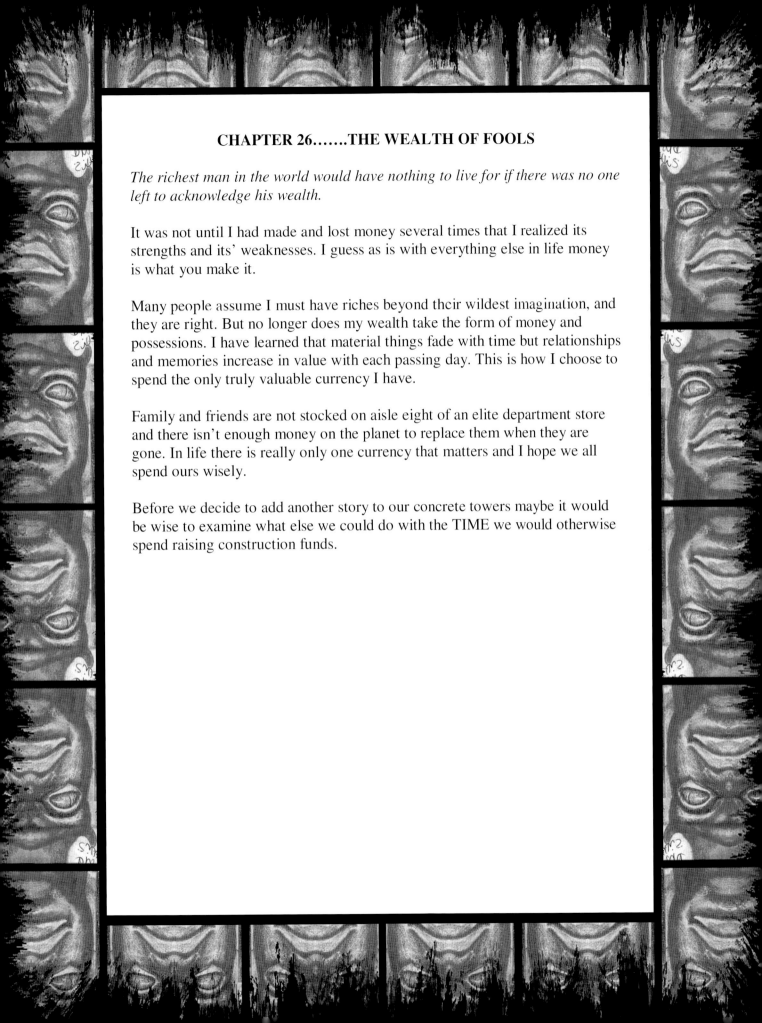

CHAPTER 26.......THE WEALTH OF FOOLS

The richest man in the world would have nothing to live for if there was no one left to acknowledge his wealth.

It was not until I had made and lost money several times that I realized its strengths and its' weaknesses. I guess as is with everything else in life money is what you make it.

Many people assume I must have riches beyond their wildest imagination, and they are right. But no longer does my wealth take the form of money and possessions. I have learned that material things fade with time but relationships and memories increase in value with each passing day. This is how I choose to spend the only truly valuable currency I have.

Family and friends are not stocked on aisle eight of an elite department store and there isn't enough money on the planet to replace them when they are gone. In life there is really only one currency that matters and I hope we all spend ours wisely.

Before we decide to add another story to our concrete towers maybe it would be wise to examine what else we could do with the TIME we would otherwise spend raising construction funds.

CHAPTER 27............AN ISLAND OF MY OWN

When we first started traveling I hoped that we would eventually find a place that suited us well enough to hang up our packs and settle down. At the time I was not sure what I wanted to do with the rest of my life but I was pretty sure I wanted to do it far away from the rat race of my former homeland.

Much like many of my other favorite finds; it was a chance meeting that led us to the place that I would one day call home. On our first stop in Asia we met a young German couple who lived in France and we decided to team up with them for a trek through the mountains of Chang Mai, Thailand.

We spent several days hiking and camping in the jungles of Chang Mai and we built an incredible friendship. When our trek was over we discussed our future travels and plans. Fralek and Anita described an incredible island in the South China Sea that they had heard amazing things about and encouraged us to tag along.

We were planning on heading for Cambodia next but we were having the time of our lives with our new friends and their description of the island peaked our interest. As a result, we decided to accompany them and see what the little island they spoke so highly of had to offer.

It took me about six seconds to fall in love with the place once we arrived. The tropical setting, incredible prices and friendly people made it feel like paradise. There were miles of abandon beaches, several secluded and quaint fishing villages and enough modern convenience to suit every indulgence. It was the first place where every concern just seemed to melt away.

We all recognized what a special place it was and we made the most of each day. Whether it was exploring the jungles for waterfalls or snorkeling through mine fields of jelly fish we had a great time doing any and every little thing. Over the next few weeks as we traveled together our friendship and our love for the island blossomed.

However eventually it was time for Fralek and Anita to return to the hustle and bustle of Paris. That meant it was also time for us to head toward Cambodia and the ancient ruins of Angkor Wat. We never liked leaving a place that had good friends but this time it was particularly difficult. Something about that island captured our hearts, we had never been so happy and the thought of leaving just didn't sit well…..so we decided not to.

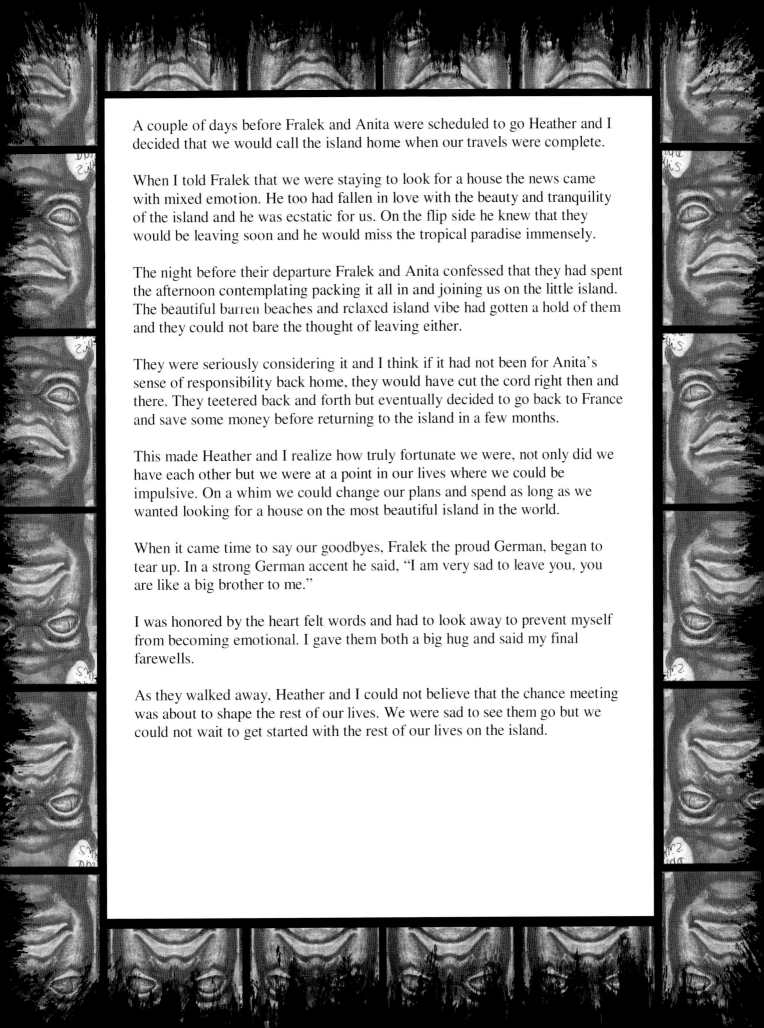

A couple of days before Fralek and Anita were scheduled to go Heather and I decided that we would call the island home when our travels were complete.

When I told Fralek that we were staying to look for a house the news came with mixed emotion. He too had fallen in love with the beauty and tranquility of the island and he was ecstatic for us. On the flip side he knew that they would be leaving soon and he would miss the tropical paradise immensely.

The night before their departure Fralek and Anita confessed that they had spent the afternoon contemplating packing it all in and joining us on the little island. The beautiful barren beaches and relaxed island vibe had gotten a hold of them and they could not bare the thought of leaving either.

They were seriously considering it and I think if it had not been for Anita's sense of responsibility back home, they would have cut the cord right then and there. They teetered back and forth but eventually decided to go back to France and save some money before returning to the island in a few months.

This made Heather and I realize how truly fortunate we were, not only did we have each other but we were at a point in our lives where we could be impulsive. On a whim we could change our plans and spend as long as we wanted looking for a house on the most beautiful island in the world.

When it came time to say our goodbyes, Fralek the proud German, began to tear up. In a strong German accent he said, "I am very sad to leave you, you are like a big brother to me."

I was honored by the heart felt words and had to look away to prevent myself from becoming emotional. I gave them both a big hug and said my final farewells.

As they walked away, Heather and I could not believe that the chance meeting was about to shape the rest of our lives. We were sad to see them go but we could not wait to get started with the rest of our lives on the island.

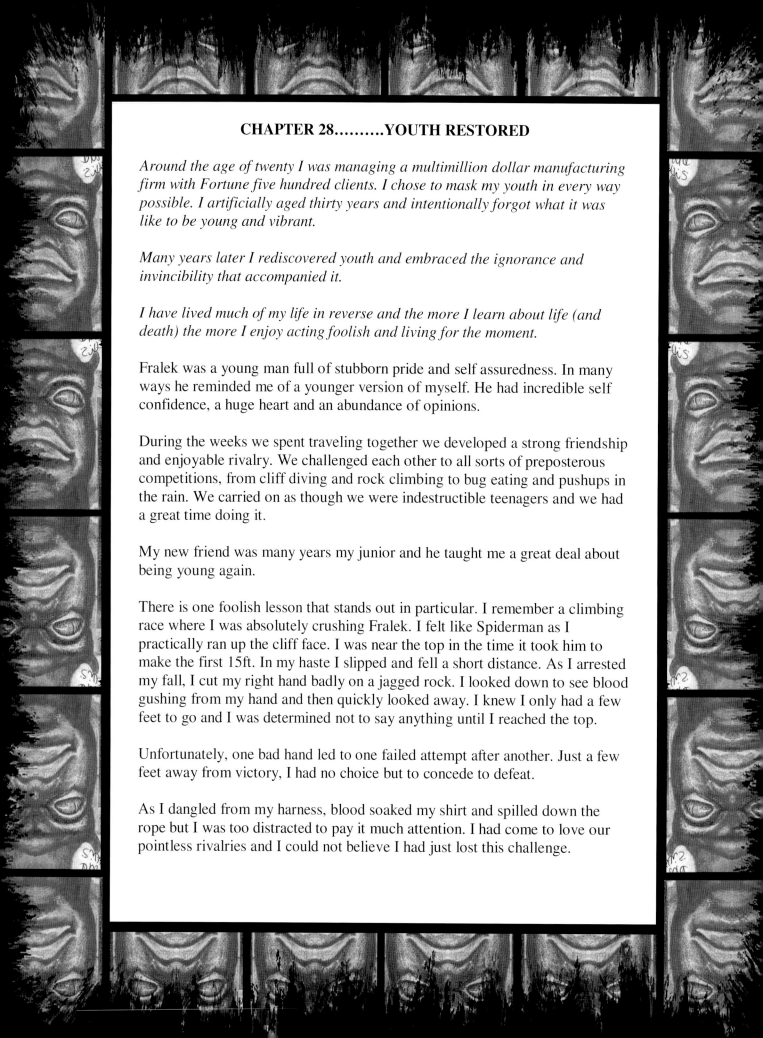

CHAPTER 28..........YOUTH RESTORED

Around the age of twenty I was managing a multimillion dollar manufacturing firm with Fortune five hundred clients. I chose to mask my youth in every way possible. I artificially aged thirty years and intentionally forgot what it was like to be young and vibrant.

Many years later I rediscovered youth and embraced the ignorance and invincibility that accompanied it.

I have lived much of my life in reverse and the more I learn about life (and death) the more I enjoy acting foolish and living for the moment.

Fralek was a young man full of stubborn pride and self assuredness. In many ways he reminded me of a younger version of myself. He had incredible self confidence, a huge heart and an abundance of opinions.

During the weeks we spent traveling together we developed a strong friendship and enjoyable rivalry. We challenged each other to all sorts of preposterous competitions, from cliff diving and rock climbing to bug eating and pushups in the rain. We carried on as though we were indestructible teenagers and we had a great time doing it.

My new friend was many years my junior and he taught me a great deal about being young again.

There is one foolish lesson that stands out in particular. I remember a climbing race where I was absolutely crushing Fralek. I felt like Spiderman as I practically ran up the cliff face. I was near the top in the time it took him to make the first 15ft. In my haste I slipped and fell a short distance. As I arrested my fall, I cut my right hand badly on a jagged rock. I looked down to see blood gushing from my hand and then quickly looked away. I knew I only had a few feet to go and I was determined not to say anything until I reached the top.

Unfortunately, one bad hand led to one failed attempt after another. Just a few feet away from victory, I had no choice but to concede to defeat.

As I dangled from my harness, blood soaked my shirt and spilled down the rope but I was too distracted to pay it much attention. I had come to love our pointless rivalries and I could not believe I had just lost this challenge.

As I began the repel down my mind was occupied with our next competition. Before I reached the bottom I had convinced myself that not only could I compete with a mangled hand, but I could win.

Once on the ground, I was disappointed to see that the cut ran diagonally across all four fingers. Nonetheless, I was still determined to take the evening bowling title. We bandaged my entire hand with the exception of my thumb and climbed on our motor bikes to make the long ride back to town.

Over dinner the girls tried to get us to scrap the whole bowling idea and take them to a local discotheque. We would have none of it as we began to review the rules for the coming contest.

When we initially agreed on the rules I was not injured and knew that I could easily hold my own. Now that my bowling hand was bandaged up like a mummy, one rule in particular gave me reason for concern. That rule clearly stated that if a bowler rolled a gutter ball he would be required to drink one shot of the local rice whisky. This was a penalty I knew I would never have to endure with all five digits, but now it was pretty much a foregone conclusion.

When we arrived at the bowling alley the girls excused themselves for the discotheque and Fralek and I settled in for a long night of competition. My goal soon changed from winning, to avoiding as many gutter balls as possible.

Fralek agreed to give me a few practice shots and I picked up a ball with my left hand. Ball after ball and try after try I found the gutter. I briefly contemplated giving up but decided that conceding to Fralek twice in one day was far worse than a few shots of gut burning rice whisky. I plucked my right thumb into the lightest ball I could find and prepared for battle.

My very first shot rolled straight and true and the match was on. At first I thought I stood a chance using only my thumb. But it didn't take long for thumb fatigue to set in and the gutter balls weren't far behind. Amazingly, the pain in my hand was less and less prominent with each shot of whisky. Unfortunately, I also noticed that as the pain numbed, the gutter balls increased.

Laugh after laugh we just kept bowling until it was obvious I was soon to be down two events to zero. Eventually Fralek took pity on me and each time I rolled a gutter ball he would join me in a shot of whisky.

We had intended to play only three games but Fralek just kept ordering more booze so we always had an excuse to stay for one more game. When it came time for the alley to close, we bribed the owner to let us stay. I don't remember how many bottles of whisky we drank or how many games we played. I just remember that the two of us were so shit face drunk on rice whisky that we could barely find our lane let alone roll a ball down it. I can't recall what we talked about but I do remember that our laughter was the only thing that rivaled our drunkenness.

When the discotheque closed the girls found us barely able to speak and laughing like school children humped over on the steps in front of the bowling alley. They scraped us off the concrete and took us home.

In my life I have seen most of the wonders of the world, the majority of the planets ancient ruins, the artwork of histories masters and just about everything else on my list. I enjoy intellectual conversations and I appreciate the finer things in life, but sometimes there is nothing better than acting foolishly and living for the moment.

I would have never guessed that bowling with a German would go down in my memory banks as one of the best learning experiences of my life. In retrospect, I suppose my travels have taught me that there is a time and place for everything.

I have learned to enjoy all the different aspects of my life as they unfold in front of me and I have come to sincerely appreciate every opportunity to truly be young again. From playing the broom game with my South African friends on the beach to limbo dancing for my dinner in Nicaragua each experience has taught me that getting older doesn't have to happen on the inside.

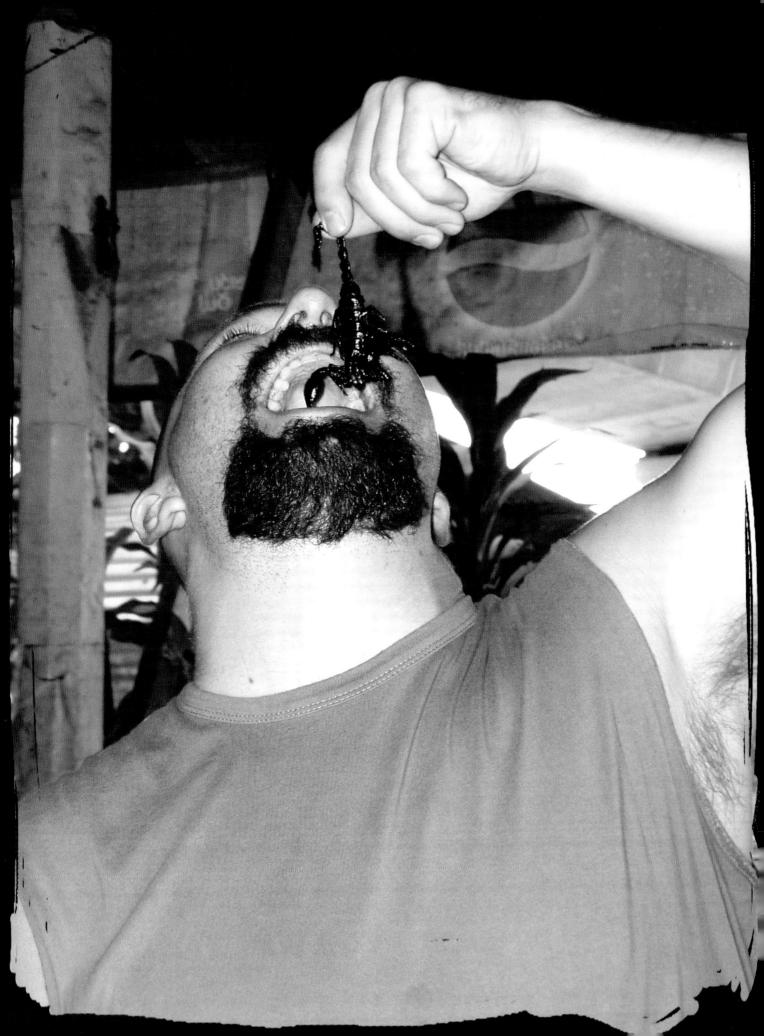

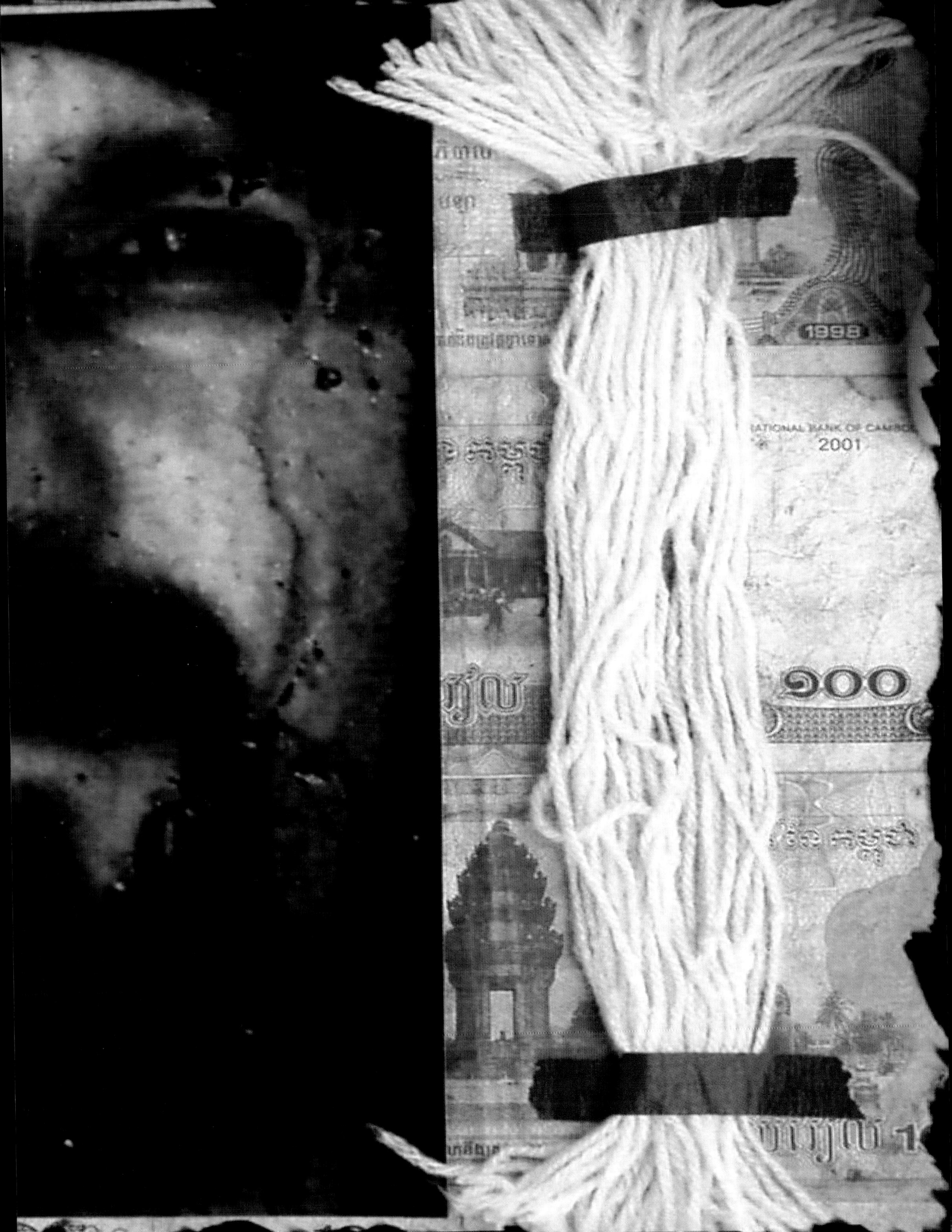
1998
2001

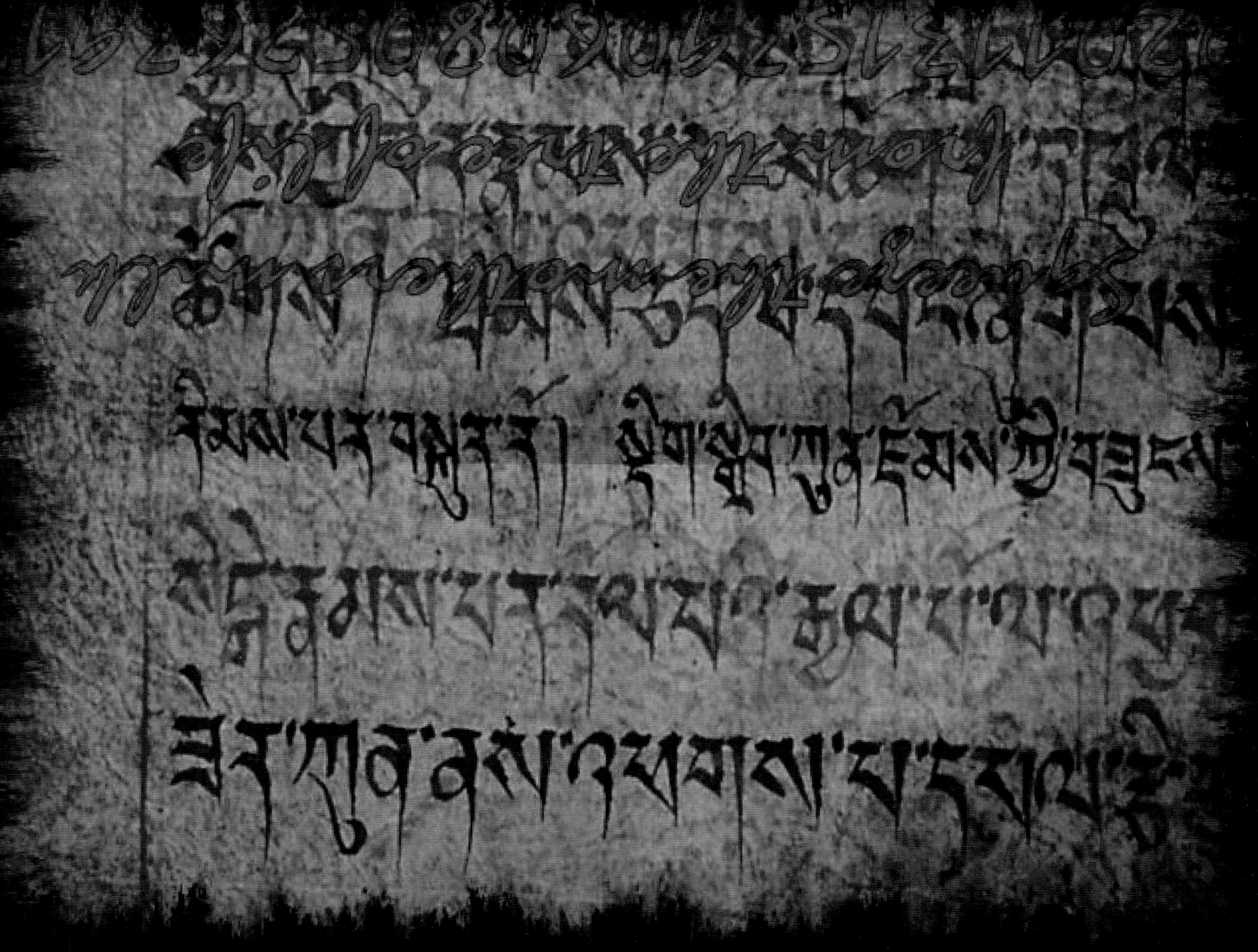
ཞིམ་པར་བསྐུར་རོ། །ཕྱིག་སྒྲིབ་ཀུན་ཇོམས་ཀྱི་བཟུང
ཟེར་ཀུན་ཞེས་འཕགས་པ་དཔལ་ལྡི
Squeeze the mother's milk
from the tree of life

ESSENCE
OF SELF-
LESSNESS
LIES DEEP
WITHIN
THIS CUL
TURE AND
IT'S VAL
UES AND
BELIEFS
AS WELL
AS MANY
OF IT'S
PEOPLE -
BUT LET US
NOT FORGET
EVEN THIS
SOCIETY IS
GOVERNED BY
MAN NOT
BY ANY

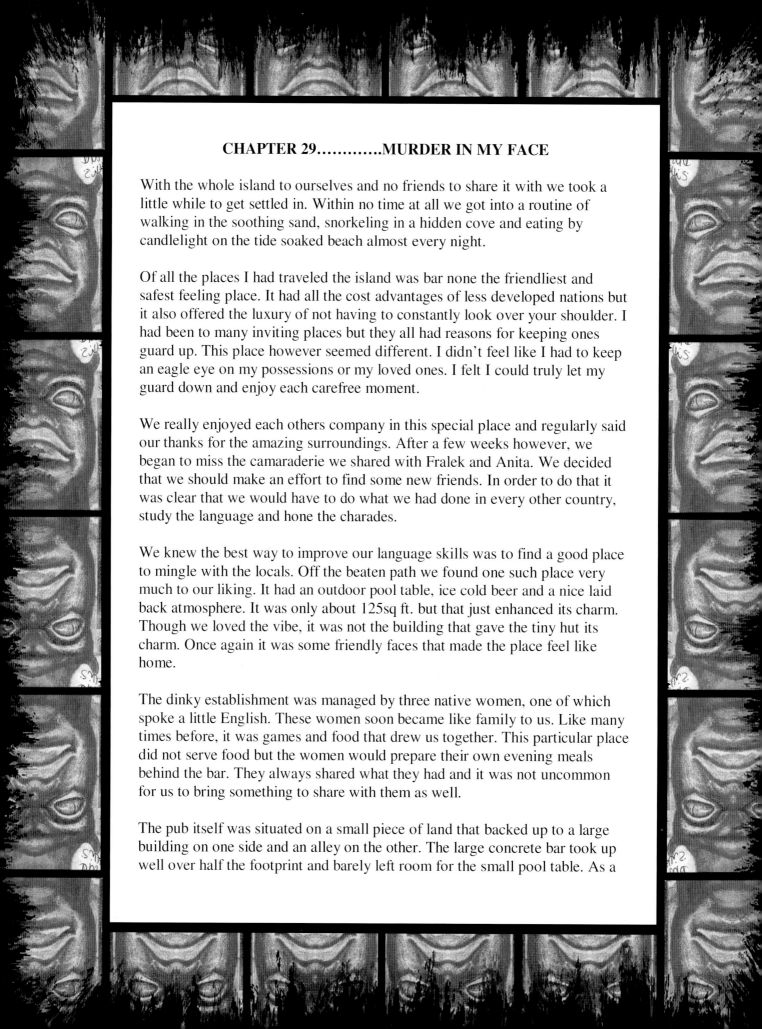

CHAPTER 29………….MURDER IN MY FACE

With the whole island to ourselves and no friends to share it with we took a little while to get settled in. Within no time at all we got into a routine of walking in the soothing sand, snorkeling in a hidden cove and eating by candlelight on the tide soaked beach almost every night.

Of all the places I had traveled the island was bar none the friendliest and safest feeling place. It had all the cost advantages of less developed nations but it also offered the luxury of not having to constantly look over your shoulder. I had been to many inviting places but they all had reasons for keeping ones guard up. This place however seemed different. I didn't feel like I had to keep an eagle eye on my possessions or my loved ones. I felt I could truly let my guard down and enjoy each carefree moment.

We really enjoyed each others company in this special place and regularly said our thanks for the amazing surroundings. After a few weeks however, we began to miss the camaraderie we shared with Fralek and Anita. We decided that we should make an effort to find some new friends. In order to do that it was clear that we would have to do what we had done in every other country, study the language and hone the charades.

We knew the best way to improve our language skills was to find a good place to mingle with the locals. Off the beaten path we found one such place very much to our liking. It had an outdoor pool table, ice cold beer and a nice laid back atmosphere. It was only about 125sq ft. but that just enhanced its charm. Though we loved the vibe, it was not the building that gave the tiny hut its charm. Once again it was some friendly faces that made the place feel like home.

The dinky establishment was managed by three native women, one of which spoke a little English. These women soon became like family to us. Like many times before, it was games and food that drew us together. This particular place did not serve food but the women would prepare their own evening meals behind the bar. They always shared what they had and it was not uncommon for us to bring something to share with them as well.

The pub itself was situated on a small piece of land that backed up to a large building on one side and an alley on the other. The large concrete bar took up well over half the footprint and barely left room for the small pool table. As a result the outdoor pool table infringed on the alley a bit, but there was not a lot of traffic so it wasn't much of a problem.

Pim was the youngest of the three women and though she didn't speak much English she shot a hell of a game of pool. Pool was a great way for us to communicate without struggling too much with the language barrier so we played often. On a particularly relaxed night Pim and I were fiercely locked in battle while Heather was visiting with the others up at the bar.

With my back to the street I leaned over the pool table to make my next shot. As I did I heard the familiar sound of children playing with fireworks in the alley. However the cadence wasn't quite right and it seemed uncomfortably close so I turned around to get a better look.

As I looked into the alley I saw a flash of light and heard another pop. Before I could really figure out what was going on I noticed a local man running right towards me. It seemed as though he was running toward our little bar for cover. When he got within about five feet of me I saw him look up the alley at a second man who emerged from behind some boxes.

From only a few feet away the second man began to run down the alley while firing shots. The first shot struck the man standing right in front of me in the head. I could see the life draining from his disfigured face as I grabbed Heather and Pim and drug them behind the concrete bar for cover.

The rest of the shots fired in rapid succession as the assailant fled down the alley. When I stood from behind the bar I could see the man laying dead only a couple of feet from our pool table. My first instinct was to stay under cover until the coast was clear but the local women popped right back up rather un phased by the whole ordeal. All around me I could see other patrons and shopkeepers going about their business as though nothing had happened.

I thought maybe it would be wise to get the hell out of there but I assumed since I was the closest witness the police would want to talk to me. While I waited for them I was consoled by the women at the bar.

They assured me that this was nothing to be concerned about. This had nothing to do with me and there was no reason to be alarmed……this sort of thing happened all the time. In fact, they said that the next time it happened there was no reason to go diving behind the furniture. This was a local gang on gang crime and I had the whitest face on the island. There was no way that I could be mistaken for a rival gang member.

I assured the ladies that it wasn't the intent of the gunmen that concerned me; it was the quality of his marksmanship.

They went on to explain that every so often one of the local factions would deface one of their rivals publicly. Such humiliation could not be tolerated and the person that lost face would be bound by honor to kill the other man. In turn, the rival gang would kill the shooter and all would be forgotten.

The women said that there was talk of a drug deal gone bad a couple of nights earlier. A man stormed into a public place accused a rival gang member of stealing from him and belittled him in front of several colleagues.

Everyone was expecting this exact outcome and in a couple of days the shooter would be killed and the whole thing would be over with.

Equipped with this new knowledge, I was increasingly nervous about speaking with the police. I knew if I left the scene it would only take the cops about five minutes to track down the only bright white, bald headed, goatee brandishing witness on the island so I decided to stay put.

However, I was faced with a big moral dilemma. Should I tell the cops what I saw or should I keep my damn mouth shut? As I was toiling over exactly what to say and what to omit, the police arrived on the scene. I thought I would have a little more time to polish my story as they put up the crime scene tape, outlined the body and started their forensic investigation.

To my surprise they arrived in an unmarked SUV, rolled the back window down, dropped the tailgate and crudely wrestled the body into the back. One officer then returned to the vehicle and the other shoved the dead mans' legs in like a sack of potatoes so he could get the tailgate up. In less than two minutes total they had come and gone and were never to be seen again.

About three days later the women at the pub informed us that the shooter had been killed and the whole ordeal was completely finished. The island that I viewed as virgin paradise clearly had a dark underbelly and its own system of justice.

With our illusion of purity shattered we were forced to decide if this was still the place we wanted to call home. We knew that we would never again have the same sense of complete safety. But on the other hand we knew we wouldn't have to worry about random drive bys, car jackings, sidewalk muggings and kidnappings either. The crimes here were specific in nature and as long as you didn't get caught in the crossfire the place still seemed safer than most major cities around the world.

We were no longer sure if this was the island for us but we had a few more places to check out before we would have to pull the trigger. We had plans to visit Cambodia in a couple of days and then we would return to the island for a short time before heading to Nepal. Maybe one of these places would provide a more suitable home.

One thing we knew for sure is that apparently there is no Shangri La, no perfect city filled with peace and splendor. Even the ancient Buddhist city of Lhasa in Tibet had fallen to violence. We would have to make do with less than perfect regardless of our final destination.

We had a lot to think about over the coming weeks and deciding where to spend the rest of our lives would not be easy. The island had a special place in our hearts but being so close to a brutal murder forced us to take our blinders off. If we had read about the murder in the paper we probably could have easily dismissed it, like we do with the countless murders that occur each day in our own country. Witnessing it first hand however, forced us to deal with the reality of man.

Kindness and compassion are not the paths chosen by all, even in a Buddhist culture. In life there seems to be a balance of all things. Equal and opposite conditions that make our planet what it is. There is day/night, hot/cold and of course good and evil to name but a few. Our island was no exception to this rule. We would just have to decide which way it was poised to lean, and that decision would have to wait until we returned from Nepal.

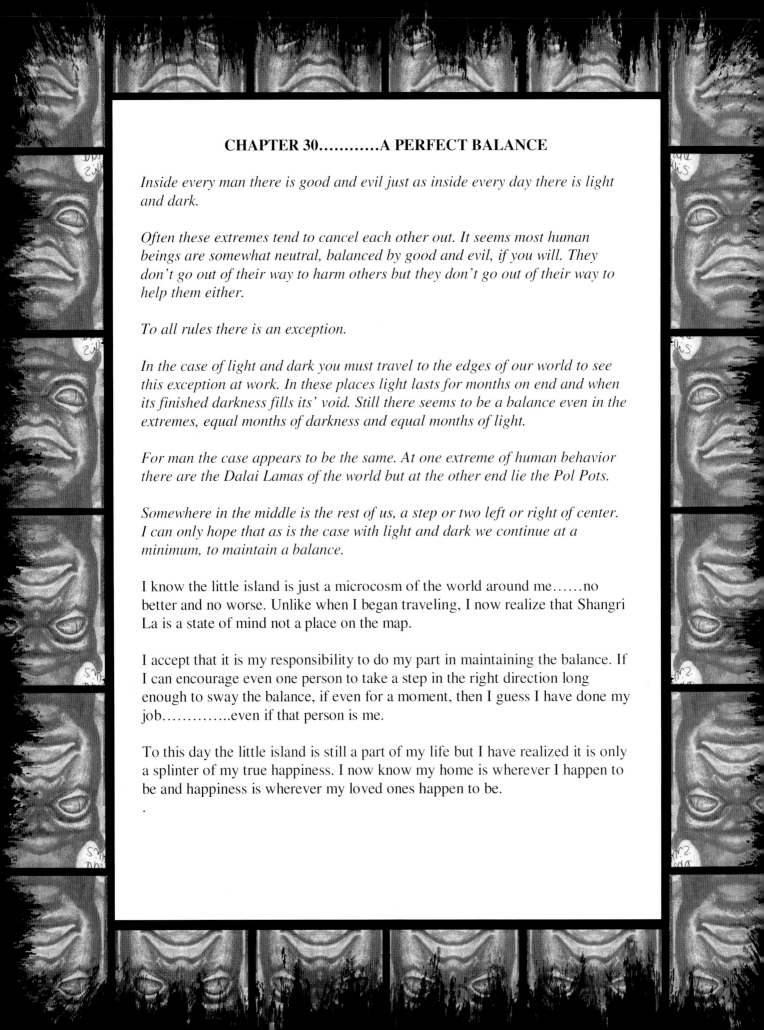

CHAPTER 30............A PERFECT BALANCE

Inside every man there is good and evil just as inside every day there is light and dark.

Often these extremes tend to cancel each other out. It seems most human beings are somewhat neutral, balanced by good and evil, if you will. They don't go out of their way to harm others but they don't go out of their way to help them either.

To all rules there is an exception.

In the case of light and dark you must travel to the edges of our world to see this exception at work. In these places light lasts for months on end and when its finished darkness fills its' void. Still there seems to be a balance even in the extremes, equal months of darkness and equal months of light.

For man the case appears to be the same. At one extreme of human behavior there are the Dalai Lamas of the world but at the other end lie the Pol Pots.

Somewhere in the middle is the rest of us, a step or two left or right of center. I can only hope that as is the case with light and dark we continue at a minimum, to maintain a balance.

I know the little island is just a microcosm of the world around me......no better and no worse. Unlike when I began traveling, I now realize that Shangri La is a state of mind not a place on the map.

I accept that it is my responsibility to do my part in maintaining the balance. If I can encourage even one person to take a step in the right direction long enough to sway the balance, if even for a moment, then I guess I have done my job..............even if that person is me.

To this day the little island is still a part of my life but I have realized it is only a splinter of my true happiness. I now know my home is wherever I happen to be and happiness is wherever my loved ones happen to be.

.

328

QUESTION THAT MAY NEVER BE ANSWERED - GOOD AND EVIL ARE TRULY AT WORK HERE WHY MAN DOES THE THINGS HE DOES IS A

The Killing field Monks of Siem Reap, Cambodia have erected a huge Temple in one of the fields used to murder one and a half million men wom en and Children.
In the interest of saving bullets the Victims were beaten against trees until Dead Sort ed by race education and Wealth and Killed.

A holiday from our holiday in Kho Samui we have lost track of time.

Kho Samui Thailand September Tenth 2003

We have decided to stay on the Thai Isles for a while. It is the low season and for the most part we have the run of the place it is without question the most relaxing place we have been to date.

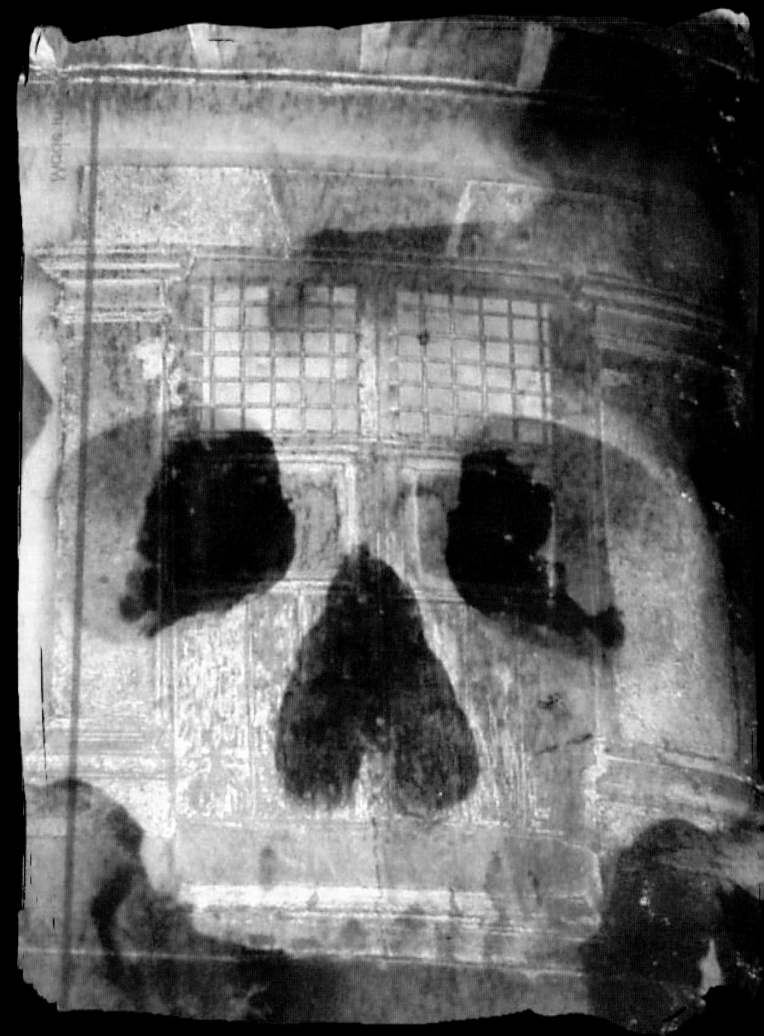

The poison that eats at men's minds, runs through the veins of each and every one of us. What can be said, but to let each man manipulate the delicate pink matter and incubate a vision of repulsive power. Let him create a vision unlike himself yet in his own likeness and let him tear that image apart like flesh from the bone before it can be destroyed by another. — How can such madness permeate modern society and how can such peril always be the fault of another. Where is our responsibility to our fellow man, and how do we prevent ourselves from engaging in the wars of others at the request of our enemies, who really capable

DREAMLAND 03

DEMI
GOD

BANGKOK 03

BANG

DREAMLAND 03

DREAMLAND 03

PHUNG 03'

THINK YOU UNDERSTAND
THINK AGAIN
WWW THROUGHTHEEYESOFMADNESS COM

44251126

MALASIA

Look where it is
You will find nothing
It has not been
If you look where I left it
And you will find much less, but look where
And you will find much less

CHAPTER 31.......DECEPTION IN KATHMANDU

Before we left for Nepal Heather made arrangements with an Everest guide team over the internet. She selected a company with a very professional and well organized web page that boasted several impressive testimonials. While these types of sight unseen arrangements always proved a bit trying, Heather always did a good job with the research and they typically worked out well in the end.

With our plans set we decided to celebrate our upcoming adventure. The night before we were to leave our little paradise in the South China Sea we decided to treat ourselves to a nice dinner out. We foolishly traded our favorite restaurant for a new place on the beach that specialized in seafood. I ordered a fresh seafood concoction that came served in a huge conch shell. Halfway through the dish I got so sick that I could barely walk home.

The next day I felt even worse as we boarded the plane for Nepal but my excitement kept me motivated. When we hit the ground in Katmandu I didn't feel much better, but I was eager to meet our Everest guides so I put on a smile as we disembarked.

We had made arrangements for our contacts to pick us up at the airport in Katmandu, but when we got off the plane they were nowhere in sight. All we saw as we exited the airport was an abundance of men with machine guns. By now we were pretty much used to that and we barely raised an eyebrow.

Outside the airport we were approached by two scraggly young men who introduced themselves as members of our guide team. They immediately reminded me of a couple of stoned surfers, but with each word that passed their lips I began to think stoned surfers would be an improvement. They seemed harmless enough but they were incapable of carrying on a serious conversation. They giggled sheepishly at everything I said and avoided eye contact at all costs.

I could not figure out how they knew who we were and their lack of professionalism started to give me some concerns. As a result, I asked them a few basic questions to assure they were who they claimed to be. They seemed to know all about our itinerary and the agency they claimed to work for.

Once I was sure that they were actually with the guide team, we agreed to follow them out to the parking lot. When we got to their car we both stopped and stared in awe. It was the most abused and battered piece of junk I had ever seen. It was a small two door compact that had been smashed in every conceivable way. Every inch of the car had some sort of damage and it was rusted so badly that I was surprised it didn't fall apart before our very eyes.

I knew Nepal was one of the poorest nations in the world so I tried not to pass judgment on the boys based on the caliber of their automobile. However, I couldn't help but question the success of their organization based on the tired old jalopy they sent to pick us up. Once inside the car my confidence plummeted even further. It was filthy, littered with garbage and a thick dust covered every surface.

On the way to the office I started to warm up to the awkward duo a little. Despite their lack of outward intellect they were very friendly and seemed to mean well. Still I could not imagine putting my life in their hands.

I wanted to give them the benefit of the doubt and I hypothesized that perhaps their talents were masked. Maybe they possessed incredible mountaineering experience and knowledge that didn't show up in everyday conversation. I decided to test the theory.

I threw out a few Everest inquiries but every question was met with an incoherent diatribe. Their English was fine, but I still couldn't understand a word they were saying. I couldn't even get a commitment on simple yes or no questions. I tried to give them a couple of easy ones but when they didn't even know the elevation at base camp, I knew I was in trouble.

Sensing that I was onto their lack of knowledge the boys explained that they were just porters and all of our questions would be answered at the office by their boss and the experienced Sherpa that would lead our trip. This made a little more sense to me and potentially even explained the sorry excuse for an automobile that we were riding in. Perhaps the enterprising young men struck a deal with the company to pick clients up at the airport in a bid to earn themselves a few extra bucks…………. I could respect that.

Feeling a little better I decided to quit pressuring the lads and enjoy some friendly chatter on the way back to the office. I had planned to give the esteemed owner of the vehicle some good hearted ribbing for his obvious lack of driving skills. All I had to do was determine which of the challenged young men owned the car and I could start poking some fun. I asked which one of them was the proud parent of our fine transport vehicle and the answer I got sent my alarm bells back to full tilt.

They laughed awkwardly and said, "This isn't our car, the owner of the company just lets us use it to pick up clients."

That being said, my only hope was that the owner was an enlightened man free of lavish material things and ignorant to the effects of corporate image. Perhaps he was still a genius when it came to mountaineering.

As we drove through the streets of Katmandu it was unlike anything I had ever seen. First of all, it was absolute chaos. There seemed to be no rules of the road whatsoever. The only thing that determined right of way was the volume of your horn. There were people pulling wooden carts, motorcycles, animals, cars and foot traffic all sharing the same crowded streets. Traffic moved in any and every direction and no one seemed to notice the mayhem that surrounded them.

Despite the traffic it was clear that this was a magical place. Ancient prayer flags and hand painted mandalas occupied every corner. Buddhist and Tibetan influence could be seen sprinkled in with Hindu and Nepalese works of art. Nothing about the place was ordinary and I could not take my eyes off of it.

The downtown area reminded me of a sorcerers' lair. There were dozens of shops with all sorts of artifacts and handmade items that I couldn't wait to explore. The city seemed like it was a million years old and I expected magic dragons and mystical holy men to appear around every corner. It was simply the most whimsical city I could ever imagine and I loved it. I was more excited about exploring the city than I was about conquering the mountain that made it famous.

Eventually our chariot rattled to a hobbled stop and we all got out. Once outside I was reminded of how sick I was. I was so dizzy I could barely stand and I was having a hard time not vomiting in front of our young hosts. I wanted to meet the owner and the Sherpa and then I wanted to find a hotel and get some sleep. The boys wanted to chatter on about the city but I insisted we get moving.

As the dynamic duo led us through the ancient city streets we passed one established guide service after another. We could see huge offices with climbing gear stowed everywhere, massive wall charts and maps, radio antennas, computers and dozens of ground support personnel. This was obviously a place where people knew the art of climbing.

Unfortunately, we didn't stop at any of those places. We just kept going and going, further and further into the back alleys of Katmandu. When the boys announced our arrival in front of a completely abandoned building I knew we were screwed. They led us up flight after flight of pitch black stairs through shambles and ruin until we reached the "penthouse suit."

We approached a big metal door with several paddle locks on the outside. The door and the locks were the only things remotely new in the entire condemnable place. The boys apologized for the lack of lighting but assured us that the office would have electricity. While one of the boys fumbled with the keys the other went on and on about how great it was that they had electricity.

I remember thinking to myself………. you know you are in trouble when the primary marketing campaign for a business is "We have electricity!" Not only was I a little more than suspicious about the quality of service available at this fine establishment but I was also getting nervous about more immediate concerns. For instance, why were there three huge locks on the outside of the door……and why was the door solid steel……. and if the boss and the Sherpa were inside then how did the locks get locked…… and why were we in an abandoned building so far from town?

I probably would have just left right then and there if not for the inept nature of the two boys. I was quite convinced that if in fact they did plan to kidnap us I would simply blow the frail misfits out the window with a powerful gust from my air filled cheeks. Additionally, Heather had made some sort of agreement with these people over the internet and I wanted to get it sorted out before we were charged for a service that I was 99% sure we were not going to be using.

Before we entered the room, I asked the bungling duo where their boss was. They said he was waiting inside. When I asked how he managed to lock the paddle locks from the inside the thought honestly had not occurred to them. They quickly deduced that he must have stepped out.

Once inside, they escorted us to the "lobby." The lobby consisted of an empty room with two cobbled together chairs that had obviously been assembled from bits and pieces of debris from the lower floors. After about ten minutes of this charade my patience had reached an end. I told the boys we were going to our hotel and we could discuss the "contract" later.

As if by telepathy one of the boys claimed he had "just spoken with the boss." He claimed he would be arriving any minute. I raised my wrist and showed the boys the minute hand on my watch. I told them that they had exactly five minutes to produce the boss and the Sherpa or we were gone. For the first time, they actually seemed motivated to do something. After some banter back and forth in Nepalese; one of the boys reluctantly stood guard while the other ran down the stairs to retrieve their boss.

Unfortunately, before the deadline had expired, the winded boy returned and declared, "Mr. Shatar will see you now." He led us into Mr. Shatars' office which consisted of a homemade desk, an honest to goodness chair, a light bulb on a wire and little else. Not one map on the wall, not one route book, not one scrap of paper and not one computer were anywhere to be found.

Behind the finely crafted desk sat a young man not more than nineteen or so years in age. This was the infamous Mr. Shatar, who had so graciously agreed to see us. From behind the desk he looked me in the eye as he stood up and aggressively stuck out his hand. Like a used car salesman he said, "So, you must be Mr. Garner?"….. As if he had so many clients there might be some confusion.

When I took his hand I made it a point to squeeze it extra firmly and hold it long enough to make him a little uncomfortable. I immediately distrusted the little charlatan and I wanted him to know that I wasn't going to be putting up with any bullshit.

It was going to take a miracle to get me to cross the street with this guy let alone trust him to lead me up the worlds' deadliest mountain. At this point my only objective was to figure out his scam and get the hell out of there with as little money lost possible.

I did not know if this was some sort of extortion outfit or if these buffoons actually intended to lead us through the death addled Himalayas. As Mr. Shatar began to explain their services I started to put the pieces together.

I asked him some simple technical questions to see what he knew about Everest. When he didn't know the elevation at base camp I knew they were all full of shit. When I pointed out that I was not comfortable being led by people with no knowledge of the mountain whatsoever, he insisted that he employed one of the best Sherpas in Nepal. He claimed his only responsibility was running the business end of things. I told him that unless they produced this all knowing Sherpa in the next five minutes they weren't going to be seeing any green backs from me.

His comedic henchmen left to find the Sherpa as I impatiently began to grill Mr. Shatar about the finer points of business. While he was much sharper than his colleagues, it was clear he was no businessman. I asked him how much

climbers insurance was and he had no idea what I was talking about. I rephrased the question. "How much is the insurance to guarantee us evacuation and medical treatment if we are injured or experience severe AMS?"

His response was illogical and absurd. He said that no one that ever climbed with them got hurt so they didn't need insurance. When I asked him how they knew that they weren't going to be hurt in advance he replied, "When you have the kind of experience with the mountain that we do you just know..........our Sherpas can tell if there is going to be a problem before we even leave."

I just wanted to walk out right then and there, but I knew that they probably had some way of causing me grief and getting even more money out of me if I didn't figure out the best way of dealing with the whole mess. While we were waiting for the Sherpa that could predict the future I thought we might as well just cut to the chase.

I asked the nervous young man about his background in business and I enquired about his education in the field. He was quick to point out that in fact he did have a degree in computer science. That didn't really answer the business question but it did explain where the website came from. With that out of the way I thought I might as well see how high his sights were set.

I dove headlong into his fiscal expectations from our little transaction. I started by asking what their cancellation policy was. He pulled out a form that he had obviously printed from his website. He smugly showed me the clause that said they will retain 50% of the total fee if a client cancels the trip prior to departure and a 100% after departure. He claimed that they had already incurred some significant expenses and the fifty percent would barely get them in the clear.

Our trip wasn't for several more weeks and I knew that the only expenses that they had incurred were a gallon of gasoline and forty cents or so in labor for the services of the bungle brothers. I didn't say anything, but there was no way in hell that I was going to pay him 50% of a substantial guide fee for a cast of misfits that probably couldn't FIND Everest, let alone climb it.

He could tell I was getting a little agitated and he assured me that once I met the Sherpa all my concerns would be alleviated. His faith in the Sherpa made me start to think that maybe these knuckleheads were actually trying to run a legitimate business. Maybe they weren't necessarily con men. Nonetheless, they were definitely incompetent with regards to the business of mountaineering and there was no way in hell that the testimonials on their website were legitimate. But maybe, just maybe, the humble Sherpa was in fact an incredible mountaineer who teamed up with the three stooges to handle the high tech world of internet marketing.

I had incredible respect for the Nepalese Sherpas and I wanted nothing more than to believe that this whole thing could somehow be resolved favorably. I was relieved when one of the boys stuck their head in the office to announce the Sherpa had arrived.

Mr. Shatar told us to wait in the lobby for the Sherpa. Once the Sherpa answered all of our questions we were free to return to his office and get things scheduled. When we entered the "lobby" we saw a portly man in his thirties sitting in one of the makeshift chairs with his feet propped up on the other. He was reading a paper and he didn't look up at us or move his feet so we just stood patiently and waited for the Sherpa to arrive.

After about five minutes, Mr. Shatar returned to see if we were getting everything straightened out with the Sherpa. When we told him that he had not yet arrived he laughed and gestured to the arrogant man reading the paper. When he introduced us, the man with his feet hoisted up on the chair barely looked up from the paper. I told him we had a few concerns about the trip and he did not reply. He was either deaf, non English speaking or the rudest son of a bitch I had ever met.

I dove straight into my line of questioning (during which time he never once looked up).

"Where can we get climbers insurance?"

………………………………………………Don't know I don't use it.

"What strategy do you recommend for acclimatization?"

………………………………………………Go slow.

"What do you do to treat cerebral edema?"

……………………………………………… I usually recommend eating a lot of cornflakes. They are light but they give you a lot of energy.

"What is the elevation at base camp?"
…………………………………………….It's pretty high.

"Yes, but what is the exact elevation?"
....I don't know, but its high.

"Have you ever summitted?"
....Yes.

"How many times?"
....Quite a few.

"OKAY, I think we're done here!!!"

Without saying another word I went into Mr. Shatars' office and he followed close behind. Still unable to distinguish if they were con men or simply the dumbest business men I had ever met I thought a white lie would be in order. I did not want them to think that we were in the country alone so I told Mr. Shatar a bit of a fib.

I said that after we had booked our trip with him we learned that some of our friends were also planning to be here in the morning. They had previously lived in Katmandu for a number of years and had friends at the embassy who said they could make guide arrangements for us.

I was terribly sorry about the cancellation but there was no way I was going to travel with a man that treated cerebral edema with cornflakes. If he would like I could have my friends talk to their buddies at the embassy and we could meet in the morning and work out a fair way to settle this whole thing.

At this point, the talented Mr. Shatar became visibly nervous and I could tell he definitely did not want any officials involved in his "business." I was extremely polite when I gave the young upstart his options. I could pay him for the gas that his thoughtful apprentices used to skillfully collect me from the airport and we could call this a lesson learned or we could sit down over a nice dinner with my friends and their colleagues and go over all the legal details to assure we both reached an agreement that was fair.

This was a far cry from the thousands of U.S. dollars Mr. Shatar expected, but all of a sudden he seemed very willing to negotiate. He said that he had to pay the boys and the Sherpa for their time and there were paperwork fees and gas to consider. He figured three hundred dollars should about cover it.
I told him that he could take what money I had in my pocket now, or we could just sort it out tomorrow. I pulled about sixty dollars out of my pocket and stuck my hand out. He readily accepted it and then shook my hand as though we were now esteemed colleagues.

I think I probably could have just left without paying him a cent but I figured sixty dollars would let him think he got away with something and assure me that we would never be hearing from Mr. Shatar again.

CHAPTER 32............AN AGING WARRIORS' FATE

There is no shame in having your enemy unaware that he has been defeated......and there is no pride in winning a battle that didn't need to be fought.

In my younger days there is little doubt that I would have picked up one of the bungle brothers and used them like a cricket bat against the side of Mr. Shatars' head.

When I was younger, I took up every cause no matter how big or small. I looked for battles at every turn and I was never satisfied with a silent victory. I let the smallest issues consume my energy and I felt an unbearable shame if I didn't fight at every opportunity.

As I have aged I have realized that there are very few geriatric warriors with bones still strong enough to take the battlefield, but there are plenty of aging generals with minds sharp enough to change the course of history.

I now believe fighting the right battles with the right tools is the right thing to do only when diplomacy is no longer an option. I realize a concession at the bargaining table is a victory in a battle that is never fought

I know he who has the energy left to fight for his beliefs when the stakes are high did not fall in vain to his own arrogance when the stakes were low.

I now recognize choosing ones battles plots ones course, but choosing all battles seals ones fate.

If I must, I will fight and die with honor, but I will do neither for foolish pride.

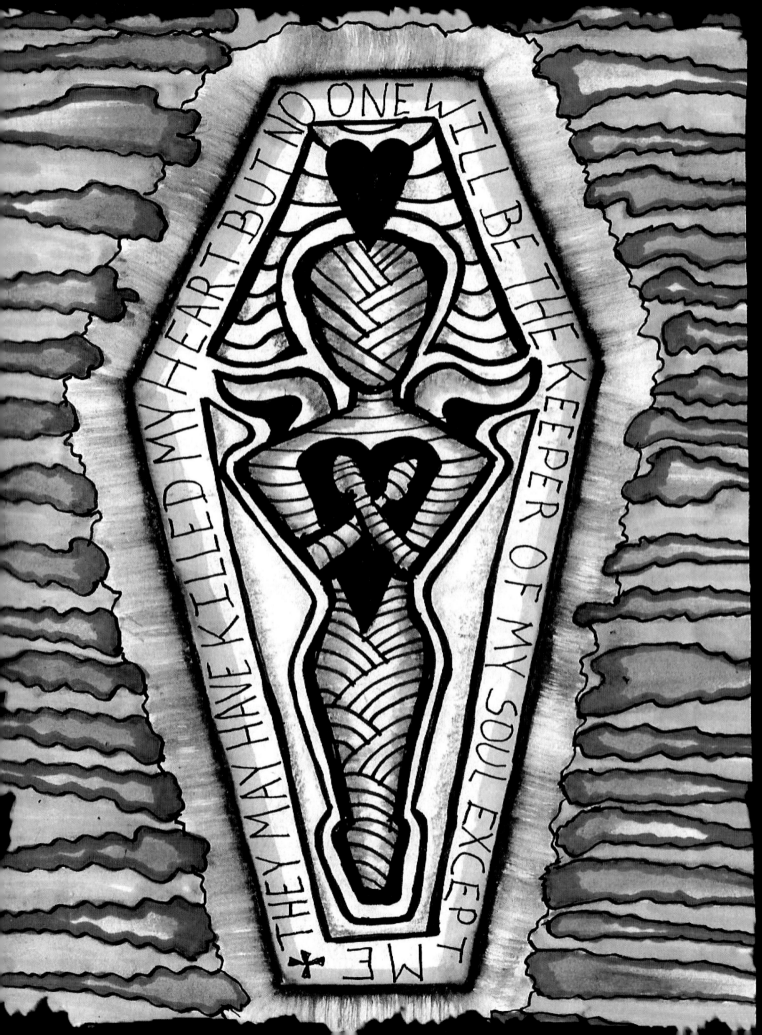

PISS
ON
The
Line
That
others
Worship
AND
SEEK
Strength
Within

The Balanced Capitol — Tacos for the soul

Today is August 16th the Maddening is getting thicker with each day, like the foam that forms on semi frozen flat beer poon on the gel on a slackers back. It is becoming increasingly harder to choose sides all sides seem equal yet horribly in balanced. Everyone is seeming yellow and black or some- thing just like that. Most of them are already here but some are still waiting for me at the gathering place. The place where they force the maddening. I cant watch T.V. without my head hurting on the inside.

It's about nine o'clock on a perfect fall evening in Greenwich Village. I am getting used to calling diffrent cities home, and while Seattle will always have a special seat at my already full table, I am starting to get the travelers soul. Hang my hat where I am and live for the moment. I am pretty sure I won't see a full life so I better get it right and I better get it right quick. There may be no tommorow and I'm leaving with no regrets. From Height Ashbury to Soho and from Heyd Lake to Tulsa I have found adventure and I have truly lived a full life. I have done just about every thing I have ever wanted. There is not a single tangible possesion outside my reach and I have found that I don't really need many any way. Some pencils, a pen or two and someplace to scratch an about all I really need. The things that are really important to me are the people I choose to spend my time with, th SOW. in printicular. So when my time comes, please preserve these pages, but do not shed a tear I have already won the game.

THE PLACE
Restaurant & Bar

310 West 4th Street
ONE OF MY FAVORITE EATS
IN THE VILLAGE · DINNER

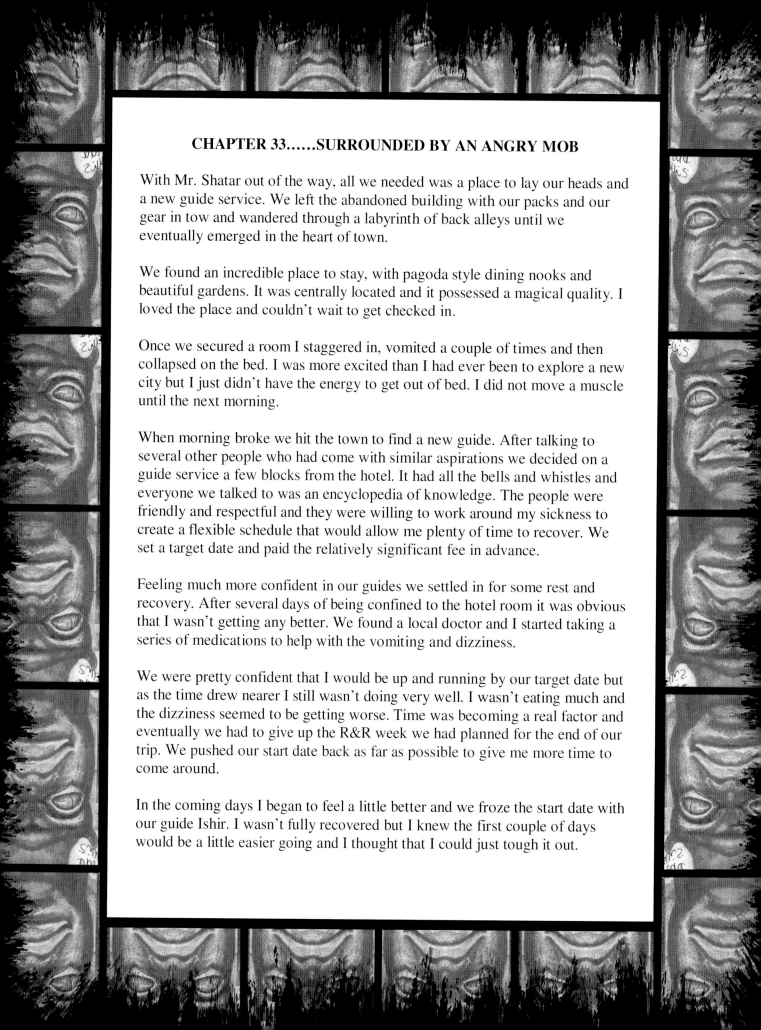

CHAPTER 33......SURROUNDED BY AN ANGRY MOB

With Mr. Shatar out of the way, all we needed was a place to lay our heads and a new guide service. We left the abandoned building with our packs and our gear in tow and wandered through a labyrinth of back alleys until we eventually emerged in the heart of town.

We found an incredible place to stay, with pagoda style dining nooks and beautiful gardens. It was centrally located and it possessed a magical quality. I loved the place and couldn't wait to get checked in.

Once we secured a room I staggered in, vomited a couple of times and then collapsed on the bed. I was more excited than I had ever been to explore a new city but I just didn't have the energy to get out of bed. I did not move a muscle until the next morning.

When morning broke we hit the town to find a new guide. After talking to several other people who had come with similar aspirations we decided on a guide service a few blocks from the hotel. It had all the bells and whistles and everyone we talked to was an encyclopedia of knowledge. The people were friendly and respectful and they were willing to work around my sickness to create a flexible schedule that would allow me plenty of time to recover. We set a target date and paid the relatively significant fee in advance.

Feeling much more confident in our guides we settled in for some rest and recovery. After several days of being confined to the hotel room it was obvious that I wasn't getting any better. We found a local doctor and I started taking a series of medications to help with the vomiting and dizziness.

We were pretty confident that I would be up and running by our target date but as the time drew nearer I still wasn't doing very well. I wasn't eating much and the dizziness seemed to be getting worse. Time was becoming a real factor and eventually we had to give up the R&R week we had planned for the end of our trip. We pushed our start date back as far as possible to give me more time to come around.

In the coming days I began to feel a little better and we froze the start date with our guide Ishir. I wasn't fully recovered but I knew the first couple of days would be a little easier going and I thought that I could just tough it out.

Before I knew it, launch day had arrived and we were in our room taking inventory of our gear. While I checked our supplies Heather went down to the lobby to cash some traveler's checks and settle our bill.

I was busy prepping my pack and reviewing the gear so I didn't notice that she had not yet returned. After thirty minutes or so I started to become concerned. I was going to go to the lobby and look for her but she had taken the room key and I couldn't lock the room without it. My concern grew as I waited. I determined that I was going to give her another fifteen minutes or so and then go on the hunt.

When she finally came back to the room she was frantic and she had a look on her face that I recognized immediately. In our ten years together we really only argued about one thing, it wasn't money, it wasn't lifestyle, and it wasn't politics or religion. It was car keys.

She misplaced the car keys so frequently that at one point, I actually started a log of how much of our lives had been wasted looking for the damn things. I knew it only made things worse but it was the only way I could keep from getting completely frustrated with the situation.

It was not uncommon to find that she had left the keys in the refrigerator as she grabbed a snack on the way out the door, or locked them in the trunk of the car in her haste to pack. They were never really lost; they were just in some obscure place that you would never expect keys to be. Eventually, I bought her a bag with a special insert for the keys but, despite my efforts, she still lost them.........frequently.

There was a certain look that she got when she didn't want to admit that they were gone again……and that was the look on her face now. Only we didn't have any car keys in Nepal so I wasn't sure exactly what had gone missing.

I could immediately tell she was upset and rather than get angry I tried to console her. A million times she had lost the keys and a million times we had found them.

She began to cry as she said, "I think I have done something bad." I know she expected me to be upset but for some reason I just knew that whatever it was, it could not be that big of a deal. I squeezed her in my arms and told her not to worry; we would fix whatever it was.

As her story unfolded I realized it was a little more serious than I anticipated but I still wasn't that concerned.

Apparently the front desk had run out of money and in order to cash the travelers checks she had to walk across the street and go to an independent money exchange kiosk.

When she returned from the kiosk she bumped into Ishir in the lobby and visited with him for awhile before going to the counter to settle our final bill. When she went into her money belt to retrieve the cash she realized that our passports were not in their normal spot. In a panic she rushed across the street only to find that the currency kiosk had closed for the night.

Normally this would not have been a reason for panic but we had already pushed our meeting with the mountain to the last possible minute and we were scheduled to be on a plane out of Katmandu at 6:00am the next morning. The kiosk would not be open before our flight was scheduled to leave and we couldn't leave without our passports.

Complicating matters was the current political climate in Nepal. The country was in a state of civil unrest which increased the number of road blocks and document checks. It just wasn't a good idea to go traipsing around with no passport. To make matters worse, tensions between the Maoist and The King's Army were at an all time high and the military had imposed a curfew.

Ishir had told us that the penalty for breaking the curfew was quite severe. He did not specify the exact nature of the punishment but it was clear that it was something best avoided. Now that it was past the curfew retrieving the passports was starting to seem somewhat impossible.

While I was thinking about the curfew I also started to think about the other things that Heather had lost. Every time something was missing it was never in the place that she thought she may have left it. In fact, many times she inadvertently dropped the item in the bottom of her cluttered backpack and just overlooked it in the mess.

I knew we would find it and I couldn't stand to see her so upset. I sat her down and walked her through several scenarios where she thought she lost something important only to find it hours later.

She started to calm down and we began unpacking our gear. She pulled the most likely pack from under her bed and began to tear through it. As I was unpacking one of the other bags the phone rang and Heather answered it. Without saying a word she set the phone down and made a bee line for the door.

When I stopped her to ask where she was going she said some guy called about the passports and she was going to meet him a couple of blocks away. Her renewed franticness made it hard to get any sense out of her, but I knew one thing for sure. She sure as hell was not going to go out after dark, past the curfew, by herself in a city on the brink of civil war to meet some guy who just happened to call her on the telephone.

I had to calm her down all over again and get the rest of the story. Apparently when she realized the kiosk owner had left for the night she started reaching out for help to anyone who would listen. She informed the military guards in front of our hotel. She informed the security guards at the hotel, she informed the carpet salesman near the kiosk, she informed the hotel staff and she informed some other shopkeepers that she visited on the way to the kiosk.

This mystery man on the phone could be one of a hundred different people. I could not believe that she spent so much time stirring up the entire town before even giving me a chance to solve the problem without making it a national incident.

As my blood started to boil I realized that it was partly my fault. Even though I wasn't the angry or yelling type I did let my frustration be known every time she lost the damn car keys. If she wasn't worried about what I would say she probably would have come to me first.

I didn't like anything about this situation. The Kings army had about 84,000 soldiers and the Maoist army had about 83,000. It was clear that the people of Nepal were spilt between the causes. You never knew who you were really talking to regardless of the uniform they were wearing at the time. The possible scenarios of who the guy on the phone was were endless and I didn't trust anyone whose political intentions were unknown.

When I asked her about the phone call I was very specific.

"Did the man say who he was?"

....No.

"Did he say that he had the passports?"

....No, he said he knew something about them.

"Did he say exactly where to meet him?"

....No, he said he would be across the street from the hotel by a fountain.

I wished we could just roll back the clock an hour and start over. What could have been a very simple matter to get my arms around was now a cloak and dagger mystery of epic proportion. I asked Heather to wait in the room while I broke the military curfew and went to talk to the unknown man.

I was very specific in my request. Do not, under any circumstances, leave this room. Do not go out into the streets regardless of what anyone claims over the phone and do not broadcast to anyone else that I am breaking the curfew.

If I am not back in an hour, call the front desk and ask them to look around out front, but don't tell them that I have left the hotel. Just say that I came down to use the internet and ask them if they can see me anywhere.

If I am not back in two hours, call the front desk and have them connect you with the closest thing to an embassy they can find.

I will keep an eye on my watch and I will be back in less than two hours unless something bad happens. If I don't come back at all and you can't get help from the embassy contact Ishir and find out who can be trusted and send them looking for me, but don't leave the room. Hopefully the guy will know where to get the passports and I will be back in a jiff but give me at least an hour before you do anything.

That being said I went down the stairs and out into the street. I figured at the first sign of the Military or the Maoist I would beat feet back to the hotel and deal with the whole ordeal in the morning.

As I crossed the street in front of the hotel I could see a dark skinned man sitting on the side of a poorly lit fountain. As I got closer I noticed he was darker than most of the Nepalese people and I assumed he must be Indian. He seemed very nervous about being out on the street and I couldn't blame him.

He wasn't wearing a uniform and his expression was hard to read so I had no idea who he might be.

He was surprised to see me. I think he was expecting a beautiful young auburn haired woman and not a gruff bald man with a scowl on his face. When I realized he was just as nervous as I was I dropped the scowl and introduced myself. I explained that it was my girlfriend that he talked to on the phone.

The man explained that he owned a shop near the currency kiosk and he knew where the owner lived. He said that Heather had told him that we were scheduled to leave in the morning and we needed to retrieve our travel documents tonight.

He said that if I would like to follow him he would take me to the mans' house and we could retrieve the documents. I asked him about the curfew and he said that we could go behind his shop and take the back way through the alleys to avoid drawing attention to ourselves. It sounded like a bad idea but I did not have a better one and I agreed.

I was very suspicious of a man who would risk his own neck to help a complete stranger. I had surmised that he was expecting a healthy tip when we retrieved the passports. A tip seemed only fair. I had been through so much already that giving up on Everest the night before we were supposed to leave did not seem like a very attractive option. Tipping this guy was way better than losing all the money we had spent on the guide service or the cost of new plane tickets. Still I doubted his motives a little and I was reluctant as I followed the man behind his shop and into the darkened alley.

As we made our way down the alley suddenly I heard someone right behind us. With a clenched fist I spun around and drew my arm back. As I lunged forward out of instinct, I saw the frightened eyes of a dainty Nepalese man with a motorcycle helmet on his head.

He was the most innocent human being I had ever seen and he was scared to death. Before I could say anything the shop owner grumbled at him in Nepalese. It was clear that the two men knew each other. The shop owner introduced me to his assistant Bingi and then explained that Bingi lived in the back of the shop. When he saw me following his boss into the darkened alley he thought he should investigate. This did not explain the motorcycle helmet on his head but it was not really an appropriate time for questions so we just kept moving.

We cleared one city block then another and then another. We were deep into a maze of identical box like apartment buildings and I was completely lost. I kept looking at my watch to make sure I could make it back to Heather before the two hour deadline expired. I knew it would take me almost two hours to find my way out of the labyrinth so I figured that once we got the damn passports I would have to convince one of the men to lead me back to the hotel.

My main concern however was to avoid being caught out past the curfew with no passport. Also high on my list was avoiding being hoisted onto the bayonet of a Maoist incensed with my ties to the capitalist nation of my countrymen. Hovering around third place was eluding the muggers and thieves that I was sure lurked around every dark corner. As I took inventory of my concerns suddenly making it back before the deadline seemed a little less important. I just wanted to make it back.

I was starting to get nervous about the distance we had traveled into the back alleys. I asked the shopkeeper how much farther we had to go. His answer did not exactly fill me with confidence. His exact words were, "I think the man we are looking for lives somewhere around here."

I then asked him if he had been to the man's house before, …………………………… he said, "No, I don't even know the man."

This made me not only nervous but confused so I asked him how he knew where to find the man's house. He said that the two of them left their shops at about the same time every night and came down the same road until the man from the kiosk turned off at about where we were standing.

I wondered how we were going to find this man with no idea what his house looked like but unbeknownst to me the shopkeeper had a plan.

We rounded the corner and the shopkeeper said, "I think this is it." I breathed a sigh of relief, thinking that we could get the passports and get the hell out of there before any one of a dozen or so nefarious things could happen.

I asked him which one it was as I looked at a U shaped dead end that housed three to four hundred identical apartments.

The shopkeeper didn't answer; he just began to yell aggressively into the heavens. I couldn't understand a word of his Nepalese rant. I thought that maybe the guy had lost his mind. When I figured out his plan I was pretty sure that in fact he had.

Window by window and door by door he began to yell and scream until light after light came on all the way up and down the five story section of apartments. Tenant after angry tenant came to the window and the man yelled at them all. Maybe it is just the way the Nepalese communicate but it sure did not seem to be going well. After waking at least a dozen tenants in the first small section we moved to the next section and the shopkeeper repeated the routine.

Eventually, after several sections, it seemed that someone knew the man we were looking for. They directed us to a section of the complex near the center of the U. As we approached the building it was clear that it was not like the rest. Every door and window was heavily fortified. There were huge metal bars that guarded more huge metal bars that guarded huge metal doors.

The shopkeeper began his usual screaming and yelling routine, only this time it met with much different results. Shortly into his rant the people from near by buildings began to empty into the street. They wasted no time surrounding us and it did not take long for me to notice that most of then were holding sticks and clubs.

For some reason I trusted that the shopkeeper had been acting in my best interest but it was obvious that this was now well out of his hands. I looked at Bingi and I thought he might cry. He was now holding his helmet in his hand and his head was hanging like he knew our fate had been sealed.

The shopkeeper's rants now became more frantic and more insistent. As the crowd closed in around us it was clear that there was no way in hell I was going to talk or fight my way out of this jam.

As the mob began yelling violently and closing in I held my hand out in front of Bingi and gestured for his helmet. I took the helmet from him and buckled the chin strap. When I gripped the buckled strap firmly in my hand Bingis' eyes swelled to the size of walnuts. He looked like a frightened fawn when he realized what I intended to use the helmet for.

At this point the insane shopkeeper was on his own. I pulled Bingi to my side and planned to protect him as long as I could. It was clear that this mob was not giving any racial preferences and Bingi was probably going to be the first to go. I knew my efforts would be futile but I thought a flailing motorcycle helmet might buy Bingi and I a few more seconds while the shopkeeper tried to negotiate some sort of favorable outcome.

I knew if I started swinging it was going to be all over, but the mob just kept getting closer and closer and angrier and angrier.

Just as the levy was about to break a light at the top of the building came on. This particular apartment was again different from the rest. It had a big balcony out front that was enclosed in thick metal bars. Behind those bars were two large steel doors with tiny windows near the top at about head height.

You could tell that there were several locks as the person on the other side took their time opening the door. When the doors finally swung open the mob looked up in unison at the man standing on the balcony. I could tell that the man was clearly upset but at least he seemed composed. I don't think it took him long to figure out that his mob had us well in hand and it was clear that they were waiting for his instructions on what to do with us.

I knew the man on the balcony was not to be taken lightly and I studied him carefully as he combed his hair back with his hands. As he began to interrogate the shopkeeper it was clear that he meant business. For once the shopkeeper lowered his voice and spoke in a more civil tone.

The men exchanged quite a bit of dialogue and it was absolutely killing me that I couldn't understand a word of it. My fate was entirely in the hands of my questionably skilled negotiator…..and I had little control over the situation. When I could take it no longer I interrupted by asking the shopkeeper what in the hell was going on.

He explained that the man on the balcony was indeed the man we were looking for. He was a very wealthy man that most likely kept large amounts of cash in his home and he did not like the fact that we had paid him a surprise visit.

He employed many of the less fortunate people in the neighboring apartments. Their job was to watch his house in shifts and summon reinforcements if anyone came to do him harm. This mob was no accident. They were his body guards and at the first sign of trouble they would do what they were paid to do.

I told the shopkeeper to apologize on my behalf and forget about the passports. The shopkeeper looked me square in the eyes and said, "We are not leaving here without those passports."

Before I could reply he started in with the man on the balcony again. When I insisted on being kept up to speed on the rapidly exchanging dialogue the shopkeeper told me that the man did not have our passports.

That was good enough for me but not for the shopkeeper. He continued to badger the man on the balcony until he said something that I could tell really incensed him. At that point both men started to get angry and tensions soon mounted. My next update from the shopkeeper was that the man refused to go unlock his kiosk so we could look for the passports.

I didn't blame him one bit. Some strange foreigner had just shown up on his doorstep in the middle of the night with a crazed accomplice and demanded to be taken to where he kept the money.

I told the shopkeeper to stop hounding the man before he got us all killed, but he just wouldn't listen. He looked at me and said, "you need our help and you are going to get it." He then turned and began to yell at the man on the balcony some more. Finally the angry man on the balcony threw his hands in the air and slammed the doors. As he went back into his house I surveyed the men surrounding us and noticed that their numbers had increased substantially.

I queried the shopkeeper to find out what had just happened. In a very, I told you so kind of tone, he said, "he is going to help us." I could not believe that was the case. I expected he would lead us to a nice quiet alley and stone us to death. I was shocked and skeptical when I saw the man emerge from his fortress. He spoke a few words to the mob and they seemed to dissipate.

About half of them surrounded the man and the other half surrounded us. I looked at the shopkeeper and said, "Now what?" He looked down at the motorcycle helmet gripped tightly in my hand and said, "Everything will be fine if you just relax." Apparently he had come to the same conclusion as me, if I started bashing people with Bingis hat our night was going to end badly.

The shopkeeper carried himself with a sense of pride as we made our way back toward the kiosk. Periodically the two men would exchange some seemingly harsh words but we were headed in the right direction so I felt a little better.

I noticed that block after block the mob increased in number. It was obvious that this guy had hired people to watch over his entire route between the shop and his home. I imagined that they had probably sat idle for ages just waiting for a night like tonight.

I knew that the shopkeeper claimed that everything was going to be fine but I also knew one wrong glance or threatening gesture and that mob could explode in an uncontrollable frenzy. Each time new people joined the mob, the tension escalated tremendously. Before long we were surrounded by a virtual sea of people.

I was so worried about the mob that I had forgotten all about the curfew as we approached the main city street. We were impossible to miss and within seconds the entire mob was surrounded by armed soldiers. Chaos erupted as the indignant kiosk owner babbled away about the crazed man and the foreigner. He yelled at the military soldiers and aggressively gestured toward me. The shopkeeper soon started to interrupt and the military men began wading through the crowd, heading in my direction.

I just didn't know how things could possibly get worse…………. and then I saw Heather standing on the sidewalk in front of the hotel. I just wanted to worry about getting myself out of this mess and now there she was standing on the street surrounded by security guards.

I was starting to get a little panicked. I just wanted to explain the whole ordeal to the military but now I was worried about Heather. Did someone take her out of the room? Had they forced her out into the streets? Did they know that she was associated with the curfew breaking man at the heart of all the chaos? Was she being arrested?

Just as I started to ask the shopkeeper to translate for me I saw Heather waving in my direction and guess what was in her hand. That's right, the passports. As I stood there absolutely dumbfounded, the sea of people began to part. One of the guards started to make his way toward me. He was a military man that worked part time as a guard at our hotel. I recognized him because we had previously shared some friendly conversation outside the hotel.

He said, "Your girlfriend found the passports." She came down and told us that you had gone looking for them and we sent a patrol out to find you.

I thought, perfect……. exactly what I asked her not to do.

Give me two hours…….don't tell anyone that I went out against the curfew and don't under any circumstances leave the room.

I looked down at my watch and confirmed she was a perfect three for three.

The ruckus with the mob and the military took quite some time to settle down. When the smoke cleared I was very worried that everyone was going to be punished for helping me. I talked to the guard that I knew and explained what a risk these people had taken to help a man they didn't know. I explained how grateful I was for their efforts and basically begged for forgiveness. After some serious scolding the military agreed to let them off the hook. I think the guy with the kiosk or possibly even the shopkeeper had some serious juice in that town and that probably helped as well.

When order was restored I went to thank the shopkeeper who was over talking to Heather. I asked him to translate for me while I thanked the owner of the kiosk. He was happy to do so. When I had the two men together I thanked them sincerely and reached into my pocket for the much deserved tip. I held out a hundred dollars American for the shopkeeper and he refused to take it. I held out another hundred for the kiosk owner and he stuck his hand out to accept the reward but the shopkeeper promptly slapped it away.

I did not know who this shopkeeper was but he had balls that's for sure. He scolded the kiosk owner until he lowered his hand and somewhat begrudgingly extended it for a shake. I shook his hand and thanked them both again for their extraordinary efforts. The shopkeeper looked me in the face and said, "When you are asked about the people of Nepal you tell them that we are kind and fair."

That was a request I intended to honor………………

I could not believe how badly I misjudged this man. He didn't help me because he wanted something from me; he helped me because he believed it was the right thing to do. He put himself at considerable risk for someone he didn't even know and he expected nothing in return. I was embarrassed that I had the audacity to try and pay him off, but I could tell he didn't hold it against me.

As I wished him well he asked if he could speak with me in private for a minute. Of course I accepted the invitation.

He pulled me to the side and said, "Will you do something for me?"

I replied, "Sure, what is it?"

……………………………. "Please don't beat her too badly," he said in a soft voice.

He was serious and I couldn't figure out what he was talking about. I assured him that it wasn't in my nature to beat the woman I loved but I could tell that he didn't believe me.

He leaned in and said, "She told me that you were going to kill her." I laughed and explained that it was just an expression in English. I told him it wasn't meant to be literal.

He said, "I know, but for me, please don't beat her too badly."

I felt about one inch tall as the man left convinced I was a wife beater.

As the shopkeeper left I turned to face Heather who was standing on the curb trying to look cute. I walked up to her and said, "Where were they?"

She said, "They were on the bed, I accidentally flipped the blanket over them when I was putting my backpack under it."

I was just happy to see that everything worked out, I put my arm around her and we walked up the stairs to the hotel together.

On the way up she said, "No speech?"

I answered, "I am too exhausted for a speech but I'll give you one in the morning if you like."

She declined the offer and we never spoke of it again.

CHAPTER 34.......BAFFLING ARROGANCE

Sometimes my own arrogance baffles even the amazing me.

I would help a man I never met.

I would help a traveler from another country avoid harm.

I would give of myself and expect nothing in return.

…………So why then, is it so hard for me to accept that others would do the same?

At times I am ashamed of my skepticism and distrust in others. I am embarrassed that I am always questioning the motives of those that seem all too willing to help.

I am mortified that I could believe I am the only one who puts the greater good above my own self interest and I am shocked that I can still be so ignorant after learning so much.

I know I have lived a unique life but I also know I do not have a monopoly on character. Sometimes I just wish I wouldn't forget so easily.

Sometimes my own arrogance baffles even the amazing me.

THE CAROUSEL
OF LIFE SPINS IN
MY   NAME ONCE AGAIN
THE   ARCADE OF TIME
GIVES   NO PRIZES THERE
FOR YOU MUST LIVE FOR THE
THRILL OF THE GAME. IN
THE END   THERE IS NO
VICTORY O   NLY A GAME
PLAYED WELL. THE CIRCUS OF
THE UNKNOWN HOLDS A NEW
CLUE TO   MY UNSOLVEABLE
RIDDLE D   NO ONE BEFORE
E AN   VERY FEW SINCE
HAV E RIDDEN IN THIS PA
TIC   LAR PAR

Once again I have included som[e]
door photos. These two are from Ant[i]
gua Guatemala. The city with the mos[t]
magical doors in our world. Doors mea[n]
so much to me because they symboli[c]

choices   and
new   places
and new   experie[nce]
They   portra[y]
the   many
corridors   of th[e]
human   mind
Many   peopl[e]
believe   that
Safety   exists
in their   World
If they   do not
open   unknow[n]
Doors   than
Surely   No hor[ror]
Can   be
be-   Sto[ry]

upon them. For me just the opposite
is true. Every day that passes with[out]
out a new door opening is one more
day closer to death and extinction

of my spirit. I travel the globe
to assure a ready supply of new doors.
If I move swiftly into new territory

each day

I can keep
soul
tact

e-
my
suirs.
Some
I may
be
to
some
for
as
as
my
but
day
wi
for

my
in
and
vade
pur
with
effort
still
able
open
doors
others
well
for
self
his
I

ight my self, In order to become
even stronger so that I may some
day fight again for the others. Let
my hand be guided by my actions alone
and I will emerge a different man.

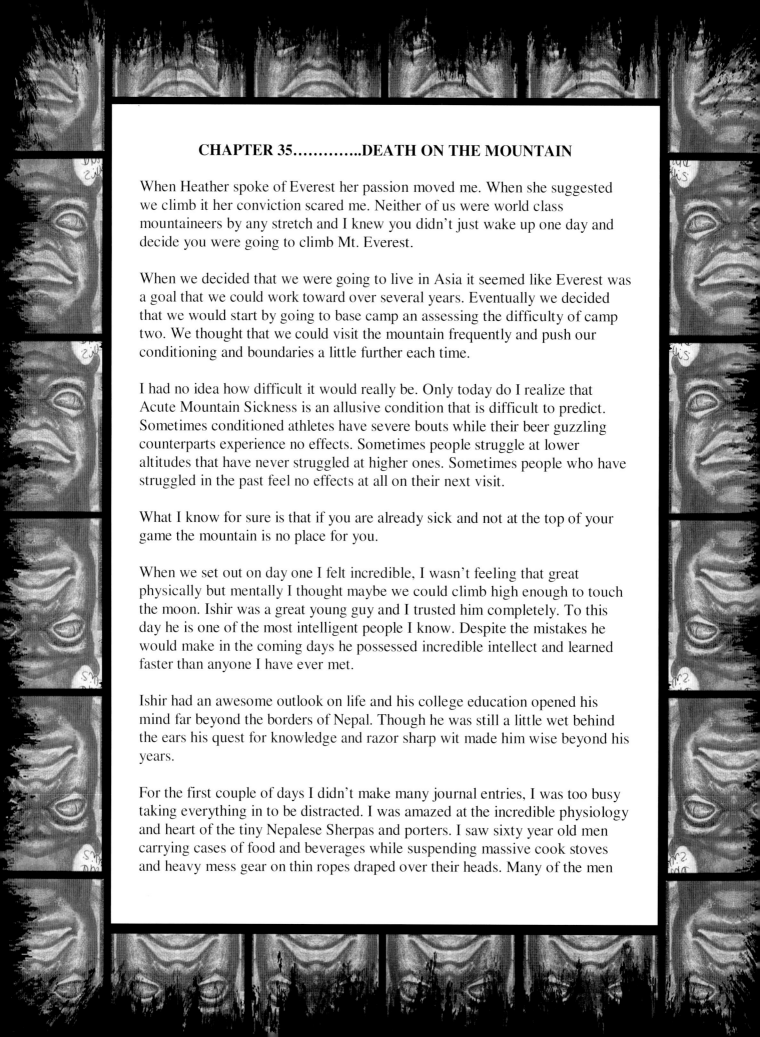

CHAPTER 35…………..DEATH ON THE MOUNTAIN

When Heather spoke of Everest her passion moved me. When she suggested we climb it her conviction scared me. Neither of us were world class mountaineers by any stretch and I knew you didn't just wake up one day and decide you were going to climb Mt. Everest.

When we decided that we were going to live in Asia it seemed like Everest was a goal that we could work toward over several years. Eventually we decided that we would start by going to base camp an assessing the difficulty of camp two. We thought that we could visit the mountain frequently and push our conditioning and boundaries a little further each time.

I had no idea how difficult it would really be. Only today do I realize that Acute Mountain Sickness is an allusive condition that is difficult to predict. Sometimes conditioned athletes have severe bouts while their beer guzzling counterparts experience no effects. Sometimes people struggle at lower altitudes that have never struggled at higher ones. Sometimes people who have struggled in the past feel no effects at all on their next visit.

What I know for sure is that if you are already sick and not at the top of your game the mountain is no place for you.

When we set out on day one I felt incredible, I wasn't feeling that great physically but mentally I thought maybe we could climb high enough to touch the moon. Ishir was a great young guy and I trusted him completely. To this day he is one of the most intelligent people I know. Despite the mistakes he would make in the coming days he possessed incredible intellect and learned faster than anyone I have ever met.

Ishir had an awesome outlook on life and his college education opened his mind far beyond the borders of Nepal. Though he was still a little wet behind the ears his quest for knowledge and razor sharp wit made him wise beyond his years.

For the first couple of days I didn't make many journal entries, I was too busy taking everything in to be distracted. I was amazed at the incredible physiology and heart of the tiny Nepalese Sherpas and porters. I saw sixty year old men carrying cases of food and beverages while suspending massive cook stoves and heavy mess gear on thin ropes draped over their heads. Many of the men had no shoes and their backs were hunched from years of abuse. Some of them were surely twice my age yet they blew past me like I was standing still. The children in the mountain villages warmed my heart and the wrinkles on the faces of the elderly told a thousand stories. By day two I was already really struggling, but the incredible views and amazing primitive culture kept me going. At this point I already knew that I was going to have trouble but as with everything else in my life I assumed focus, relentlessness and determination would carry me through.

I could literally write chapters about the first two days, but I will pick up on day three where my journal entries start to provide a glimpse of how serious things would eventually become.

DAY 3

After reaching Shangboche my spirits were pretty high but my body was beginning to show signs of trouble. I remember things being a little slow going on the way up and I know I struggled with the altitude a bit more than the others. However all things considered I didn't feel too bad considering how sick I had been.

I went to bed around 8:30pm with the usual plugged head, sore throat and aching muscles. I remember thinking that though our small stone encampment had no means of heat I was grateful that it had glass in the windows as this was a first.

By 10:00pm I was vomiting quite a bit and had developed a splitting headache. I could not get to sleep despite my best efforts.

The night air was absolutely chilling and the temperature was around zero degrees Celsius. My hacking cough and crud filled lungs made it hard enough to sleep but the freezing cold seemed to make it impossible. I just could not seem to get warm and by midnight I was wearing 5 shirts, a fleece jacket, 2 thermal arctic down coats, 3 pairs of pants, 2 fleece lined hats, multiple socks and a thermal down sleeping bag.

Just past midnight, I had developed such a fever that my whole body began to convulse with violent tremors. I could not get warm under any circumstances. Heather stayed awake with me nearly all night and we contemplated waking our guide around 3:00am. By 4:00am the convulsions and shaking were so violent that I felt I was at risk of serious harm from the fever alone. Despite the fact that my fingers and toes felt like they were about to fall off from the cold,

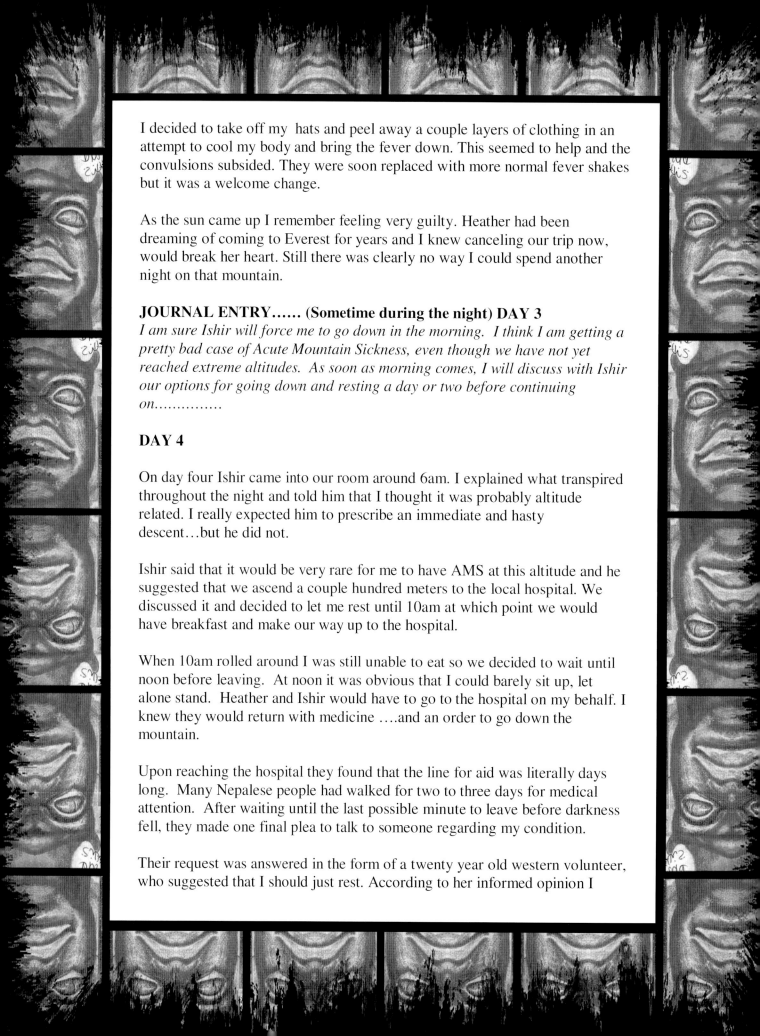

I decided to take off my hats and peel away a couple layers of clothing in an attempt to cool my body and bring the fever down. This seemed to help and the convulsions subsided. They were soon replaced with more normal fever shakes but it was a welcome change.

As the sun came up I remember feeling very guilty. Heather had been dreaming of coming to Everest for years and I knew canceling our trip now, would break her heart. Still there was clearly no way I could spend another night on that mountain.

JOURNAL ENTRY…… (Sometime during the night) DAY 3
I am sure Ishir will force me to go down in the morning. I think I am getting a pretty bad case of Acute Mountain Sickness, even though we have not yet reached extreme altitudes. As soon as morning comes, I will discuss with Ishir our options for going down and resting a day or two before continuing on……………

DAY 4

On day four Ishir came into our room around 6am. I explained what transpired throughout the night and told him that I thought it was probably altitude related. I really expected him to prescribe an immediate and hasty descent…but he did not.

Ishir said that it would be very rare for me to have AMS at this altitude and he suggested that we ascend a couple hundred meters to the local hospital. We discussed it and decided to let me rest until 10am at which point we would have breakfast and make our way up to the hospital.

When 10am rolled around I was still unable to eat so we decided to wait until noon before leaving. At noon it was obvious that I could barely sit up, let alone stand. Heather and Ishir would have to go to the hospital on my behalf. I knew they would return with medicine ….and an order to go down the mountain.

Upon reaching the hospital they found that the line for aid was literally days long. Many Nepalese people had walked for two to three days for medical attention. After waiting until the last possible minute to leave before darkness fell, they made one final plea to talk to someone regarding my condition.

Their request was answered in the form of a twenty year old western volunteer, who suggested that I should just rest. According to her informed opinion I would probably be better in the morning. They begged her for some antibiotics and something to help with my fever but their request fell on deaf ears. The volunteer told them that if I was too sick to come myself, they should hire porters to carry me up the mountain where I could wait in line until a doctor was available to treat me in person.

When they returned with the news I wanted so badly to go down…but it was Heathers' dream and I could not be the one to make that decision and still live with myself. Everyone except me was quite confident that I would be fine in the morning. I was quite confident that when the next morning came and they saw how sick I was, we would definitely be going down.

JOURNAL ENTRY…… DAY 4
Today I could only keep down a partial bowl of oatmeal and less that a cup of water…there is still talk of going up higher in the morning…I will surely need more food if I am to go on……………

DAY 5

On day five an Australian doctor traveling through Namche heard of my condition and came to see me. She gave me some medicine that brought my fever down considerably. I was still in some trouble but at least I wouldn't be getting brain damage from overheating my noodle and that made me feel a little better.

Later that day we heard that one of the Japanese climbers in our camp (a man whom I will call Hiroshi) contracted AMS at the very same altitude. This seemed to make Ishir very nervous. Upon hearing the news he left to radio Kathmandu regarding my condition. When he returned he was very somber. He told me that a helicopter had been placed on standby for my evacuation. By the look on his face I knew things must be pretty serious.

Ishir gave me some Diamox to combat the AMS and we discussed our plan for the following day….yet for some reason…..still no concrete decision to go down.

JOURNAL ENTRY…… DAY 5
Today I could only keep down about a cup of water and a half bowl of chicken soup…I am very worried about dehydration, but all the food keeps coming back up…I am very weak and shaky…but still there is talk of going on, where the air is thinner and the temperatures much colder………

DAY 6

JOURNAL ENTRY…… (Sometime during the morning) DAY 6
*I was up most of the night with dry heaves and fluid filled lungs... I HAVE
HAD IT….. WE ARE GOING DOWN…..I AM PULLING THE PLUG…………*

On the morning of day six when Ishir came to our room he seemed very
concerned about the fact that my ability to eat and drink had diminished to
zero. The Diamox he gave me seemed to help with my crushing headache but I
was getting weaker and weaker by the minute.

Around eight o'clock Ishir left to call for an evacuation. By this time I had
started to get a bit delirious but I still knew an evacuation was the right thing to
do. The helicopter would not take long to arrive and I would finally be getting
off the mountain and getting the medical attention I needed.

About two hours later Ishir returned with some….interesting news.
Apparently when he called to put the chopper on standby earlier, he told the
evacuation team that my primary symptoms were high fever and extreme bed
shakes. This was not a problem for the evacuation, but it was a problem for the
insurance company. The carrier for our climbers insurance used an "internal
disease clause" to dispute the cost of the emergency AMS evacuation. They
claimed that this type of sickness was not covered.

Ishir explained that due to a recent dispute between the air carrier and the
insurance company, the rescue team would make the evacuation but we would
have to pay the estimated cost up front. We did not have $4,800 in cash on
hand and I could barely blow snot bubbles let alone negotiate in Nepalese.

We discussed it and decided to make a bid for the lower elevations of Pakding
on foot rather than spend crucial time arguing between the insurance company
and evacuation team.

As we set out for Pakding I knew I needed to eat and drink as much as
possible. Eating and drinking, as well as descent, are the primary keys for
combating AMS. However I was completely unable to do either….three potato
chips and a couple of teaspoons of water came swirling back up.

Three days had passed and all I could get down was one bowl of soup, a little
oatmeal and a couple cups of water…most of which did not stay down. Of all
the stories I had heard, it was when people quit eating and drinking on the

mountain that they got into serious trouble. Despite all this I was determined to make it to Pakding which was only two hours away.

At this point my body and my mind were beyond fatigued. I was starting to get a little loopy and I can only recall a few strange events about the decent.

Here is what I remember ……...

Most of the trip is a bit foggy like getting really drunk and having your friends tell you what you did the night before. I do remember being pretty much completely oblivious to everyone else on the trail. One hundred percent of my focus and energy was on moving forward, which apparently I was doing quite slowly.

I remember the trip taking a lot longer than I expected. In the end I think the 2 hour trek ended up taking nearly 8 hours. I am not sure what happened to the other 6 six hours but I do know that Heather and Ishir kept nagging me to stop and rest. According to them I refused, claiming that if I rested for even a single minute I would not be able to restart my engines and continue.

At one point I also remember seeing fish flapping in the trail with no water to support their breathing. I looked around for a stream or river to throw them into, but when I could not find water I realized that the fish were just a strange delusion. Just my mind playing tricks on me…This happened several times but by the third time or so, I was hip to it and just kept going.

Another weird thing I can remember is seeing all the skulls. Something we had witnessed a couple of months earlier in Cambodia was now happening all over again in Nepal. When I looked at the rocks I saw hundreds of skulls from the killing fields. I remember thinking that it was quite peculiar that so many skulls had been left on the mountain. Eventually I realized this too was just a delusion.

The last strange thing I remember is crossing the long suspension bridge over the Dudkosi River at Josale. I remember walking forever and ever, but it was like I was going UP on an escalator headed DOWN. I just couldn't make any headway. It was like walking into a really strong wind.

With no progress in sight I began to hear bells ringing behind me and someone yelling in Nepalese. I didn't really have the strength to turn around but when I opened my eyes I realized that I had just been standing there motionless for quite some time. The others, who had long since crossed the bridge, thought I was just resting. What they didn't realize is that I had fallen completely asleep. It took a whole string of yaks and a determined Nepalese woman to wake me up and get me moving again.

There are also several things about the trip to Pakding that I don't remember.

Here is what the others told me…………..

Heather said that by this time they were all very concerned for my survival. I was delirious, babbling in my responses to them, and staggering badly like a drunk. She said they had to form a skirmish line between me and the edge of the cliffs so I didn't walk right off the edge. They said that they were going to call for a porter assisted evacuation but that I refused stubbornly and insisted I was fine…yet another bad decision on all of our behalves.

They said that I collapsed on some rocks and just laid there motionless for awhile. I do remember lying on some rocks, but no collapse…I guess this occurred several times.

Eventually I regained my senses and started to have some logical thoughts.

Here is what I remember………………..

After stumbling along for several hours and dropping in elevation, all of a sudden a strange thing happened. Suddenly I could think a bit more clearly and I was filled with energy compared to earlier. Almost instantly, and all at once I felt more awake, I can't really explain the feeling…I was just a different person than the man who left Namche in the morning. The effects of AMS were losing their grip on me and as they did I started to realize how serious my condition had been and probably still was.

At dusk we reached Pakding where we ran into some friends from France, Jerry and Andra. Jerry is an experienced mountaineer who has made 16 different climbing trips to Nepal. This includes leading 3 teams in assaults on the Everest Summit.

As we pieced together my symptoms it was obvious that I shouldn't have started out sick in the first place. It seems that what had everyone so confused about my sickness was that in addition to AMS I had also contracted a severe viral infection while on the mountain. The combined symptoms masked the tell tale signs of AMS and Ishirs' lack of experience recognizing the symptoms only made it worse.

As it turned out Jerry had the viral portion of my sickness, which caused him to call their efforts off as well. Apparently the severe viral infection swept the mountain and forced the hasty retreat of many climbers and hikers.

It somehow made me feel better to hear that an experienced mountaineer like Jerry was so weak that he had to hire a horse guide to get him down. …..It made me feel like less of a failure.

What didn't make me feel better however was what Jerry told me next.

He and Andra were called in to check on a man who reportedly had AMS and had collapsed outside of Namche. He was making his way down the mountain when he just fell down. By the time they had arrived the man had been placed in a Gamow bag to simulate lower altitudes, but he had stopped breathing all together inside the bag. By the time the chopper arrived he had been dead for twenty minutes. That man was Hiroshi, the man who got AMS the same day, in the same place, under the same conditions that I did. The man who made essentially the same bad decisions but suffered much greater consequences.

In a few days I would be meeting my family on the island and Hiroshi would be going home to his in a box. The only person more shaken by the news than me was Ishir, who now could not apologize enough for not spotting the signs earlier.

The fact that I had a pre-existing sickness and serious viral infection to go along with the AMS seemed to stump everyone. I had no hard feelings towards Ishir or anyone else. Ultimately, I should have pulled the plug sooner myself.

In fact I was definitely part of the problem. I explained my symptoms accurately but I did so with a pretty serious game face. I tried to play down the seriousness of it all….which I realize now was pretty stupid.

I gave Ishir a pep talk and then begged him to get me the rest of the way down that God forsaken mountain. All I could think about was getting to Kathmandu to a warm bed and some real medical care. I knew if I could make it through one more freezing night in the Himalayas I could reach Katmandu by the following night.

DAY 7

JOURNAL ENTRY...... DAY 7
We left Pakding at dawn today to reach Lukla in time for the last flight to Kathmandu. I didn't sleep much last night as my lungs still have a lot of fluid in them and my hacking cough pretty much kept everyone up. I think the locals here will be glad to see me go.....................

When I woke up on day seven all I could think about was getting to someplace warm. I could hardly wait; even as bad as I felt my primary interest was for a hot shower and warm bed.

Unfortunately the mountain was not finished punishing me yet. The trek to Lukla was fairly short but again it seemed endless. When we finally reached the airport we saw the last scheduled flight of the day departing just as we hit the air pad.

Ishir knew he needed to get me back to Katmandu so he went to speak with the man who managed the airport. He explained my condition and begged the man to arrange another flight. The man agreed to arrange a flight for us and even agreed to let us transfer the money that we had spent on our return tickets to pay for it. We were now scheduled to leave at one o'clock and I could not believe Ishir pulled it off. I thanked him repeatedly and then collapsed in a corner while we waited for the plane.

At 12:30, one half hour before our plane was to depart, the mountain had its last word. A storm front moved into Lukla and the airport was closed until morning. I was not going anywhere.

DAY 8

JOURNAL ENTRY...... DAY 8
We awoke this morning at 6 am and rushed to the airport for a flight out. But it was not to be.............

On the morning of day eight a storm had now moved into Kathmandu. There would be no flights going that direction until the storm clouds lifted. Once again my hopes of warmth and medical care were dashed.

Around noon Ishir finally had some good news. The fog in Katmandu had lifted and we could put the Himalayas in our rearview mirror. I had never been so happy to get on an airplane in my life. As we flew over the worlds' most amazing mountain range, for once I was happy to say goodbye.

DAY 9

JOURNAL ENTRY...... DAY 9
With the right drugs, a warm room and some fluids, I am feeling a bit better. Now the only life threatening ailment I have is an acutely damaged ego.

I have learned to have a great respect for the Himalayas, but I still will not accept defeat. Even as I write these words, we are planning our return trip to accomplish what we set out to do.

Next time I will be in better shape and better health... and I will be ready. Unfortunately I know the mountain will too.

Ahhh.....there is that glorious arrogance again. Now the only question that remains is have I learned anything in the years that have passed since penning those boastful words, and have I gone back to battle the mountain once again?

CHAPTER 36............UNREALITY

Sometimes life's lessons force us to acknowledge things we hoped weren't true. How we deal with this shifting of our reality is what defines our very nature.

Reality isn't always real. Sometimes if you believe in something enough the unreal becomes real. A good analogy is the music industry. Some zealous adolescent with an air guitar and a bad haircut thinks he is a rock star. He only knows one reality and before you know it he is selling out arenas.

Unfortunately that same idea also works in reverse. This is best witnessed in professional fighters. I can't count the number of times I have seen an incredible unbeaten fighter transform before my eyes. One round (or one punch) can change their perception of reality and you can actually see it in their face when it happens.

Fighters who believe they are unbeatable often are, but when they get their first glimpse of vulnerability their reality is shattered and many of them never recover.

Everest taught me that I too have boundaries. I can't always just try harder, focus more and work longer to conquer every obstacle. Sometimes the world will beat me.

However, thankfully I am still under the illusion that life has an infinite number of rounds. I believe that no matter how badly I have been beaten I can still come back to win the fights worth winning.

The mountain might have forced me to acknowledge something that I had hoped wasn't true but it also forced me to rewrite my reality. My new version is more robust, more adaptable and more likely to bring me success regardless of a single defeat or victory.

Ultimately Everest left me with only one question...............is this a fight that is important to win?

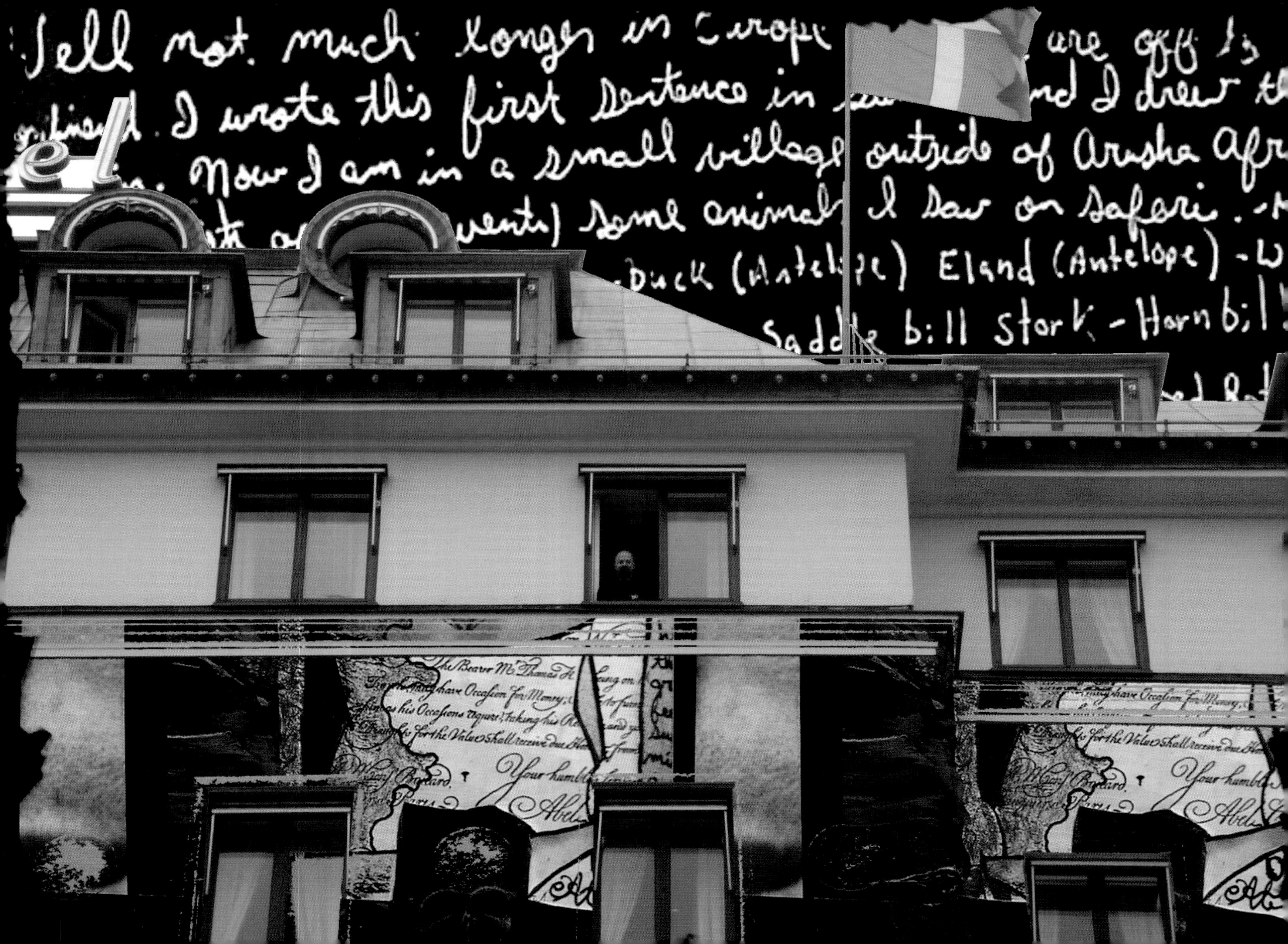
Well not much longer in Europe
are off to
I wrote this first sentence in
and I drew th
Now I am in a small village outside of Arusha Afr
some animals I saw on Safari.
Duck (Antelope) Eland (Antelope)
Saddle bill Stork - Horn bill
The Bearer Mr Thomas
may have Occasion for Money
his Occasions require, taking his
for the Value shall receive due
Your humble
el

BEWARE OF !
ALTITUDE KILLS
GO SLOWLY
AVOID ALTITUDE SICKNESS
_KUNDE HOSPITAL

Have you traveled these corridors before, the boundries of what you consider so naive isolation from danger will deliver child for danger is everywhere. And waiting your fate. Seek it out stare it down, and let it too yourself with battle, a Baptism with fire is the only way first haircut. The fear of fear is the worst kind. strengthening ourselves with lifes trials is what allow ten mile hike with three men. The firs an ex-fire fighter who had been draf salesman and former stock broker. H the world until and dran spent

XMNOVWACCDEPGH

You walk gingerly with in
he safety. You assume that self
from harm. Not so my foolish
to arrive   will only seal
at it is   like to feel fear. Harden
are for   the inevitable. Do children not fear their
to   live you must die a little first.
          continue. I recently went on a
          marine seargeant. The second
the   Dallas Cowboys. The third was a
been   raised Mormon and Isolated from
thirties   when on his wedding night he had sex
alcohol for   the very first time ever. Subsequently he
going   twenty five years addicted to
alcohol   and getting married and divorced
s. On this   hike I wanted to set the pace a
beach. after   a short time I realized that though
nine and   fire fighter were firmly in tow
was no   where to be found. I told the others to
and I drop   back to see what the hold up was. When
the salesman he was slowly but
aking progress. I assumed he had
and couldn't keep the pace.
careful questioning I learned that
all problem was fear. But Con what
actually terified that he might fall
rocky beach. Though I found this
I soon learned he had
a serious injury
strangeness

Call Craig
Refinement
Career
for notes
travel
Craig
A Place
A Place
Mon Tuesd

CHAPTER 37.........THE LONG LONELY ROAD HOME

After leaving Asia we spent a couple of incredible months in Australia and New Zealand. As we headed toward North America we were forced to deal with the fact that our travels would soon be coming to an end. The South island of New Zealand provided us with a great opportunity to just relax and figure out our next move.

At this point I had business contacts all over the world. If we wanted to keep working we could do it virtually anywhere. Conversely, if we wanted to stop working we could do that just about anywhere as well.

We loved the little island in the South China Sea but the entire world was now at our disposal and we really enjoyed traveling. We were thrilled to have infinite choices and it seemed like we would be happy with any of them.

At this point I thought our relationship was the utopia of relationships, we shared in all major decisions, encouraged each other to pursue independent passions and shared most of the same beliefs and values. I could not recall a handful of bad days in the ten years we spent together and it was rare for us to argue about anything.

The trip taught me that little things like looking for the car keys were pretty insignificant in the grander scheme of things and it taught Heather that I would be there for her no matter what. We both grew as people but more importantly we grew together. We learned a great deal from each other during that trip and most of all we learned that our love and friendship was all that really mattered.

We loved each other dearly (or so I thought) and I knew our relationship was one in a million. We had suffered many hardships throughout our lives together and I thought our bond was unbreakable.

When we returned to the States an unforeseen series of events would prove that to be untrue. It would not be long before our traveling days together would be over. Worse yet, we would never speak to each other again. To this day it breaks my heart to say those words.

Eventually my travels and my life would go on without Heather. In those years I would fill the journal pages that will some day reveal the next chapter of my life.

I learned almost as much from losing Heather as I did from knowing her and as I visited the rest of the world I carried those lessons with me. My evolution as a man and a human being was far from over when we parted ways and though I had a hole in my heart I forged ahead.

I have continued to explore my world both literally and figuratively and I will continue to do so as long as there are still things on this planet for me to learn. I have realized that I don't need to travel to exotic places to have incredible experiences but I still can't resist the temptations of far away lands.

Today, I am a student of the world and my home is wherever I happen to be. In the years that have passed since this chapter of my life ended I have learned a lot more about myself. My views today may not be exactly the same as they were then, but I tried to share a snapshot in time of a man working his way through life's challenges.

I am sure twenty years from now I will look at these words and be embarrassed by their naiveté................but I guess that's what growth is all about.

Thank you, for sharing a slice of my life, I hope you enjoyed the ride.

among ... is ... in
from every corner of the building

waiting for an ...
to turn them
into a new
version of
former selves
want so
to ...

Journal Entry Mothers DAY nineteen hundred and ninety nine: I recently recounted a story to a close friend and business partener. We were discussing defining moments in our lives. I spoke of being raised by the perfect combination of parents. My mother the compassionate and caring one, and my father the strong non-emotional type. I recalled coming home from kindergarten on my second or third day of school. At dinner I was obviously displeased with my new experience. My mother inquired as to my troubles. I told her each day a boy in line while waiting to get into school would punch me. She immediately told me to tell a teacher. With out hesitation my father said stand up and come here. He taught me to fight that day and I became the forbidden stop on every bullies train. I had decided that Dad was the strong one. About one or two months later was waiting outside the house for my mother and I was assaulted by a huge rabid Dog. My mother left from the house befor the dog could attack me and bludgened it with our discarded   christmas tree.
om   could
k   some
s   of
                                       own.
                                       I could
                                       not
                                       loose.

We were driving South around the
of NewZealands South island when u
a Sign that said cave 34 kilometer.
were game for some adventure so w
the main road and followed the sic
in pursuit of some remote cave e
ation.

In no time we arrived in a tiny vi
with one small tavern and a g
store. We entered the general st
asked for directions to the cave.
learn cavewas the name of the

which we are still following some ten
days later. We have just arrived _____ in Franz
Joseph and intend to _____ climb
the glacier in the _____ morn
_____ ing. It is the only _____ glacier
this close to the Ocean _____ in the
world. The landscape _____ here is
quite unlike anything _____ I
have ever seen. Snow capped _____ mountains
line the coast, and this island _____ has the
strangest combination of _____ plants
and tree I have ever seen. _____ ET. of
has huge ferns the size
large trees, and a very _____ It's
strange palm like tree. _____ rain
Covered with peculiar _____ ter _____ tains
as well, a combination of moun _____ look
and hills peppered with what _____ mounds
like massive ant or termite _____ remind
which are heavily forrested. They _____ of Tecal
me of the un-excavated ruins _____ but to
in Guatemala. I can't help _____ one would
wonder what _____ unearthed
find if they _____ tree -
these giant _____ amids
covered pyr _____ to re
I am starting _____ with
start my struggle _____ multi
myself and my
mate calling and
responsibility to this world
as our journey draws close
to an end North America awaits just
weeks away and so does reality
which I may not accept

NEW ZEALAND LIFE

46
A
♣

DEVIANT PEOPLE

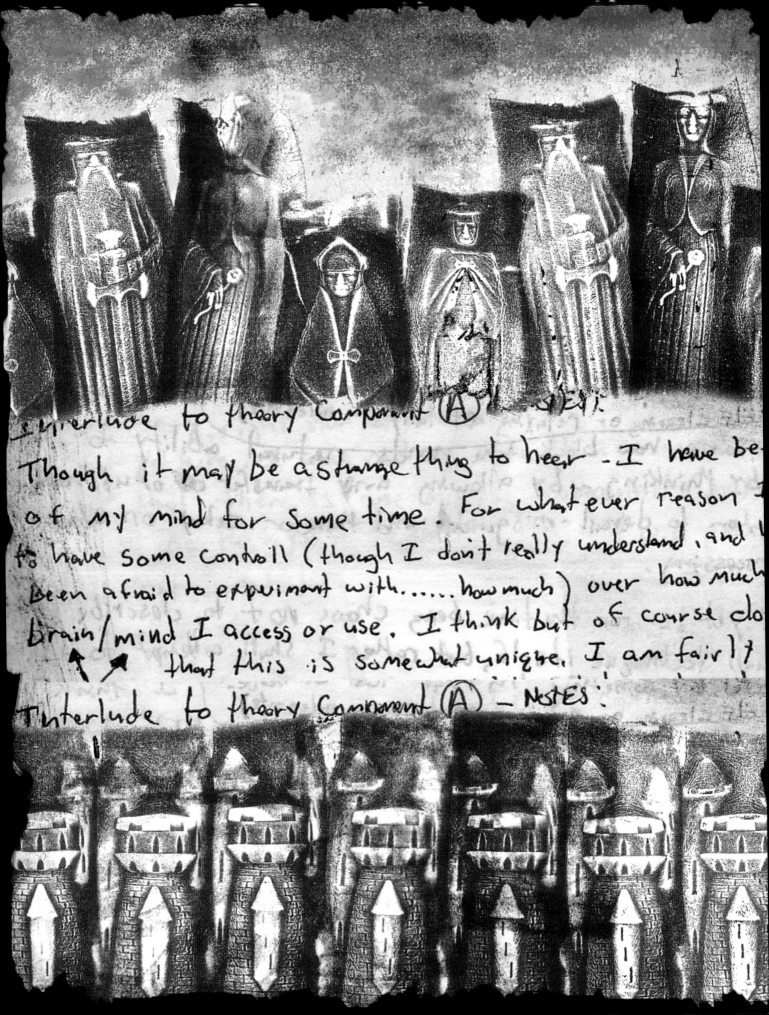

Interlude to theory Component (A) ...(E4):

Though it may be a strange thing to hear - I have be
of my mind for some time. For whatever reason
to have some controll (though I don't really understand, and
been afraid to experiment with......how much) over how much
brain/mind I access or use. I think but of course do
↑ ↗ that this is somewhat unique. I am fairly
Interlude to theory Component (A) - NoteS.

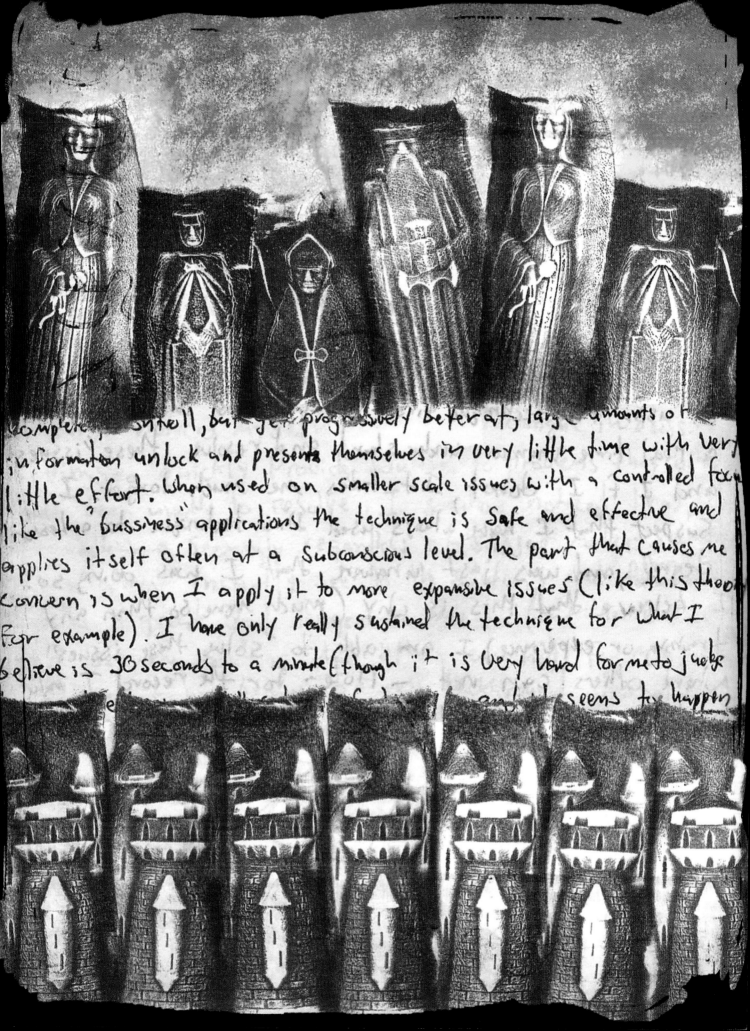

complete, small, but get progressively better at; large amounts of information unlock and presents themselves in very little time with very little effort. When used on smaller scale issues with a controlled focus like the "bussiness" applications the technique is safe and effective and applies itself often at a subconscious level. The part that causes me concern is when I apply it to more expansive issues (like this theory for example). I have only really sustained the technique for what I believe is 30 seconds to a minute (though it is very hard for me to judge ... and it seems to happen

Lady Liberty
holds a key,
For what
she does not
know. Find it
and follow the
virtual rabit hole,
To unlock a tale —
that I have told.

G.D. Garner

CHAPTER 38.........WHAT I WANT

At this point in my life my priorities have changed. I no longer covet great things for myself and I no longer expect to one day save the world.

I simply want to touch a few lives and have those that I have touched, touch a few lives of their own. I want to give the gift of self awareness, compassion for others and the confidence to steer ones' life.

I want to provide opportunity for a handful of people who aren't in a position to provide it for themselves. I want to take the time to equip young people with the tools needed to move mountains but I want them to choose which mountains to move. I want the gifts that I give them to assure they always choose wisely.

I want to spend the time necessary to build character and forge change in a few people brave enough to try and I want to teach them that trying is all it takes.

..........................and I want you to help.

Here is how you can do that……………………..

If you found this book to be anything other than total rubbish, tell a friend to buy a copy. Give one as a gift or buy two for yourself (one for the throne room of course).

If you thought it was an unreadable piece of crap, use it for kindling and buy another to level the legs of your dining room table…….but buy another.

If I must I will forge ahead alone but with your help I can touch more lives in a more significant way.

A portion of the proceeds from this book are going to be used to set up an educational fund for a handful of children that I know have the character to "pay it forward." These children don't lack ambition or intelligence they just lack opportunity.

My efforts to help the world are going to be spent mentoring self perpetuating change in a handful of families that I know will be the first ripple in a very big pond. Twenty years from now I don't want to write about the incredible changes in their lives, I want to write about the incredible changes they inspired in the lives of others.

I don't intend to dedicate my life to fund raising, feeding the world or saving the planet. I just want to take small continual steps in providing an adequate education and true belief in the possibility of change for a handful of people who can in turn start a cascade of self help and awareness.

I am not looking for a handout I am asking for a hand. I will put in the time but I need you to help with the means.

Thank you in advance and may your vision clear to allow you to see "Beyond The Eyes Of Your Madness," whatever it may be.

Sincerely, G.D. Garner

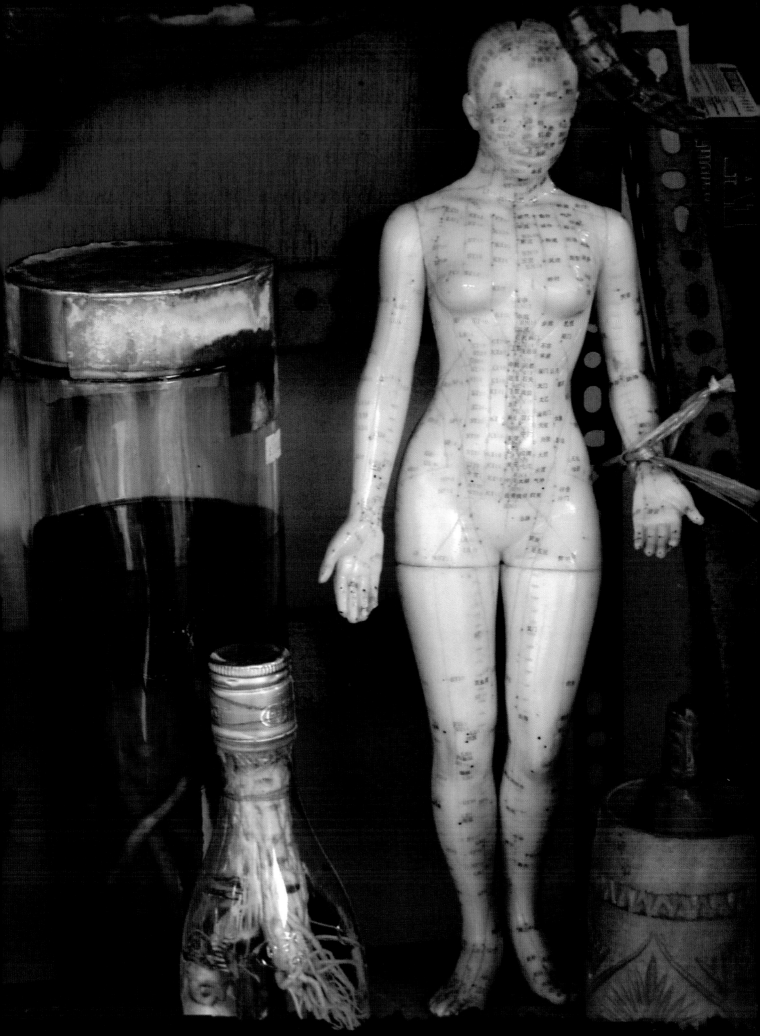

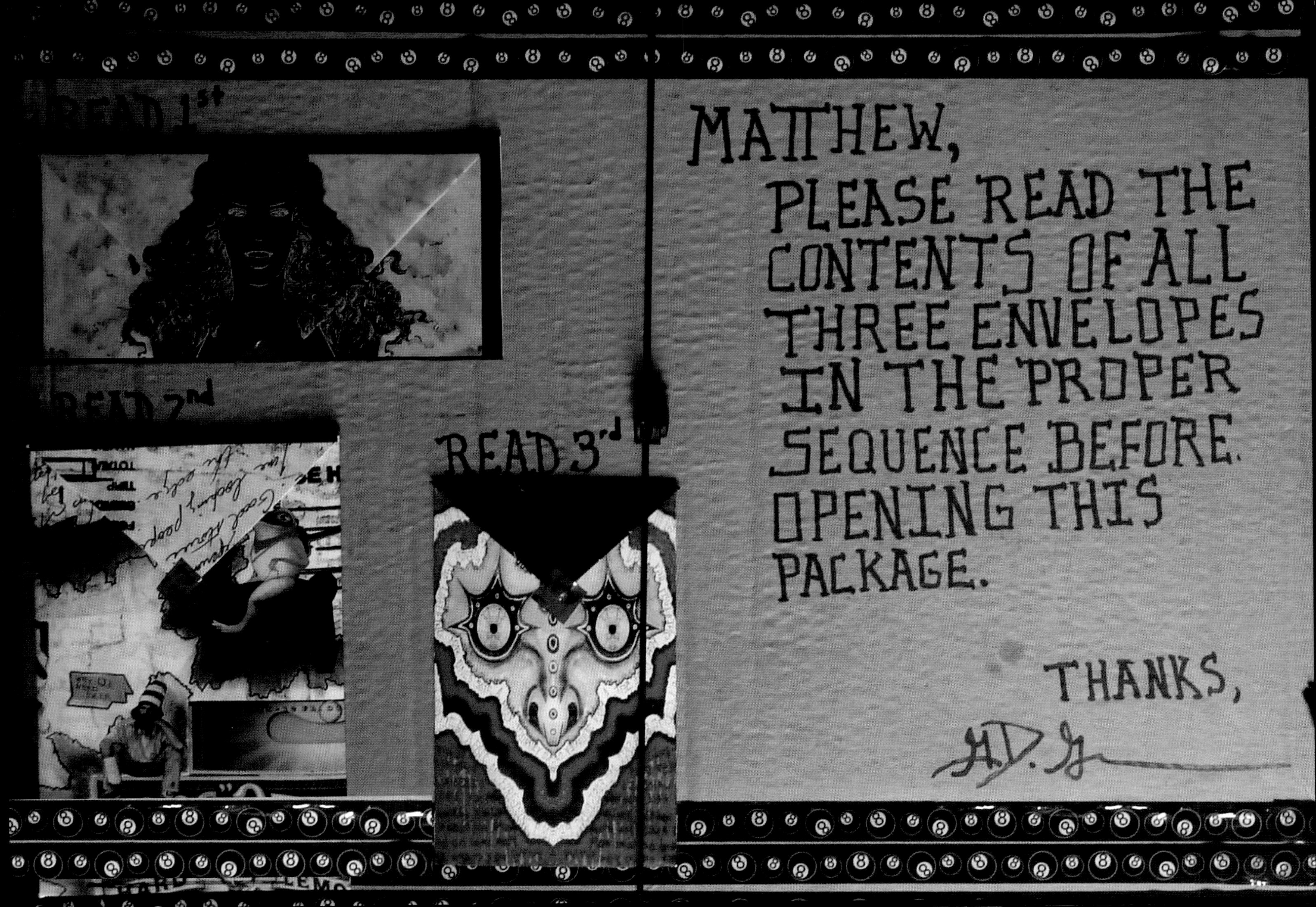

MATHEW,
PLEASE READ THE
CONTENTS OF ALL
THREE ENVELOPES
IN THE PROPER
SEQUENCE BEFORE
OPENING THIS
PACKAGE.

— THANKS,

A.D.G.

READ 1st

READ 2nd

READ 3rd

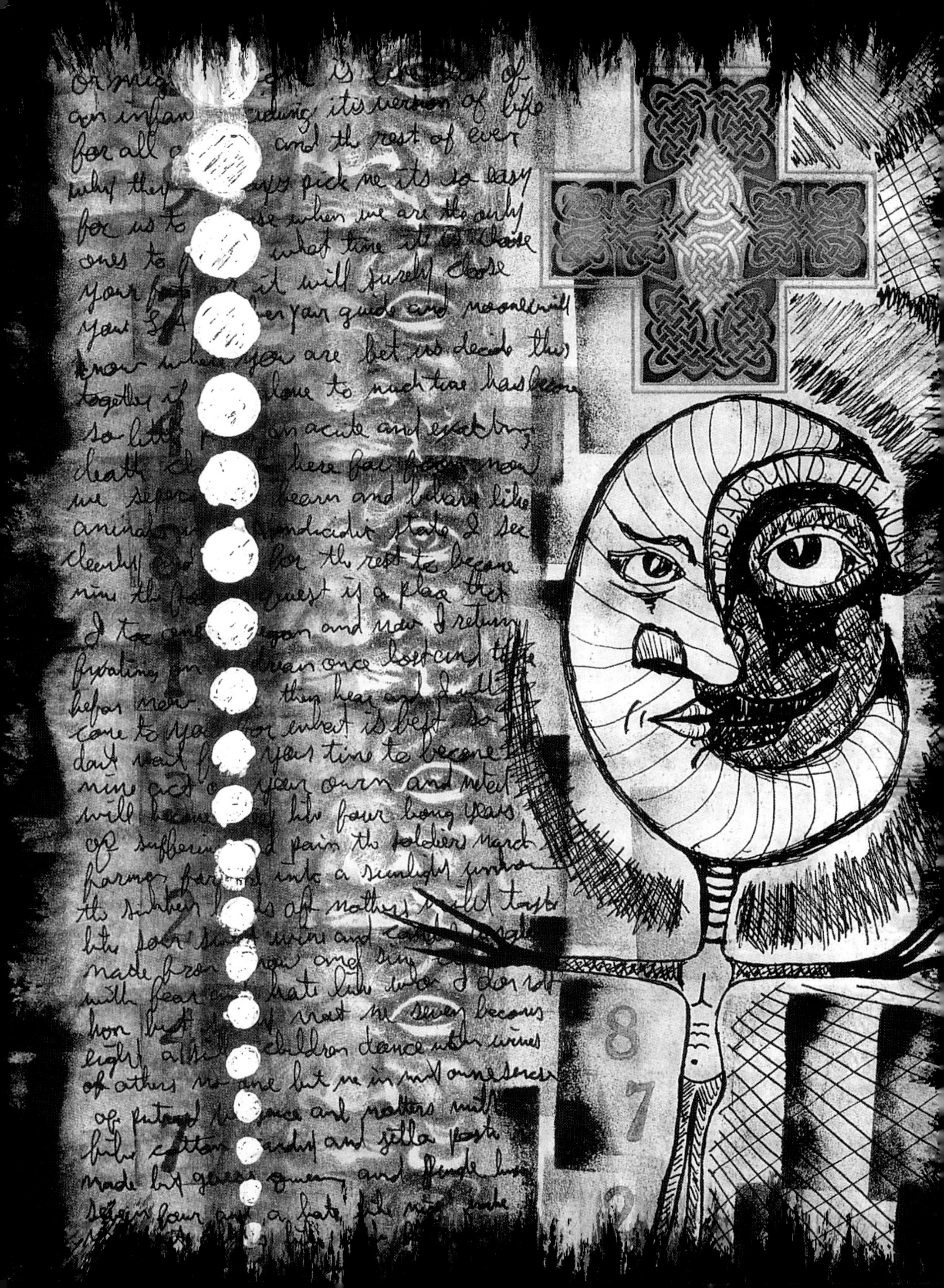

CHECKMATE

Journal Entry April 22... A CONSTRUCTED... IN PRESER... OF

A longer day with less Time I am waiting for the fine line that seperates madness and gen... To disolve and let me choose my path. Each day the line gets thicker pushing me closer to one extreme. But while I remain trapped within the line I gain nothing. No closer to freedom. I would not wish this fate upon the scurge of our time nor would I change existence as it has chosen to present itself to me. There are far too many others clam... for my attention. Less overtly than usual but just as frequent, do they no underst... the process that allows each of us to evolve. Evolution and time wait... picking fruit makes little... no mouths. Yet still... and day out the... like it was their last with no sense of... march forward waiting to explode into a vision... and return to the earth as creatures with a... understanding. This continues to puzzle me as it always... I don't expect to understand their ways only their... they must have reasons for what it is they do. But... intend to abort in this fashion or do they have no... like canned peas on the shelf of a country store forgotten... a waste of something so important. I guess it is... than except their fate. So let us continue on our path... of proclamation and of thoughts of fortitude... heirs to a throne since forgotten and you are... So Bless the acts of those who do not choose, but follow in the... of those who came befor, because if not for them then you would... seem generic. Seen the the same with no way to Yourself from those who are inseperable and that would slowly mind and defeat your will. So take nothing for granted each bite of life as though it would be your... because eventually it will be so of poison and of no longer more insanity no today because is your day.

Sense for those who h... they pick Day pick each purpose of their ancestors greate... has b... reasons surely do they really choice but to expl... one. It seems such easier to be differ... to glory. Our visi... are the only rema... reason we contin... footstep... surely seperat... poison... and s... last stalk...

chose no by every for we the only

Journal Entry date - UN-KN-OWN

A moment of freedom surrounded by
nothing at all for this instant only
I have let go. My objective now is
to write freely and ignore time. I will
not wait to seize the precious fruit
held at bay by thieves and murderers
alike. Each day is to special to live
for the next and the only crime I can
commit is to let even a single moment
drip from the ends of my fingers
like melted ice through
my bones. While others
watch I will do,
and when I do
I will do
with passion
as though
I have
never
done
before.
Because
each
day
is
mine
for the
taking and
to waste just
one moment
be to destroy
a gift so rare
so rare
my focus
on every breath
and every beat
of every waking
hour in every day
that she wakes at
my side. I will see
us through to the other
side and we will cross
through this world and the
next as the heart that beats
in two bodies as both...

more processing capability indicate t
by mentally and physically over

informat
do not
humans
able to
I h
wo tenths of
could b
d) by
ws of
reason
their
glimpse
wo te
uld b
y the
tech

their availa
glimpses I
two tenths o
be easily c
amount of inform
ero" I dono
humans
ilable brain
es I have be

small perc
that
we is
ty
over
ble
through
the
with
nfin
small
ability
ive the
pro
is my
into u
a
dicate
over
this
with
all perc
that
is in
indic
lly
cess
is u
tured in
mall p
I hypoth
use such an integrate
process capability. I be

[illegible]-21-99 LUX

[illegible] the future
waiting on ten
[illegible] in the year two
[illegible] better not be
[illegible] better be living
[illegible] with the planning
[illegible] to embrace the plan.
[illegible] certainly has been
[illegible] journey, each
[illegible] little more
[illegible] and each night
[illegible] thankfull.
[illegible] used to the
being one step ahead but it
make it any easier for those who
[illegible] wait. Days past and they return
[illegible] more in a direction I have long
[illegible]. I'm at the [illegible] coffee shop
[illegible] I met a young lady who took
[illegible] her dream. She owns this place
[illegible] years is selling to pursue her
[illegible] a fashion designer. How many die
[illegible] too long at each pitstop and
[illegible] followed their dream. Probably
[illegible]. What does the dying man
[illegible] anything more than goodbye
[illegible] life to the fullest. He has
[illegible] life and his
[illegible] I hope I
[illegible] the last night

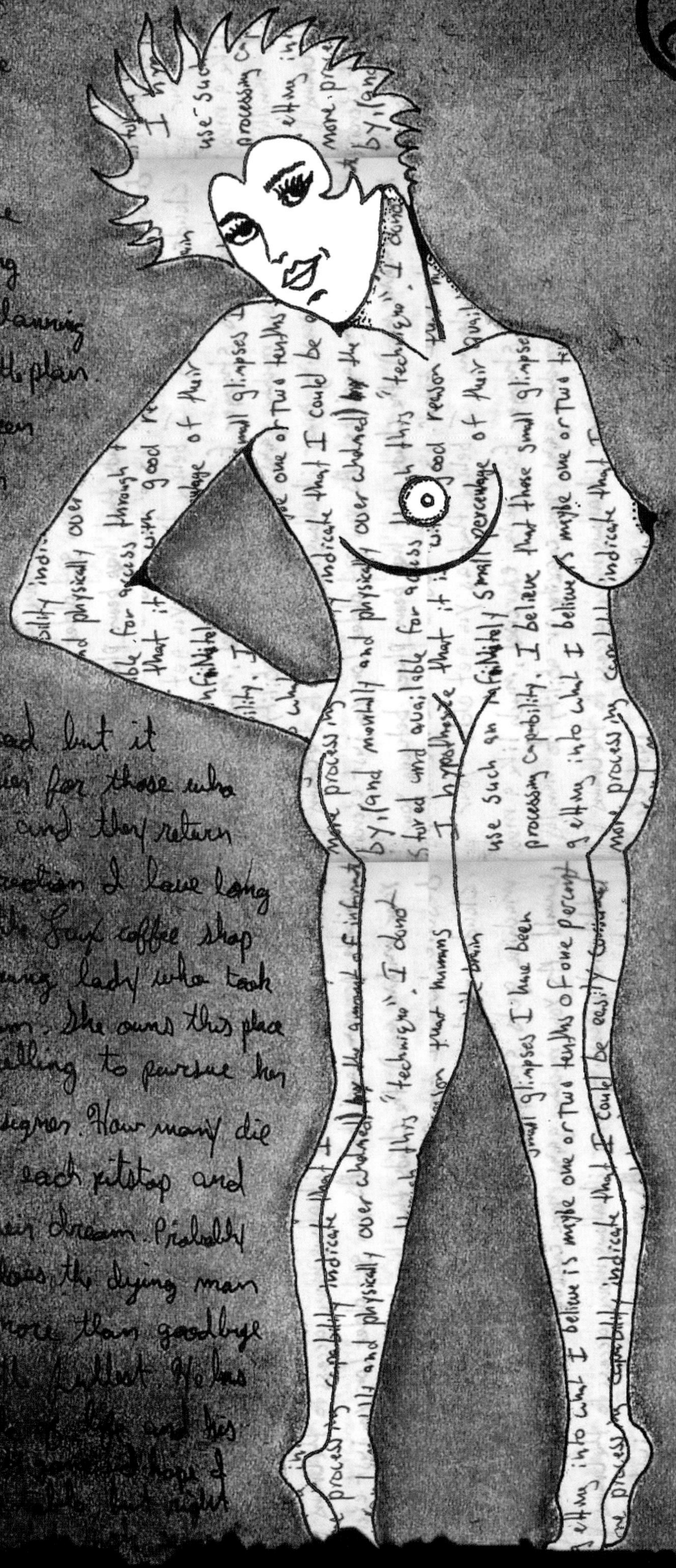

CHAPTER 39..........A PARTING MESSAGE

411633221611454533441433431235324211223311153346114412

254212353215163311154125434115323326331543332333151144223321254
5451333123532151432253133

254212353215163311154142114541331543123532153435321544331221254
545433331235321532443135254414

313544354121114341331235321541254633212541164116333513232535324
34116354333221532461343111533423515411633221143321145

313544354145353536423515463325221144443545354414331516334526123
532

421146254525111542112233432125454545331131123532254422251522453
343

4125463343262544432125411611443111141125444341123532

1533113113331235443146122135153143

41163315333212545451333114125463342351513152545452511442233

4116331533321254545133311412546334235154341153344144116

41163315333212545451333114125463342351543254626452522254112

4116331533321254545133331254242252232454122163525223343

41163543332216352522334346111213333244423515142523254414

453341453514252214322531331235321516114431133241453341411633111
3434115112241434133331512353215331233

434111154121163315332543411115413331133241334431211633153341254
6334341114431434341254545

CHAPTER 40.......A FINAL FAREWELL

4611254

5463342

1115332

1334545

Where Madonna Laid her head
My Message is being Spread
Ask Gigi to play her game
Use these cards.......
To Stake Your claim - Ady

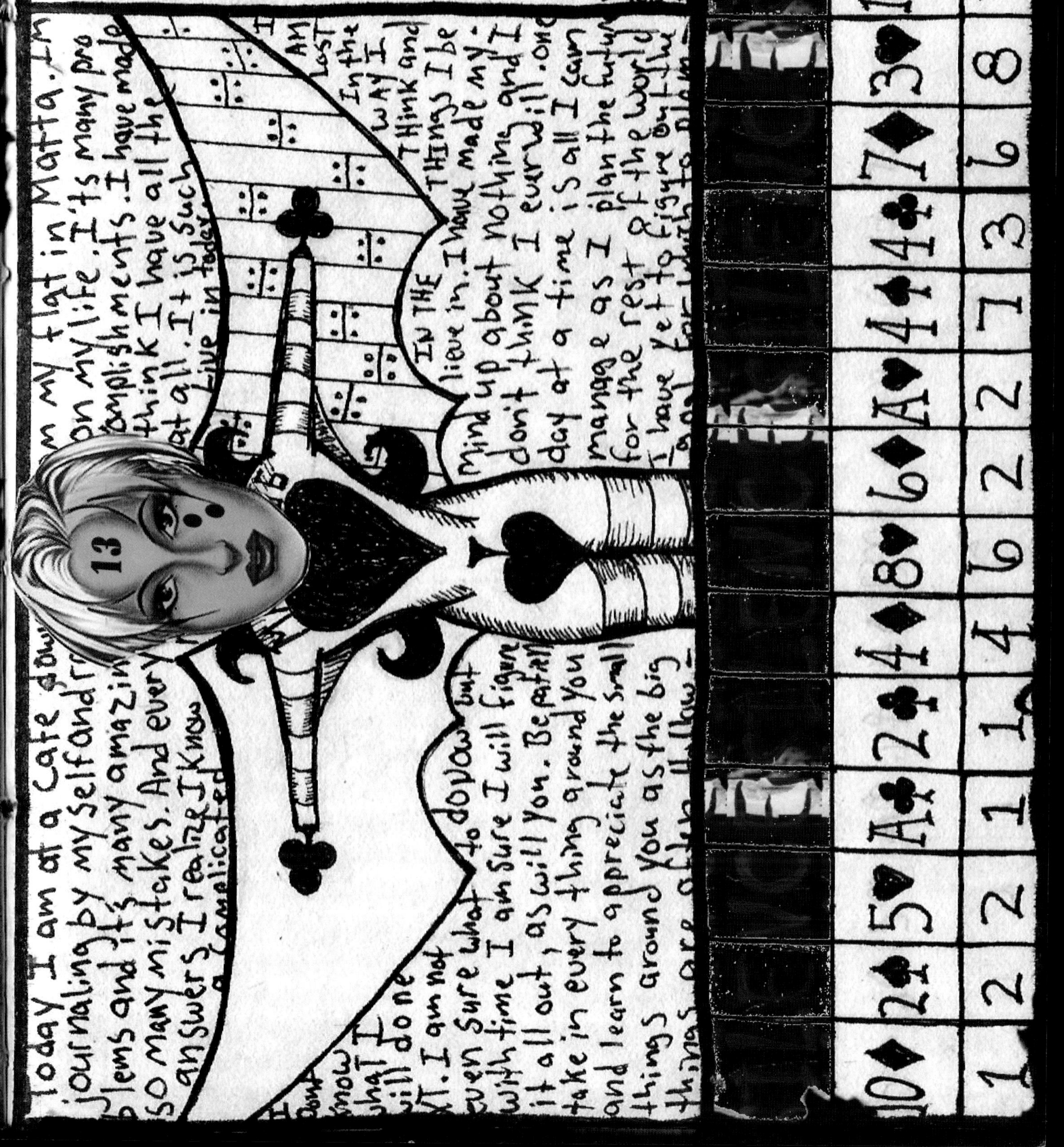

Today I am at a cafe dow
m my flat in Malta. I'm
journaling by myself and r
on my life. It's many pro
blems and it's many amazin
complishments. I have made
so many mistakes. And every
think I have all the
answers I realize I know
at all. It is such
a complicated
Live in today.
I AM LOST In the WAY I THink and THINgs I be
IN THE
lieve in. I have made my-
Mind up about nothing and I
don't think I ever will. one
day at a time is all I can
manage as I plan the future
for the rest of the world
I have yet to figure out the
goal for with to plan -
I Dont know what I will done
xt. I am not
even sure what to do now but
with time I am sure I will figure
it all out, as will you. Be patient
take in every thing around you
and learn to appreciate the small
things around you as the big
things are often Hollow -
13
10♦ 2♠ 5♥ A♣ 2♣ 4♦ 8♥ 6♦ A♥ 4♠ 4♣ 7♦ 3♥ 10♥ 5♣ 10♠ 7♥
1 2 2 1 1 4 6 2 2 7 3 6 8 3 2 1 3

IT WAS ALL JUST A DREAM

you   cant

114336   3345282543